LOUISIANA REDEEMED

FRANCIS TILLOU NICHOLLS
Governor of Louisiana, 1877 - 79
(Second Term 1888 - 92)

Louisiana Redeemed

The Overthrow of Carpet-bag Rule, 1876-1880

BY

GARNIE W. MCGINTY, PH.D.,

Professor and Head of the Department of Social Science,
Louisiana Polytechnic Institute

A FIREBIRD PRESS BOOK

PELICAN PUBLISHING COMPANY
Gretna 1998

Manufactured in the United States of America
Published by Pelican Publishing Company, Inc.
1000 Burmaster Street, Gretna, Louisiana 70053

To

The Memory of my Mother

MAUDE LESHE MCGINTY

CONTENTS

Chapter		Page
I	RECONSTRUCTION IN LOUISIANA	1
II	THE CRITICAL ELECTION OF 1876	25
III	THE RETURNING BOARD AND THE ELECTORAL COUNT	55
IV	DUAL GOVERNMENT	86
V	THE TRIUMPH OF NICHOLLS	123
VI	A NEW CONSTITUTION AND A NEW ADMINISTRATION	152
VII	THE LOTTERY FIGHT	181
VIII	COMMERCE AND TRANSPORTATION	194
IX	AGRICULTURE AND NEGROES	209
X	EDUCATION AND HEALTH	228
XI	THE SIGNIFICANCE OF THE CHANGE FROM RADICAL TO DEMOCRATIC RULE	245
	BIBLIOGRAPHY	249

* * * *

MAPS AND GRAPHS

	Page
The vote by parishes in the Election of 1868	8
The vote by parishes in the Election of 1872	16
The vote by parishes in the Election of 1876	52
Table I—The total cases and total deaths of Yellow Fever	238
Table II—The number of new cases and number of deaths of Yellow Fever, Daily report made	238

PREFACE

Much has been written on what happened in the several southern states during Reconstruction but very little has been done on the changes that took place after the Democrats ousted the Republicans from control. Reconstruction in Louisiana lasted longer than in any other state, and three students, Dr. W. M. Caskey, Dr. Ella Lonn, and the late Dr. J. R. Ficklen, have written about it. Louisiana had suffered for fourteen years preceding 1876 when the courage and tact of Francis T. Nicholls drove the carpet-bag government from the state. It is the purpose of this study to relate the steps by which the native Louisianians regained control of their government, despite the tremendous problems that faced them, and then to trace the process of readjustment through each of the years of Governor Nicholls' first administration, 1876-1880.

The change from Radical to Democratic rule constitutes an important period in the history of Louisiana. The events during this transition cast their influence far into the post-Reconstruction years. The political technique used was to be effective for some time. Likewise, the political controversies that arose between factions of the Democratic party have been revived frequently in campaigns until recently.

The research for the study has been no easy task. Extricating the facts concerning the election of 1876 and the Returning Board count of the votes were difficult but the period of dual government was equally as baffling. The author was handicapped in getting at the inside story because of the dearth of source material. Most of the political leaders did not commit their thoughts and actions to writing. A colored attorney, who was a page in Packard's legislature, leaped to his feet and shouted "men did not commit such bargaining to writing" when questioned in 1932. Practically all of the personal papers of Governor Nicholls were destroyed in October, 1931, by fire in the attic of his home,

Ridgefield. In the absence of the personal papers of the leading participants of the period, the highly partisan contemporary newspapers have been the principal source of information. The other printed accounts were biased and the persons interviewed, who lived during the period, were not entirely free from prejudice. Even the government reports, such as the census of 1870, were inaccurate.

The material for this study is to be found in the Harper Memorial Library of the University of Chicago, the Newberry Library of Chicago, the Library of Congress, the Library of the Louisiana Historical Society, the Howard Memorial Library, the Public Library of New Orleans, the Library of the University of Texas, the Library of the Louisiana State University, the Library of the Louisiana Polytechnic Institute, the Public Library of Monroe, the Archives of the City of New Orleans, the Hayes Memorial Library, Executive Documents in the Possession of the Secretary of State (Louisiana), and the scrapbooks and letters at Ridgefield (home of Francis T. Nicholls). The author also talked with three of the children of Francis T. Nicholls, and with others who lived through the period studied. In addition the files of the New Orleans Times-Picayune, the Shreveport Times, and some parish weekly publications were consulted. He is grateful for the many acts of kindnesses and courtesies extended by the staffs of all the libraries mentioned which are too numerous to list.

I have incurred many obligations during the progress of this work. I am especially appreciative for a grant-in-aid from the Social Science Research Council which helped finance the research. The Southwestern Social Science Quarterly has kindly given me permission to include material in chapters 7 and 10 which appeared in that publication. Finally, I owe much to my wife, Zoe Heard, for her encouragement and sacrifice.

Louisiana Polytechnic Institute,   G. W. M.
Ruston, Louisiana,
September, 1941.

CHAPTER I

RECONSTRUCTION IN LOUISIANA

RECONSTRUCTION in Louisiana lasted from 1862 to 1877, and therefore covered a longer period of time than in any other state.[1] As soon as Federal troops occupied New Orleans, May 1, 1862, many Union men became interested in restoring Louisiana to the Union. Meetings were held and several Union Associations were organized in New Orleans with the approval and encouragement of General Butler, commander of the occupying army. President Lincoln held that a state could not secede, and on this theory rested the efforts to restore Louisiana to the Union. The President directed General Shepley, the provisional military governor, to order an election for Congressmen from the first and second districts. The election was held December 3, 1862, and resulted in the selection of Benjamin Franklin Flanders from the first, and Michael Hahn from the second district. These gentlemen took their seats, but the term for which they were chosen expired March 4, 1863, and no successors were chosen. At that time, there was no legislature in the state under Federal control and no United States Senators were chosen. Unfortunately the Unionists in Louisiana soon split into two bitterly opposing factions—the Free State party and the Conservative Union party. The former favored the abolition of slavery, the registration of all loyal citizens who had resided one month in the parish and six months in the state, and the drafting of a new state consti-

---

[1] Reconstruction in Louisiana has been the subject of three studies: John R. Ficklen, Reconstruction in Louisiana (Baltimore, 1910); Ella Lonn, Reconstruction in Louisiana after 1868 (New York, 1918); W. M. Caskey, Secession and Restoration of Louisiana (University, Louisiana, 1938).

tution by delegates elected for the purpose. The Conservative Union party considered the constitution of 1852 still valid and desired to proceed with the election of state officers. This faction called an election for November, 1863, but General Shepley blocked it in New Orleans. The leaders then declared Dr. Thomas Cottman and A. P. Field elected to Congress from the first and second districts, respectively, but these gentlemen were not allowed to take their seats.[2]

The Unionists in Louisiana held an election for governor and lieutenant-governor February 22, 1864. The Federal administration and the more conservative faction of the Free State party supported Michael Hahn for governor; the radical wing of the Free State party nominated Benjamin Franklin Flanders, who was a friend of the negroes; the Conservative Union party chose J. Q. A. Fellows, an advocate of compensation to loyal men for the lost slave property. The election, held only within that portion of the state under control of Federal troops, resulted in a decisive victory for Hahn.[3] Governor Hahn resigned when he was elected to the United States Senate in February, 1865, and was succeeded as governor by the lieutenant-governor, J. Madison Wells. President Johnson recognized Wells as the Governor of Louisiana.[4]

In the meantime, President Lincoln worked out his general plan of Reconstruction which recognized the validity of the state constitution of 1852.[5] Despite Radical opposition,

---

[2] Annual Cyclopedia, 1865, "Louisiana", p. 509; Ficklen, **Reconstruction in Louisiana**, pp. 49-50.

[3] Phelps, **Louisiana**, p. 328; Ficklen, **Reconstruction in Louisiana**, p. 62. J. Madison Wells was elected lieutenant-governor.

[4] Ficklen, **Reconstruction in Louisiana**, p. 104. The United States Senate refused to allow Hahn to take his seat in that body.

[5] Phelps, **Louisiana**, p. 327. This plan and the one President Johnson announced are so well known that it was not thought necessary to restate them here. The essential features of each are given in almost every American history covering this period.

General Banks ordered an election in April, 1864, of delegates to the convention to revise the constitution of 1852.[6] After an extravagant and expensive session, in which considerable money was spent for wines and whiskeys,[7] the convention completed its revision of the constitution and approved its labor by a vote of 67 to 16. The document provided for the abolition of slavery, and suffrage for male whites over 21 years of age, with the legislature authorized to extend it to deserving male negroes. It empowered the legislature to license lotteries and gambling saloons, and located the state capital in New Orleans. It decreed the election of state senators for four years and representatives for two years, and provided public education for whites and negroes between 6 and 18 years of age. The governor was required to call an election for a general assembly to meet October 1, 1864.[8] This constitution remained in force until the Congressional plan of military Reconstruction superseded it in 1867.

The Confederate Governor of Louisiana, Henry W. Allen, surrendered his records to the Federal authorities at New Orleans, June 2, 1865, and the country parishes were directed to form new civil governments.[9] Governor Wells called an election for November 6, 1865, in all parishes of the state to choose the usual state officers and members of Congress. All male whites over 21 years of age and resident one year in the state who had taken the oath of allegiance of 1863 or 1865 were eligible to vote.[10]

The political situation within the state at this time was not critical, for the returning Confederates as a rule accepted

---

[6] Ficklen, Reconstruction in Louisiana, p. 56.
[7] Ibid., p. 77.
[8] Ibid., p. 79.
[9] Annual Cyclopedia, 1865, "Louisiana", p. 510.
[10] Ficklen, Reconstruction in Louisiana, p. 107.

the situation and their defeat. Bitterness against the North came later, and was the result of the radical Reconstruction policies rather than the war. However, several political factions soon appeared. The Democrats met in a convention in New Orleans, October 2, 1865, to chart their course in the election the following month. They nominated J. Madison Wells for governor; accepted the constitution of 1864 as valid until another could be adopted for the state; and asserted the right to petition Congress for compensation for freeing their slaves.[11] Other political groups were: the National Conservative Union party, which opposed negro suffrage and endorsed the candidacy of J. Madison Wells for governor;[12] the Radical Republicans, who insisted that all loyal persons should be equal before the law, and thus stood for negro suffrage; and the small group that remained loyal to Henry W. Allen.[13]

The election resulted in a Democratic legislature[14] which was probably the most representative body convened in Louisiana since 1860.[15] The legislature met in New Orleans, November 23, 1865, in extra session, and attempted to solve the momentous economic and social problems confronting the state. The Vagrant Law[16] passed December 20, 1865, was designed to force the freedmen to work. Other laws regulated the unwholesome social conditions that had arisen since emancipation. The legislature elected Randell Hunt and Henry Boyce to represent Louisiana in the United States Senate, but they were never seated because the controversy

---

[11] Ficklen, **Reconstruction in Louisiana**, p. 109.
[12] Ibid., p. 111.
[13] Ibid., p. 112.
[14] **Journal of the Senate of Louisiana, 1865**, pp. 25-27. Wells and Albert Voorhies were elected governor and lieutenant-governor, respectively, by large majorities.
[15] Ficklen, **Reconstruction in Louisiana**, p. 115.
[16] **Acts of the Legislature of the State of Louisiana, Extra Session, 1865**, p. 18.

over Reconstruction had become too heated.[17] In fact, radical Congressional Reconstruction nullified most of the work of this legislature.

The harmony existing between Governor Wells and the Democratic legislature could not, by the very nature of things, continue long. The governor, who had been a strong Unionist during the war, was disappointed by the failure of Congress to readmit Louisiana to the Union. The Democrats had accepted Wells for governor because he seemed to be the candidate most likely to meet the demands of the President. The action of Congress caused him to go over to the Radicals.[18] Most of the appointees of Wells were Unionists who were thought to be acceptable to the Democrats. Hence, the governor was disappointed when the legislature passed a law providing for a new election for all municipal and parish offices, and he vetoed the measure. It was natural for him not to desire to turn his appointees out of office, but his veto was over-ridden by the legislature. This led thirty members of the constitutional convention of 1864 to meet in the spring of 1866, and devise a plan to oust the Democrats from control and thereby win the support of the Federal government for the Unionist faction in Louisiana. They proposed to reconvene the convention of 1864, and revise the constitution according to their views. The convention had resolved that it could be reconvened on the call of the president, Judge E. H. Durell, but he refused to do so. Thereupon, the radicals met and elected a new president, R. K. Howell,[19] who proceeded to call the members of the old convention together.

---

[17] Ficklen, Reconstruction in Louisiana, p. 116.
[18] Ibid., p. 116.
[19] Judge R. K. Howell, a member of the State Supreme Court, had been a member of the convention of 1864 but had resigned before the convention adjourned, and hence could not logically be eligible to call the convention to reassemble. See Phelps, Louisiana, pp. 353-354.

Governor Wells endorsed the movement for a convention and called the meeting for July 30, 1866, in Mechanics' Institute, New Orleans. The Louisiana Democrats denounced the movement as an effort to win negro votes and formulated plans to prevent such a convention from being held. Those backing the movement for the convention counted on the Federal troops to protect them. However, these plans miscarried and the troops arrived too late to prevent the riot. The so-called riot was a fight between white men and negroes and was staged at the Mechanics' Institute, the place designated for the meeting. The fight resulted in 38 killed, 34 of whom were negroes; and 146 wounded, 119 of whom were negroes.[20] The Congressional investigating committee placed the blame on the conventionists and negroes. Nevertheless, many thought it was the result of an effort to deprive the negroes in Louisiana of their just rights. The adherents of Congressional Reconstruction used the riot to win supporters for their policy, especially in the North.[21]

The Federal elections of 1866 went contrary to President Johnson's wishes and Congress proceeded to pass over his veto a series of Radical acts instituting military Reconstruction.[22] General Philip Sheridan was appointed military governor of the fifth military district, comprising Louisiana and Texas. Sheridan appointed to office only those who could be depended upon to carry out his policy, and he refused to register voters of doubtful loyalty. An orderly election of delegates to a constitutional convention

---

[20] Ficklen, **Reconstruction in Louisiana**, p. 169.
[21] New Orleans **Times**, October 8, 1866. The **Times** condemned the manner in which the riot was reported.
[22] The First Reconstruction Act was passed March 2, 1867, and was supplemented by acts of March 23, and July 19, 1867. The provisions of these Acts are so well known that they are not re-stated. Every standard history of the period gives the essentials of the Reconstruction Acts.

was held September 27-28, 1867.[23] The ninety-eight delegates, equally divided between whites and blacks, met in Mechanics' Institute, New Orleans, on November 23, with the Republicans securely in control.[24] The framing of a contitution required almost three and one-half months, and the convention did not adjourn until March 9, 1868.

The new constitution opened public conveyances and public places to all without regard to race or color, and gave the suffrage to all male citizens of the United States twenty-one years of age and resident in Louisiana for one year, except those who had been connected with the Confederacy or who had favored secession. These last, in order to qualify as voters, had to sign a certificate acknowledging the rebellion as morally and politically wrong. The constitution contained a Bill of Rights, the first in Louisiana history, and declared the English language the official language for publishing public records, laws, and the legislative and judicial proceedings. The University in New Orleans and the public schools of the state were thrown open to all races. Representation in both houses was re-apportioned on the basis of total population, instead of qualified voters as in 1864. Only eighty-five of the ninety-eight delegates signed the constitution, but it was ratified, 51,737 to 39,076, by popular vote on April 16-17, 1868.[25] State officers were chosen at the same time and H. C. Warmoth was elected governor with

---

[23] The newspapers of the period studied contained no record of disturbances. The number of certified registered voters was 127,639 and 82,907 of these were negroes. See **Annual Cyclopedia, 1867**, p. 461.

[24] Ficklen, **Reconstruction in Louisiana**, p. 193. There were 75,083 votes for and 4,006 against the convention. The white citizens had remained away from the polls and hoped thereby to defeat the Radicals, as the law required the majority of the registered voters to vote in a valid election. They were disappointed in this move.

[25] Ibid., pp. 200-201. Several members were absent and five refused to sign.

Oscar J. Dunn (colored) lieutenant-governor. The other state officers elected were: George E. Bovee, secretary of state; Simeon Belden, attorney-general; G. M. Wickliffe, auditor; Antoine Dubuclet, treasurer; Rev. T. W. Conway, superintendent of education.

Louisiana was readmitted to the Union with five other Southern states, on June 25, 1868. Two days later the military commander of the district removed the former governor and lieutenant-governor, and placed Warmoth and Dunn in office a few days before the date of their inauguration.[26] The legislature met in New Orleans, June 29, 1868, with about half of its membership negroes. The Republicans outnumbered the Democrats 20 to 16 in the senate and 56 to 45 in the house. William Pitt Kellogg and John S. Harris were elected to the United States Senate and were seated July 18. The readmission of Louisiana to the Union brought the end of military rule, but Federal troops remained in the state ready to assist the civil authorities or the commanding general. Although the civil government was in the hands of the carpet-baggers and negroes, the Democrats worked during the summer and fall of 1868 to carry the state for Seymour and Blair, their candidates for President and vice-president. The Republicans were equally as active in behalf of their candidates, Grant and Colfax.[27] Political clubs,[28] parades, and posters were employed and the Repub-

---

[26] President Johnson removed Sheridan as military commander of the district in September 1867, and appointed General Hancock in his place. Hancock resigned as a result of being over-ruled by Grant. He was succeeded in turn by Generals R. C. Buchanan, J. J. Reynolds, and L. H. Rousseau. See Phelps, **Louisiana**, pp. 363-365.

[27] In the Presidential election of November, 1868, Louisiana gave the Seymour and Blair electors 80,225 votes and the Grant and Colfax electors, 33,225.

[28] The Democratic clubs had such names as: "Seymour Tigers", "Swamp Fox Rangers", "Seymour Infantas", and "Innocents".

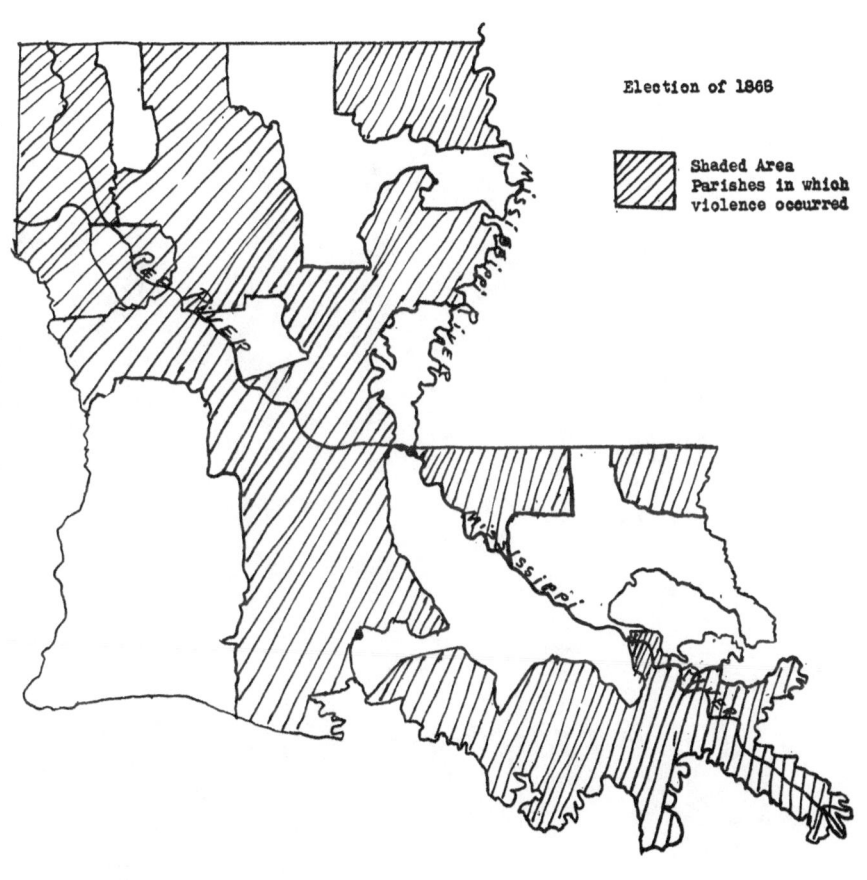

lican documents were couched in language simple enough for the illiterate negro to understand when read to him.[29]

The irresponsible and unrepresentative legislature of Warmoth's administration created a most undesirable situation. The Metropolitan Police Bill, authorizing the governor to appoint five police commissioners for New Orleans, Jefferson City, and St. Bernard Parish, enhanced the governor's power and was one cause of dissatisfaction.[30] A proposition to compel both whites and blacks between eight and fourteen years of age to attend school at least six months each year was defeated.[31] Another source of dissatisfaction was the rapid increase of the state debt during Governor Warmoth's extravagant administration.[32]

The Democratic party was greatly strengthened by a

---

[29] Some of the documents contained cartoons and illustrations whose meanings the ignorant could easily grasp; and some contained simple questions and answers that were designed to get negro votes.

[30] Phelps, **Louisiana**, p. 366. Three of the five commissioners of the board appointed were negroes and were the cause of much agitation. The Metropolitan Police cost the state $800,000 annually. See H. E. Chambers, **History of Louisiana**, 3 vols. (Chicago and New York, 1925), I, p. 669.

[31] Ficklen, **Reconstruction in Louisiana**, p. 207. Failure to comply with the provision would carry a fine of $25.00 for the first offense and $50.00 for each subsequent one. After the third offense the State Board was authorized to put the children in school for five months and charge the cost to the parents, if they were able to pay. The state superintendent of education proposed the bill, which failed to become a law.

[32] Warmoth said the state bonded debt in January, 1869, was $6,777,300, but a mass meeting in New Orleans, January 28, 1870, declared the state debt to be $28,000,000 and the debt of the city of New Orleans, $17,000,000. See Phelps, **Louisiana**, p. 367. Chambers says the total cost to the state of four years of this mis-rule amounted to the astonishing sum of $106,020,000. See Chambers, **History of Louisiana**, I, p. 667. The correct figure for the amount of the public debt was somewhere between the figures given by Warmoth and the mass meeting, as both were highly biased.

secret order, the "Knights of the White Camelia", which was organized to maintain white supremacy and to cppose the Radicals in their alleged efforts at miscegenation. Although the members denied that the organization was political, its cardinal doctrines made it impossible for the order to remain aloof from politics. The Knights of the White Camelia had its origin in South Louisiana during 1866-1868, and soon spread over the state. It probably had more members in the South than the Ku Klux Klan, but was not as well advertised. The two organizations were similar in purpose.

The carpet-bag government attempted to meet the white threat with a new constabulary law providing for a chief constable in each parish with authority to appoint all the deputies desired.[33] This law was offensive to the whites since the positions of constable and deputy constable were filled by negroes who felt their importance while holding office. The Southerners took vengeance on the negro in "riots", "political massacres", and the like. Many of these so-called massacres occurred during September and October, 1868.[34]

Reports were circulated with some evidence of truth that Warmoth exacted a signed blank resignation from every office seeker before he would appoint him to office.[35] Moreover, Warmoth instituted a Returning Board clothed with absolute authority to determine the legality or illegality of votes cast in any part of the state. Citizens soon learned it was more important to count than to cast the votes. In addition, the election laws were revised in 1870, so as to give the Republicans control of all state elections.

---
[33] Chambers, **History of Louisiana**, I. p. 669.
[34] The most notable of these outbreaks occurred in Bossier, St. Landry, and St. Bernard parishes. For a full account of them, see Ficklen, **Reconstruction in Louisiana**, pp. 226-231.
[35] Chambers, **History of Louisiana**, I, p. 668.

The legislature of 1870 was extravagant, but the session that began January 2, 1871, was even worse.[36] Expenses amounted to $958,956.50, an average of $113.00 per member per day, or a total of $6,800 for each legislator for the session.[37] The legislature made appropriations for its expenses when there was no money in the treasury and spent $7,578,148. The treasurer collected $6,616,845, but uncollected taxes and licenses due at the close of the fiscal year amounted to $5,208,738. The assessment rolls of the state for 1871 showed the amount of taxable property to be $251,296,017, with $151,089,161 of this amount in New Orleans.[38]

The Republican party in the state split into two factions, and a controversy began between them with the convening of the legislature in January, 1871. The governor and his supporters composed one faction, while the Custom House officials were the backbone of the opposition. The "Custom House crowd" had the ear of the Radicals in Congress and the United States Marshal, Stephen B. Packard, could count on the support of Federal troops to carry out his wishes, but the actual leader of the faction was William Pitt Kellogg. The two factions became so violent in January, 1872, that Congress appointed a committee to investigate their conduct. The report condemned Warmoth severely for his methods in grasping and holding imperial powers and speak-

---

[36] The total receipts of the state treasury for the fiscal year ending November 30, 1870, were $6,537,959, and the total expenditures for the same period amounted to $7,050,636. See **Annual Cyclopedia, 1870**, p. 462.

[37] Phelps, **Louisiana**, p. 368.

[38] **Annual Cyclopedia, 1871**, pp. 471-472. The auditor placed the state debt at $41,194,473. The courts were called upon twice to decide if the state debt exceeded the maximum allowed by law in 1871, and in both cases the State Supreme Court held that the legal limitation of $25,000,000 had been exceeded by legislative appropriations.

ing of his followers in the legislature as "my crowd". The report continued:

> No bill that the Governor favors can fail, and none that he opposes can pass . . . In several cases persons held seats in the House from parishes in which they were absolutely unknown. In one case a friend of the governor was elected in a private room in a New Orleans hotel, at midnight, to represent a parish a hundred miles away . . . the world has rarely known a legislative body so rank with ignorance and corruption.[39]

The National Republican party split in 1872; the Liberal Republicans met in convention at Cincinnati, May 1, 1872, and nominated Horace Greeley, for president, and Governor B. Gratz Brown of Missouri, for vice-president; the Republicans re-nominated Grant, for president, and Henry Wilson, for vice-president. The Democrats met and endorsed the nomination of Greeley and Brown. It was said that the "Republicans were running a Democrat (Grant), and the Democrats were running a Republican (Greeley)."[40]

The politicians of Louisiana lined up with the national parties. The Republicans nominated W. P. Kellogg and C. C. Antoine (colored) for governor and lieutenant-governor, respectively, whereas, the Liberal Republicans, Reformers, and Democrats put out a coalition ticket headed by John McEnery for governor and Davidson B. Penn for lieutenant-governor.[41] The spirited campaign culminated in a disputed

---

[39] For a discussion of the political factions and the report of the Congressional committee see Phelps, Louisiana, pp. 369-371.

[40] Chambers, History of Louisiana, I, p. 670. Chambers quoted this from a letter of John S. Sherman to his brother, William T. Sherman.

[41] The other Republican nominees were: secretary of state, P. G. Deslondes (colored); auditor, Charles Clinton; attorney-general, A. P. Field; superintendent of education, W. G. Brown (colored).

election. President Grant used his authority in favor of Kellogg and the Republicans.[42]

The Custom House gang began impeachment proceedings which suspended Warmoth from office for fraud in counting the votes in the presidential election of November, 1872. Pending the outcome of these proceedings, the mulatto, Pinchback, was acting governor.[43] President Grant recognized Pinchback who held office until Kellogg was inaugurated.[44]

McEnery claimed he was elected governor and telegraphed Grant to withhold judgment until both sides were heard. Moreover, a committee of one hundred leading citizens went to Washington to plead for McEnery, but the President steadfastly refused to interfere in behalf of the Democrats and supported Packard, the collector of customs at New Orleans, in his defense of the Kellogg faction.[45] A mass meeting in New Orleans, January 3, 1873, condemned carpet-bag rule and endorsed McEnery, but had little or no influence on the political situation.[46] As a result Louisiana enjoyed the luxury of two governors and two legislatures for the first two months of 1873. Finally, the McEnery faction summoned all able-bodied men from eighteen to forty-five years of age in Orleans parish to report on March 1, for the state militia. A mass meeting that day pledged support to

---

[42] House Executive Documents, 42 Congress, 3 Session, No. 91, pp. 14-20. A good account of the unusual court order of Federal District Judge Durell is found in Senate Reports, 42 Congress, 3 Session, No. 457, XVII.

[43] The lieutenant-governor, Oscar Dunn (colored) died in November, 1871, and P. B. S. Pinchback was chosen president of the Senate and ex-officio lieutenant-governor. See Phelps, Louisiana, p. 370.

[44] Annual Cyclopedia, 1873, p. 445. Miss Lonn gives the date of inauguration as January 13. See Lonn, Reconstruction in Louisiana after 1868, p. 222.

[45] House Executive Documents, 42 Congress, 3 Session, No. 91; Chambers, History of Louisiana, I, p. 670.

[46] Annual Cyclopedia, 1873, pp. 444-445.

the McEnery government and asked for martial law, or the withdrawal of Federal protection from the Kellogg faction. Five days later disturbances brought Federal troops to the active support of Kellogg.[47]

When the electoral votes of 1872 were counted, the Louisiana vote was thrown out, because Congress was unable to decide on which set of certified returns to accept. However, the majority of the Senate committee on the Louisiana question proposed a new state election as a solution to the problem. The proposal was discussed, but not acted upon.[48] Thus Congress followed the worst of three possible courses.[49] The fairest procedure would have been a new election and the second best would have been the withdrawal of support from Kellogg.

The lack of Congressional action was perhaps the basis of Grant's belief that the white conservatives of Louisiana were committing acts of violence. This belief was strengthened by a series of events in the state, beginning with the so-called "Colfax Riots" of April, 1873, in which more than one hundred negroes were killed.[50] In St. Martin parish the people pledged themselves not to pay taxes levied by the Kellogg government and resisted Kellogg's officers until Federal troops came to the aid of the latter. The political situation was unusually tense during the summer of 1874, and was increased by the large quantities of arms shipped over the state to the Black League.[51] Rumors spread of

---

[47] Annual Cyclopedia, 1873, p. 449.
[48] Senate Reports, 42 Congress, 3 Session, No. 457.
[49] J. F. Rhodes, History of the United States, VII, p. 111.
[50] House Reports, 43 Congress, 2 Session, No. 261. The riots began with the convening of a mass meeting April 1, and culminated Easter Sunday, April 13. For the President's reaction see Richardson, Messages and Papers of the Presidents, VII, p. 308.
[51] House Reports, 43 Congress, 2 Session, No. 101. The Black Leagues were composed of negroes and sprang up rapidly, succeeding the Liberty Leagues of previous years.

lawlessness on the part of the White Leaguers in all parts of the state, and parish officials resigned under their pressure.[52] The refusal of the Red River parish officials to resign, when requested by the White Leaguers, led to the Coushatta tragedy of August 20, 1874.[53] A more serious conflict was the battle of September 14, 1874, in New Orleans, where there had been considerable restlessness for some time.[54] The event was precipitated when the Federal officials seized arms shipped to private citizens on the assumption that the arms were for the White League.[55] The battle resulted in eleven killed and sixty wounded for the Metropolitan Police, and the citizens or White Leaguers had sixteen killed and forty-five wounded. The Metropolitan Police were dispersed and Kellogg took refuge in the Custom House.[56] President Grant came to the rescue of Kellogg with an order for all illegal bodies to disband and all persons to submit to the legal authorities of the state within five days.[57] Eleven companies of Federal soldiers and a Federal fleet were sufficient to prevent disturbances at the election, November 2, 1874, for state treasurer, the legislature, and members of Congress. The Democrats were confident of

---

[52] Lonn, Reconstruction in Louisiana after 1868, p. 264.
[53] Annual Cyclopedia, 1874, p. 478. The officers were overpowered by a large number of citizens and forced to resign. The six negroes were allowed to go free, and the six white men were handcuffed together and escorted by seventeen men. The six prisoners were shot and buried where they fell. The murder took place near the line between Bossier and Red River parishes.
[54] Senate Executive Documents, 43 Congress, 2 Session, No. 13.
[55] House Reports, 43 Congress, 2 Session, No. 101; W. L. Fleming, Documentary History of Reconstruction, 2 vols. (Cleveland, 1906-1907), II, pp. 144-145.
[56] Phelps, Louisiana, p. 380. The New Orleans Times, September 14, 1874, gives a full account of the battle. General Ogden, leader of the citizens, reported only twelve of his men killed.
[57] Richardson, Messages and Papers of the Presidents, VII, pp. 276-277.

victory, but were uncertain whether they would be allowed to assume office when elected. The Returning Board proceeded to count the votes in secret session from December 14 to 24, before announcing fifty-three Republicans and fifty-three Conservative-Democrats elected to the state legislature with five seats undecided.[58] The Democrats claimed they were victorious in the election.[59]

Much excitement prevailed when the legislature convened on January 4, 1875. The Conservatives profited from their experience of 1872, and quickly obtained control of the house, but their victory was short-lived, as Federal troops soon placed the Republicans in control.[60] General Sheridan assumed command, under his secret orders, and made a distorted partisan report in which he suggested the white people of Arkansas, Louisiana, and Mississippi be declared banditti.[61] The Federal House of Representatives sent a sub-committee to Louisiana to investigate affairs. This committee reported unanimously that there had been no general intimidation of Republican voters; that the election was peaceable; that the Conservatives elected a majority of the lower house of the legislature, but were defrauded by the arbitrary and illegal action of the Returning Board.[62]

The people of Louisiana were truly perplexed as to their

---

[58] House Reports, 43 Congress, 2 Session, No. 261. Dubuclet was declared re-elected treasurer and the five amendments to the state constitution were adopted .
[59] Annual Cyclopedia, 1874, p. 489. The Conservatives claimed seventy-one elected to the state legislature giving the Republicans thirty-seven. They claimed the Democrat, Moncure, was elected treasurer.
[60] See House Journal, 1875, for the record of the proceedings. See also, Phelps, Louisiana, pp. 381-382 for an account.
[61] Senate Executive Documents, 43 Congress, 2 Session, No. 13.
[62] House Reports, 43 Congress, 2 Session, No. 101. The sub-committee consisted of Charles Foster, W. W. Phelps, and C. N. Potter. The full committee numbered seven; the other four being G. F. Hoar, Wm. A. Wheeler, Wm. P. Frye, and S. S. Marshall.

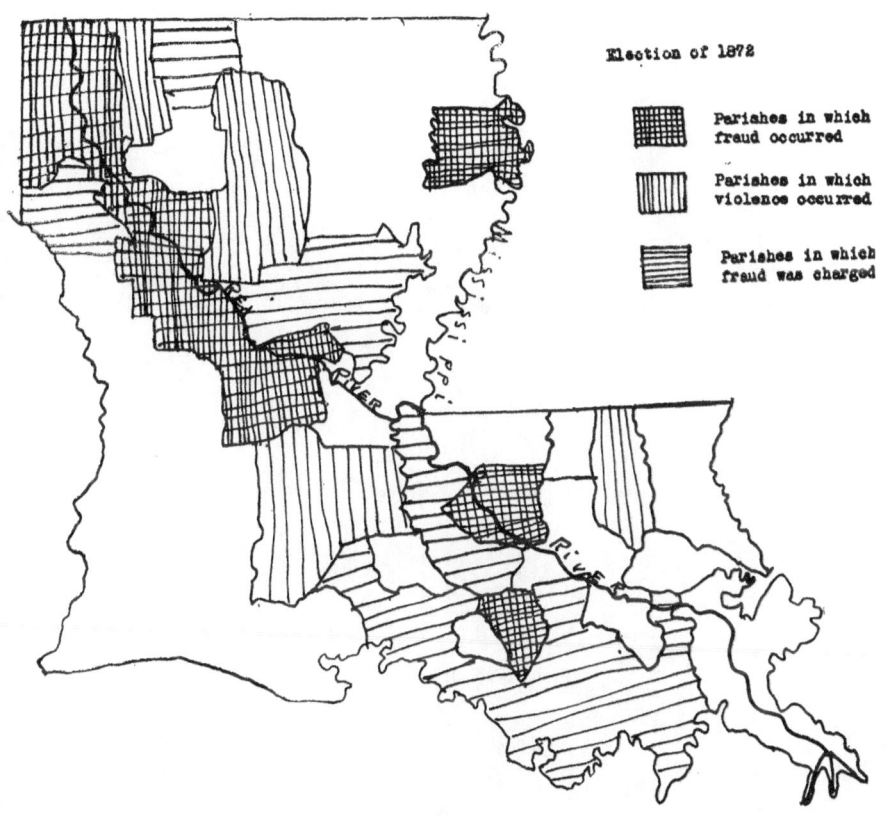

course of action by January, 1875. The overthrow of the carpet-bag government by peaceful means had proved ineffective due to the action of the Returning Board, and the attempt to throw off the yoke of oppressive government by force was nullified by Federal authorities. A compromise was suggested, and the so-called Wheeler Adjustment was the result.[63] The compromise seated sixty-three Conservatives and forty-seven Republicans in the house, and twenty-seven Republicans and nine Conservatives in the senate of Louisiana.

A group of Democrats took the position that the Wheeler Compromise only settled the outcome of the election of 1874 for the legislature, as it did not consider the election of 1872. They appealed to the Democratic-Conservative people to continue to oppose the Kellogg government and to keep the Louisiana case before Congress.[64] The impeachment of Kellogg and Dubuclet was recommended by a committee of the house[65] and that body voted February 28, 1876, to impeach the governor for high crimes and misdemeanors in office, but the senate blocked the movement.[66] An extra session of ten days, beginning March 2, 1876, proved fruitless,

---

[63] The compromise adopted April 14, 1875, was outlined by Wheeler of the Congressional Committee in Louisiana.
[64] **Annual Cyclopedia, 1875,** p. 461. The Democrats had a majority in the House of Representatives and would be receptive to a petition from their adherents in Louisiana. The Senate, with a Republican majority, could not afford to postpone the request in view of the approaching election of 1876.
[65] **Journal of the House of Representatives of Louisiana, 1876,** p. 200.
[66] **Journal of the Senate of Louisiana, 1876.** The house voted to impeach at 5 p. m. and 45 minutes later a committee appeared before the senate. The senate organized as a court and gave the house until 7 p. m. to prepare the specific charges. When the house was not ready for trial at 7 o'clock the senate dismissed the charges as a political conspiracy by a vote of 25 to 9. The next day the house adopted fourteen articles of impeachment, but the senate refused to act further in the matter.

due to the legislators' interest in the approaching political campaign.[67]

The political situation was influenced by economic and social conditions. It should be borne in mind that the negroes slightly outnumbered the whites in Louisiana[68] and before the war the more vicious negroes were sold "South". Hence, there was a large number of negroes of the criminal type in the state in 1860. The negro problem of Louisiana was further complicated by the presence of more free men of color than in any other Southern State, and these men often displayed a desire to be leaders. Before 1860 slaves were found principally on the large plantations of the river valleys and on the alluvial soil of the southern part of the state. The hill section of the north was inhabited largely by small farmers who owned few or no slaves. As the soil of the "piney woods" was not fertile, the struggle for existence there was exacting, and afforded only meager opportunities for educational and cultural growth. Here economic jealousy led to the greatest prejudice against the freedman.

Louisiana suffered more than her share of economic loss in the war for the agricultural report in 1867 shows a decline of seventy per cent in the value of the real property of the state from that of 1860.[69] The returning Confederate found the whole economic and social order upset. Without capital and labor about the only thing he could do was to grow cotton. His hardships were increased by unwise legislation which made it impossible for most of the land owners to pay their taxes. One writer in describing the deplorable

---

[67] New Orleans Times, March 3, 1876.

[68] **United States Census, 1870.** The population of Louisiana was 726,927 and 364,210 were negroes.

[69] J. L. Sellers, "The Economic Incidence of the Civil War in the South", **The Mississippi Valley Historical Review**, XIV, pp. 178-183. The banking capital of the South was reduced from $61,000,000 in 1860 to $17,000,000 by 1870 and the currency was reduced from $51,000,000 to $15,000,000 for the same period.

economic condition, stated that Warmoth's tax-gatherers forced the people into direct poverty, and Kellogg's henchmen finished the process of looting the state.[70] An example of the Warmoth regime's extravagance is furnished by twelve committees of the senate sitting after the end of the regular session. One committee drew almost $17,000 in expenses and salaries.[71] One clerk was reported as serving on three committees and drawing pay for four.[72] The journals of each house of the 1869 session showed abundant evidence of the graft and corruption. The 1869 legislature appropriated $250,000 for salaries and traveling expenses of its members and clerks and the next year the amount was doubled.[73] Printing and advertising for those years cost $183,000 and $200,000, respectively. The legislature was most generous to canals, railroads, and levees, and the interest on bonds issued to railroads reached the sum of $461,014.14. Some of these enterprises never reached the realm of reality, yet they received either direct financial assistance, or the backing of the state's credit. Needless to say, most of the funds found repose in the pockets of the grafters, and the state received no material benefit. The legislature of 1871 went beyond the bounds of all reason with thirteen subsidies[74] totaling more than $800,000 and nineteen different appropriation bills, thereby increasing the state debt four million dollars.[75]

---
[70] Chambers, **A History of Louisiana**, I, p. 678.
[71] **Journal of the Senate of Louisiana, 1870**, p. 12.
[72] Lonn, **Reconstruction in Louisiana after 1868**, p. 20.
[73] Ibid., p. 30.
[74] **Acts of the Legislature of the State of Louisiana, 1871**.
[75] The governor used the veto freely. By 1872 Warmoth had vetoed 70 bills and refused to sign 40 additional ones. He approved a bill in 1871 to purchase a site and erect a State Capitol (Act 31) that increased the state debt $1,500,000. Act 41, guaranteeing the principal and interest of the Louisiana Warehouse Company of more than a million dollars, was passed over the governor's veto. The New Orleans, Mobile, and Chattanooga Railway rceived the sum of $4,250,000 from the state plus the grant to use a part of the New Orleans levee valued at $1,000,000, and built only 70 miles of railway.

The rate of the state tax was fourteen and one-half mills on the dollar.[76] Much fertile land sold for its taxes, and many tax-gatherers bought estates for a mere pittance.[77] The state paid almost $500,000 to collect $6,500,000 in taxes in 1871; the law allowed ten per cent for assessing and collecting the taxes in all parishes except Orleans where five per cent was permitted.[78] The legislative session of 1871 cost $958,956.50, compared with a maximum of $100,000 in pre-war years.[79] The governor's message explained that the money:

> was squandered in paying extra mileage and per diem of members for services never rendered; for an enormous corps of useless clerks and pages, for publishing the journals of each house in fifteen obscure parish newspapers, some of which never existed, while some never did the work; in paying extra committees authorized to sit during the vacation and to travel throughout the State and into Texas; and in an elegant stationery bill which included ham, champagne, etc.[80]

Warmoth claimed to be honest and not susceptible to bribes, yet he testified that he made more than one hundred thousand dollars the first year he was governor.[81] As his salary was eight thousand dollars per year, it challenges one's ingenuity to explain such a disparity. The political struggle

---

[76] Senate Reports, 42 Congress, 2 Session, No. 41, part 1, p. 358. See also **Annual Cyclopedia, 1871,** p. 473, where the rate of state taxes was given as 20½ mills on each dollar.

[77] In several parishes the most fertile land sold for $1.00 per 40 acres in 1871.

[78] Senate Reports, 42 Congress, 2 Session, No. 41, part 1, p. 358.

[79] House Miscellaneous Documents, 42 Congress, 2 Session, No. 211, p. 396.

[80] Annual Cyclopedia, 1871, p. 471.

[81] House Reports, 42 Congress, 2 Session, No. 92, p. 25.

during the early part of 1873 was such that neither government made any effort to collect the taxes. McEnery forbade the citizens to pay taxes to the opposing government,[82] and Kellogg reported at the close of the year his government had collected less than half the taxes due.[83] The board he appointed to examine the state debt found it to total $53,000,000, and thought $30,500,000 should be deducted because of unwarranted guarantees, and recommended repudiation of $12,000,000 of the remainder.[84]

New Orleans was suffering as much as the remainder of the state, if not more. The city debt of $16,000,000 in 1868 reached $20,000,000 by November, 1871, and its bonds sold for three-fourths of their par value.[85] The increase in the rate of taxation was startling; in 1868, the rate was fifteen mills on the dollar; in 1869, it was twenty-three and three-fourths; in 1870, twenty-six and one-third; in 1871, twenty-seven and one-half, and in 1873, thirty; it receded to twenty-seven and one-half mills on the dollar in 1874. By July, 1874, the seven per cent gold bonds of the city had to be sold for less than half their par value.[86] It should be pointed out that the high taxes and low price of bonds were not due altogether to Reconstruction but to the depression that began about 1873.

With such conditions prevailing in the state, it was not surprising that five million, of the eight million acres of public land available for cultivation, remained unsold. The forty-seven thousand acres sold during 1873 brought the lowly sum of twelve and one-half cents an acre.[87] The people had

---

[82] Globe, **42 Congress, 3 Session**, p. 1852.
[83] **Journal of the Senate of Louisiana, 1874**, p. 5.
[84] Ibid., pp. 8-9. See also **Annual Cyclopedia, 1873**, p. 450.
[85] **House Reports, 42 Congress, 2 Session**, No. 41, p. 205.
[86] New Orleans Times, July 9, 1874. The bonds brought 48 cents on the dollar.
[87] Lonn, **Reconstruction in Louisiana after 1868**, p. 253.

lost hope, and business was disappearing. Capital could not be attracted when the government was likely to subject it to confiscation. One business amounting to $250,000 annually had decreased to a bare $20,000 and an estate that netted $70,000 in 1867 could not pay a $540 tax and insurance bill five years later.[88] Citizens representing all professions agreed that political and economic conditions were deplorable. Immigrants avoided the state, and it was said there were six thousand vacant houses and stores in New Orleans to be had for the taxes. The population of the city decreased thirty thousand in two years. Many people were on the verge of starvation.[89]

This explains why by 1875 every Conservative was resentful and weary of the Republican government as represented by Kellogg. The ignorant, unscrupulous legislators, many of them ex-slaves, enjoyed the luxury of walking on Brussels carpets, costing four dollars per yard; lounged on walnut desks which cost three hundred and seventy-five dollars each; and spat into one dollar spittoons. They drank from tumblers costing thirty-five cents each, used soap which cost a similar amount per bar, ornamented their desks with ten-dollar ink stands, used seventy-five-cent brushes to dust their shoes, and arranged their hair with a comb and brush which cost five dollars—all furnished from state taxes.[90]

Complaints against the courts for inefficiency and lack of justice were common. Some thought it useless to bring suit because they had lost faith in the integrity of the courts.[91] A judge in East Baton Rouge parish was also a member of the police jury, and as chairman of the finance committee of that body, he was in a strategic position. It is little wonder that he and his co-workers required $37,500 to

---
[88] House Reports, 43 Congress, 2 Session, No. 101, part 2, p. 239.
[89] Lonn, Reconstruction in Louisiana after 1868, p. 340.
[90] Ibid., p. 341. See also Phelps, Louisiana, pp. 367-370.
[91] House Reports, 43 Congress, 2 Session, No. 101, part 2, p. 218.

operate the parish when not one of them owned taxable property.[92]

The public school system lacked honest and efficient officials and almost ceased to exist except in New Orleans, which had a free system in 1865 with 19,000 pupils enrolled in 141 schools.[93] The state superintendent of education reported 100 schools built in 1873 which made a total of 864 schools in operation with 57,433 pupils enrolled;[94] the following year 1,039 schools were accommodating the 74,309 pupils enrolled; the next year, 1875, only 1,032 schools accommodated the enrollment of 74,846. The cost per annum for "tuition including supervision" decreased from $12.00 per student in 1873, to $11.00 in 1874, and $9.40 in 1875. The state spent on the public schools $678,473.52; $789,068.95; and $699,655.20, respectively, for those three years. The average salary per month of 1,476 teachers in 1873 was $42.50; in 1874, the 1,494 instructors drew an average monthly salary of $40.00; and in 1875, the 1,557 teachers were paid an average of $37.00 per month.[95] The money spent for public schools of the entire state makes a poor showing compared with the cost of $840,108.65 for criminal justice in New Orleans in 1875. The most disgusting phase of the educational system was its immorality and inefficiency. The parish of Concordia had $30,000 of its school funds embezzled by the senator of the district in 1873. The parishes of Morehouse, Carroll, St. Tammany, Tangipahoa, and Plaquemines

---

[92] House Reports, 44 Congress, 2 Session, No. 156, part 1, pp. 78-80.
[93] Senate Reports, 42 Congress, 2 Session, No. 41, p. 279.
[94] Reports, State Superintendent of Education, 1870-1873. The superintendent was a colored man named Brown. These figures mean little in the absence of figures on length of session, average daily attendance, etc.
[95] Reports, State Superintendent of Education, 1875, pp. 5-7. In 1873 there were 856 male and 611 female teachers. For 1874, the figures were 797 and 697 respectively. They were more equally balanced by 1875 with 797 males and 760 females.

suffered their school funds to go in a similar, or more disgraceful manner the same year. The school system was made the football of the political machine. As a rule, the members of the legislature were also members of the local school board and selected teachers that were easily managed. It was reported that teachers sublet their positions for as little as twenty-five per cent of their salaries.[96] The students had no respect for the ignorant and incompetent teachers, and the white lads of Natchitoches parish ran off the teacher and the negro children from the school.[97] In New Orleans the white children clashed with "nigger Brown", the state superintendent of education, and refused to let the sons of Lieutenant-Governor Pinchback (colored) remain at school when they were not protected by policemen.[98]

---

[96] House Reports, 43 Congress, 2 Session, No. 156, part 1, p. 145.
[97] Ibid., No. 261, part 3, pp. 320-321.
[98] Lonn, Reconstruction in Louisiana after 1868, p. 357.

CHAPTER II

THE CRITICAL ELECTION OF 1876

THE condition of Louisiana at the beginning of 1876 was deplorable. Judge Abel of Louisiana made the charge that more money had been stolen from the state treasury by officials during the eight years of carpet-bag rule than by all the "unofficial thieves, robbers, and burglars who have operated in Louisiana during the whole time since" the Louisiana Purchase.[1] The same account estimated "$100,000,000 in gold would fail to compensate for the robberies and injuries that have been inflicted upon Louisiana by the villainous politicians who have been kept in power by Grant's illegal use of Federal troops when they had been defeated at the polls." Another partisan view of the situation in Louisiana condemned the governor, the judiciary, the police department of New Orleans, the schools, the Returning Board, and stated:

> Our friends may understand how much we would like to dispense with General Grant's Governors, and have one of our own, from the fact that while the property in the city of New Orleans is valued at $118,000,000, (an over assessment) its taxes during the past ten years, together with the amount of debt for which it has been made responsible, amount to the enormous sum of $109,737,000, an amount greater than all its property could be sold for.[2]

The prevailing disorder discouraged every good citizen. The revelry of wrongs had become unbearable; soldiers rode over the state without restraint; riots were frequent and

---
[1] The Opelousas Courier, August 5, 1876, quoted from a statement in the New York Sun.
[2] A newspaper clipping in the Scrapbook of Nicholls' home. The article was entitled "The New Orleans Debt". (The clipping had no date).

blood was shed; high taxes and extravagance in public affairs knew no bounds; the records were not properly kept; finances of the state had sunk to a deplorable condition. Neither life nor property was secure. An upright and honest plantation owner, when asked if a certain property were his, replied: "I thought so once. I certainly bought and paid for it, but now I scarcely venture to say that I own anything."[3]

The economic situation was closely interwoven with the political. The Republican press accused the Democratic-Conservative party of being pledged to repudiate the state debt,[4] while the latter dismissed the charge as campaign slander. The statement did affect business, and especially the price of state bonds before the Democratic-Conservative convention declared itself opposed to repudiating the state debt.[5] Economic conditions improved during the year and the betterment was indicated in a review of the business and commerce of New Orleans, published September 1.[6] The total exports of New Orleans for the year ending June 30, 1876, were estimated at $83,984,196, and the total imports amounted to $6,547,902 with the tariff on the imports reaching $1,844,776.94.[7] Bank clearings in New Orleans, August 26, were $3,223,775.23; on September 23, the amount was $3,892,542.99; October 21, $4,838,128.41; November 18, $11,188,557.89; and December 23, $13,772,934.61—thus, quadrupling in four months.[8] It was the season of the year when

---

[3] J. A. Breaux, **Address** on "Francis T. Nicholls", pp. 4-7, on the occasion of certain mementos of F. T. Nicholls being presented to the Louisiana State Museum.

[4] New Orleans **Republican**, July 4, 1876.

[5] New Orleans **Times**, July 28, 1876. The price of bonds decreased.

[6] Daily **Picayune**, September 1, 1876.

[7] New Orleans **Times**, September 1, 1876. The data did not reveal what products originated in Louisiana, nor the amount. The writer sought specific data of Louisiana products for the period 1876-1880, in the New Orleans Custom House, but was unsuccessful.

[8] New Orleans **Times**, September 2 and 30, October 28, November 25, and December 30, 1876.

crops were sold, debts liquidated, and winter supplies purchased. Furthermore, the business of the nation was improving and the Democratic-Conservative leaders gave new hope and confidence in Louisiana. Work on the jetties at the mouth of the Mississippi River was being pushed,[9] and Daniel Dennett was advertising his ten thousand copies of "Louisiana As It Is" to inform the nation of the natural resources and the opportunities in the state.[10] Although the cotton crop looked good in September,[11] two months later it had suffered of worms, rot, rust, and drouth. Drouth damaged it twenty per cent in sixteen parishes, and the crop for the entire state was sixteen and one-half per cent less than the previous year.[12] Railroad building was proceeding within the state. The New Orleans and Texas Railway Com- was building from Vermilion to Orange, and the New Orleans Pacific Railway Company was building from New Orleans to Alexandria.[13]

The press thought education suffered because of the political turmoil. New Orleans spent $24.58 per pupil for schooling in 1874-1875; the following year, 1875-1876, the sum had decreased to $20.73 per pupil.[14] The school board of the city proposed taking over the exclusive power to examine and certify teachers because the colored state superintendent of education, Brown, had abused this power.[15] The Democratic press said:

> The disgusting mockery and shame to which our school system has been brought by the present superintendent should teach us to permit none other than the best man to be named for this office.[16]

---

[9] Opelousas Courier, May 20, 1876.
[10] Ibid., May 20, 1876.
[11] Ibid., September 16, 1876.
[12] Ibid., November 11, 1876.
[13] New Orleans Republican, August 13, 1876.
[14] New Orleans Times, January 8, 1876.
[15] Daily Picayune, July 13, 1876.
[16] New Orleans Times, July 20, 1876.

The State Democratic Convention met in New Orleans, January 5, 1876, elected four delegates and an equal number of alternates to the National Democratic Convention, and created a new State Central Committee.[17] This committee issued a platform, and passed resolutions giving the keynote of the approaching campaign:

> There must be an honest government in Louisiana—(they stated) a state the fairest among all her sisters—or Louisiana, burdened with debt, exhausted by taxation, and suffering from the supremacy of ignorance over intelligence, will become a colony for convicts and the home of depravity. The people, for whom this committee speaks, are resolved in this centennial of their liberties, to test the relative strength of intelligence and ignorance. They will use no violence, but all the means in their power will be employed to defeat the further rule of the vicious and ignorant of this State . . . what remains to be done, is the perfection of the Democratic-Conservative organization in all parishes of the State where action has not been taken.[18]

The committee resolved again to petition Congress for political relief; set the qualification for membership in the Democratic-Conservative party as opposition to the carpet-bag clique; opposed all monopolies; approved specie money; favored reduction of taxes, salaries, appropriations and the abolition of useless offices.[19] In the spring the Democrats thought they observed hopeful signs of reviving democracy over the state.[20] The Shreveport *Times* predicted the failure of the United States Senate to seat Pinchback would cause him to join the Democratic party and thus enable the Democrats to carry Louisiana by a 10,000 majority.[21]

---

[17] New Orleans **Times**, January 8, 1876.
[18] **Annual Cyclopedia**, 1876, p. 483.
[19] Opelousas **Courier**, January 15, 1876.
[20] New Orleans **Times**, April 6, 1876.
[21] Shreveport **Times** quoted by the Opelousas **Courier**, May 6, 1876.

The Republicans lacked unity, and did not mature their program as early as the Democrats. Their leader, Kellogg, found himself in an uncomfortable position at the party caucus in New Orleans. His colored partisans accused him of favoring the whites, whereas, the white Republicans objected to his giving political offices to Democrats. This friction was a factor in delaying the Republican meeting to choose delegates to the National convention until the last of May.[22] The negroes had learned their political lesson well and had twice as many delegates as the whites. The crowds, the noise, the contesting delegations, all indicated nervousness, and showed that the negroes were not altogether satisfied with what they received. The delegates selected to the National Convention were experienced leaders, and represented the two races equally.[23] The resolutions adopted took note of the centennial year, and sounded the tune of the campaign as follows:

> That the assassination of many hundreds of prominent Union men . . . the massacre of thousands of inoffensive colored citizens, the relegation of nearly all the Southern States to the control of the disloyal elements whose treason brought about the war . . . indicate grave national dangers, which demand the enactment of additional laws to secure every citizen the inalienable rights of life and liberty.[24]

The Republicans agreed on national issues, but lacked harmony on state affairs because Warmoth was a power among local politicians, and it took the entire strength of the state administration, backed by Federal authorities, to hold him down. Two candidates, Pinchback and Packard, feared

---

[22] They met in New Orleans, May 30-31, 1876.

[23] The colored delegates were Pinchback and Brown; Packard and Kellogg were the white delegates.

[24] **Annual Cyclopedia, 1876,** p. 484.

Warmoth would win the nomination for governor.²⁵ The convention for nominating state officers opened at Mechanics' Institute, June 27. The party was about equally divided between the Warmoth-Pinchback and the Kellogg-Packard groups,²⁶ and a spirited contest ensued for the temporary chairmanship, which went to Pinchback at 5 p. m. the first day. Pinchback declared on assuming the chair that he would appoint the committees according to his own sense of fairness and hoped to please both factions. The meeting place was changed the second day to the St. Charles Theater, where the disagreements and confusion grew worse, and it was July 1, before a permanent organization was perfected. The excitement reached a climax when the Committee on Credentials reported, and gave nearly all the forty contested seats to the Warmoth faction, which now had a clear majority of the two hundred and sixty-three delegates. Disorders of various types took place including free-for-all fights in which firearms were brought into play, and the policemen were called. The leaders comprehended the situation and reached a compromise that allowed certain delegations to cast half-votes. Pinchback retained the chair. The platform endorsed the principles set forth in the previous convention; approved the National Republican platform adopted at Cincinnati; endorsed the candidacy of Hayes and Wheeler; approved the debt and resumption of specie payments.²⁷ Through a compromise, Stephen B. Packard and C. C. Antoine, colored, were nominated for governor and lieutenant-

---

[25] Kellogg had declared June 23 that he was not a candidate for reelection, nor was he seeking the United States Senatorship. See New Orleans **Times,** June 24, 1876. Previous to the meeting of the convention, Pinchback made an alliance with Warmoth to be on the winning side.

[26] New Orleans **Republican,** June 28, 1876.

[27] New Orleans Times, July 2, 1876. See also **Annual Cyclopedia, 1876,** p. 484.

governor, respectively.[28] The behavior of the convention attracted the attention of the newspapers— the *Republican* lamented "nothing was done all day (June 30) but howling, raising silly points of order, bullying the chair and each other, and listening to two or three windy orations;" the *Times* observed "the same scenes of rioting, howling, and fighting of the previous day were re-enacted;" the *Picayune* commented:

> The scenes enacted within the week at the St. Charles Theater would be sufficient to cover any party with infamy were they presented to any other section of the Union but the South. There ignorance and ruffianism ran in high and unrestrained riot, and every utterance betrayed a fixed and brutal disregard of the interests of good government.[29]

The nomination of Packard and Antoine did not make for solidarity as Warmoth and Pinchback did not support the nominees. The press voiced its opinion in rather bitter terms. The New Orleans *Democrat* observed that

> Adding the prejudices of birth and sectional hate to the venom of party greed and personal ambition, S. B. Packard is, perhaps, the most complete personal and political representative of U. S. Grant that the hideous phantasmagoria of the past eight years has produced.[30]

While another announced:

> We reject Packard as a mediator; we reject him in every capacity which implies confidence, respect, or toleration.

---

[28] The remainder of the ticket was: secretary of state, Emil Honore (colored); auditor, Geo. B. Johnson; attorney-general, W. H. Hunt; superintendent of education, W. G. Brown (colored). Warmoth was to run for Congress from the first district. Pinchback remained Chairman of the State Central Committee, and Kellogg was nominated a Presidential elector.
[29] New Orleans **Republican**, July 1, 1876; New Orleans Daily **Picayune**, July 6, 1876; and New Orleans **Times**, July 1, 1876.
[30] New Orleans **Democrat**, July 6, 1876.

He is only known in Louisiana as a Federal office holder who has done his utmost to secure the interference of the General Government in our State affairs, whenever it was necessary to secure the success of his party.[31]

An impartial observer recorded this opinion of Packard:

the most dangerous politician in the state . . . He is reputed to be a man of unflinching courage, strong will, and no scruples. His single idea is to keep Louisiana in Republican hands, and his only method is to mass the colored vote . . . He has a little the air of a fanatic, but he is in reality an extremely adroit and unscrupulous politician who tolerates no rival near his throne.[32]

The Republicans held a mass meeting July 10, at Mechanics' Institute to ratify the state and national nominees.[33] The highlight of the meeting was Packard's speech praising the economy of the Kellogg administration and promising to continue its financial policy. He championed measures for the restoration of confidence and good feeling between the races. Packard desired "a peaceful and good-natured contest at the ballot box that the utmost fairness may characterize every phase of the canvass."[34] The editor of the *Times* thus expressed his attitude toward the election:

It is desirable to have a peaceful election in this State next November. We may go further and say that it is the general determination to have such an election, and a canvass which shall from its inception to its close wear all the badges of fairness, justice, and legality.[35]

The Democrats formulated plans to unite their party, and the city delegates decided it best to let the country dele-

---

[31] Daily Picayune, March 1, 1875, and July 4, 1876.
[32] Lonn, Reconstruction in Louisiana after 1868, p. 408, quoted from Nordhoff, The Cotton States.
[33] New Orleans Republican, July 11, 1876.
[34] New Orleans Times, July 11, 1876.
[35] Ibid., June 24, 1876.

gates select the time and place of the state convention.³⁶ One editor wrote:

> It is well known that the struggle in which we are about to engage will be no child's play. The Radical party will be quick to take advantage of every mistake made by our people; and to parade every weakness of their candidates and each selfish purpose that they may have in view.³⁷

The Democratic press sought to impress the voters with the importance of the election. According to the *Picayune*:

> We are now on the eve of one of the most exciting and probably most bitter campaigns we have seen in this state for years, and it behooves us not merely to lay our own plans with deliberation and judiciousness, but to closely study the tactics of the opposition in all their ramifications.³⁸

The *Times* reminded the voters that:

> No election that has ever occurred in Louisiana—not even that on secession—is fraught with weightier consequences than the election now before us. We no longer have the trade, the wealth, and the power we had fifteen years ago . . . We have property excessively taxed and without value; commerce destroyed or driven away; labor unemployed, and even life and liberty are uncertain. All this arises from the effect of bad laws, worse government and utterly corrupt rulers. Every man must feel and know that this is a battle for life and to the death . . . The governor must be a man of unsullied character, great administrative talent, one thoroughly conversant with our political wants and necessities and with all this the most popular man in the State, capable of uniting all the conservative forces in the pending battle with Radicalism.³⁹

---

³⁶ New Orleans Times, April 22, 1876.
³⁷ Ibid., July 2, 1876.
³⁸ Daily Picayune, July 2, 1876.
³⁹ New Orleans Times, July 21, 1876. See also New Orleans Times, July 15, in which a plea is made for party unity and a candidate with the respect of Democrats and Conservatives.

There was considerable speculation as to who would be the Democratic nominee for governor. Two weeks before the Democratic-Conservative Convention met in Baton Rouge, the New Orleans *Times* listed eleven likely nominees,[40] while the *Bee* named fifteen aspirants to the governorship, placing General F. T. Nicholls thirteenth.[41] Friends of L. A. Wiltz were unusually active in behalf of his candidacy, and before the convention met claimed one hundred and ten votes from the New Orleans delegation of one hundred thirty-two.[42] It would require one hundred eighty-eight votes for nomination. There were two hundred forty-three delegates from the rural part of the state. The choice of this group was F. T. Nicholls who had a strong following in the Bayou Lafourche section and was popular with the negroes, but he refused to let his name go before the convention until he was sure he could win. When the delegates assembled at Baton Rouge, it was evident the country section was for Nicholls,[43] and that the choice lay between him and Wiltz.[44]

Judge Schneider, of Bossier, was chosen temporary chairman;[45] but the organization of the convention was not completed until the third day when the committee on credentials

---

[40] New Orleans Times, July 11. The men were: L. A. Wiltz, A. S. Herron, J. McEnery, L. Texada, T. D. Manning, D. B. Penn, A. Voorhies, W. D. Spencer, J. C. Moncure, F. S. Goode, and F. T. Nicholls.

[41] The New Orleans Bee listed: J. McEnery, D. B. Penn, L. A. Wiltz, A. Voorhies, F. N. Ogden, Judge Eagan, J. C. Moncure, W. D. Spencer, T. C. Manning, L. Texada, A. S. Herron, F. S. Goode, F. T. Nicholls, General Declonet, and Colonel A. Roman.

[42] Daily Picayune, July 15, 1876, and July 22, 1876.

[43] Daily Picayune, July 25, 1876.

[44] New Orleans Times, July 25, 1876.

[45] Daily Picayune, July 25, 1876. The New Orleans Times, July 28, 1876, listed John A. "Snider" of Bossier as chairman of the convention, but this was a mistake in spelling the name.

reported. The platform was then adopted,[46] and the colored Conservatives staged a parade.[47]

The Democratic-Conservative platform was skillfully drawn with nine major planks:[48] it demanded governmental reform as the paramount need of the state; it severely arraigned the Republican party for usurpation of powers; it pledged itself to maintain the financial honor of the state and to practice economy; it approved the Texas-Pacific Railroad project; it favored free schools for all regardless of race; and it endorsed the platform and nominees of the National Democratic Convention at St. Louis. The candidate for governor was chosen on the fourth day. Wiltz led on the first and second ballots with Nicholls a close second; on the third ballot Nicholls led and McEnery withdrew. The nomination of Nicholls was made unanimous on the fourth ballot, and the other candidates were easily agreed upon.[49] Wiltz was nominated unanimously for lieutenant-governor.[50]

The leader of the Democratic-Conservative ticket was born August 20, 1834, at Donaldsonville, Ascension Parish, Louisiana.[51] His father, Thomas Clark Nicholls, was appointed the presiding Judge of the Court of Errors and Appeals in 1840, but ill health forced him to resign five years later. During his last illness, in 1846, he summoned his

[46] Annual Cyclopedia, 1876, p. 485.
[47] New Orleans Republican, July 27, 1876.
[48] Daily Picayune, July 27, 1876. See also the New Orleans Times of same date, and Annual Cyclopedia, 1876, p. 485.
[49] Daily Picayune, July 27, 1876, and Annual Cyclopedia, 1876, p. 485. The remainder of the ticket was: attorney-general, H. N. Ogden; secretary of state, W. A. Strong; auditor, A. Jumel; superintendent of education, R. M. Lusher.
[50] See Daily Picayune, New Orleans Times, and New Orleans Republican of July 27, 1876. The Picayune and Times vary slightly on the votes received at each ballot by the candidates. The Republican gives the same figures as the Picayune.
[51] Americana, XX, p. 317. See also "The Nicholls Family in America".

children and told them he was leaving little or no material
fortune, but he bequeathed them "the richest of all legacies,
an unsullied name."[52]   After his father's death, Francis lived
at "Woodlawn" with his eldest sister, Mrs. William Pugh,
until he entered the United States Military Academy in 1851,
where he graduated twelfth in a class of thirty-five in 1855.
Upon graduation he was assigned to duty in Florida where
he spent several lonely weeks before being transferred to
Yuma, Arizona.   Ill health forced Lieutenant Nicholls to resign his commission, effective October 1, 1856.   He returned
to Louisiana, studied law, and was licensed to practice by
the State Supreme Court in 1858.[53]   He then formed a partnership with his brother, L. D. Nicholls, and practiced in
Napoleonville until the outbreak of the War Between the
States.

Francis T. Nicholls was chosen Captain of the company
he organized for the Confederacy. His ability won him
rapid promotion, and at the age of twenty-nine he was commissioned a Brigadier-General.   His left elbow was shattered
by a musket ball at the Battle of Winchester, Virginia, and
the arm was amputated above the elbow.   He lost his left
foot at the Battle of Chancellorsville.[54]   His jovial character
was revealed by a remark he made while being taken from
the field, "My life ambition to be a judge is ruined, as hence-

---

[52] "The Nicholls Family in America", found at "Ridgefield", the Nicholls home, July, 1932.

[53] **Biographical Sketches of Governors of Louisiana,** (New Orleans, 1885), pp. 47-48.   Nicholls studied law at the College of Orleans, the predecessor of Tulane University.   The biographical sketch inaccurately states that he graduated, but Miss Josephine and Mr. Frank
Nicholls told the writer, July, 1932, their father did not complete
his law course.

[54] **Louisiana Confederate Soldiers and Confederate Commands,** III,
Book I, is the main source of the military record of Nicholls, whereas
the details of the woundings, etc., were supplied to the writer in conversation by Miss Josephine and Mr. Frank W. Nicholls, July, 1932.

forth I shall be a one-sided man."[55] Despite his wounds Nicholls insisted on serving and remained with the military forces until the end of hostilities.

When the war was over, Nicholls returned to his law practice in Napoleonville and formed a partnership with Desire le Blanc and Ulysses Folse.[56] It was difficult for the disabled veteran to support himself and his family after the war. His wife and children lived at "Ridgefield" with her people, but General Nicholls was too proud to be supported by his wife's family, and he remained at "Woodlawn" with his sister while trying to rebuild his law practice. During the carpet-bag regime he strove to reorganize "Democracy" in the Bayou Lafourche district. His courage, dignity, and fairness not only attracted the attention of the white people, but weakened the Republican party in that section by winning the colored people to the standard of the Democrats.

Press comment was laudatory of the Democratic-Conservative candidate. The New Orleans *Bulletin* stated:

> Since the war, General Nicholls has spoken no word and made no sign that can be construed as unfaithful to the obligations of his parole on the accepted result of the struggle in which he had engaged.

The *Bulletin* went on to say the office literally sought the man and spoke of General Nicholls as:

> Young, talented, a gentleman by birth, breeding and association; with a brilliant record as a soldier and lofty character as a man, he is in all things the ideal southerner, to whom we can yield unqualified respect and confidence and against whom his opponents can bring no shadow of charge, either of political misdeed or personal unworthiness.[57]

---

[55] Nicholls lost his left arm and left foot in battle and later lost his left eye. (The writer was not able to ascertain the exact manner in which the eye was lost.)
[56] **Louisiana Historical Quarterly**, VI, pp. 7-19.
[57] The New Orleans **Bulletin** (no date) in the **Scrapbook of F. T. Nicholls** at Ridgefield, read July, 1932.

The *Democrat* published a similar opinion of the nominee.[58] Nicholls had a high conception of his obligation.

> I shall do my whole duty to the whole people, (he stated) and when I take my oath of office, I shall cease to be the representative alone of the Democratic-Conservative parties, but will be the representative of the people—not of one set, but of the whole.
>
> I recognize, gentlemen, each and every obligation incumbent upon me under the Constitution of the United States, and all the recent Amendments, thereto, and under the Constitution of the State of Louisiana and the laws under them, and I propose, in so far as it is in my power, to enforce them without regard to race, color, or previous condition.

He let it be known that merit and ability to perform the duty would be the basis of his appointments.

> I wish it distinctly understood, that no friend of mine shall receive any appointment, at my hands by reason of that fact . . . I shall try to have official appointment in Louisiana under me, a badge and passport of integrity and capacity. I propose to bring back a proper tone in public affairs. I propose to do right myself, and in so far as I can, legally, control the doing right by other parties, I intend that others shall also do right.

He demonstrated real concern for the welfare of the negroes.

> They have no better truer friend within the borders of this State (he wrote) . . . and that fact is well known among the colored people of Ascension and Assumption, and I want you to know, that I will unflinchingly protect them in all their rights.[59]

He realized the power of the Returning Board to change or alter the election, and so he said, "I want the votes counted at once in the presence of everybody."[60] The demand for an

---
[58] Louisiana Democrat, August 2, 1876.
[59] New Orleans Times, July 28, 1876.
[60] Address of Gen. F. T. Nicholls at Baton Rouge, Louisiana, July 26, 1876. (The address was printed and distributed as a pamphlet).

honest count of votes was timely because the *de facto* governor, W. P. Kellogg, controlled the entire election machinery. Kellogg and his subordinates had already made elaborate preparations for carrying the election by fair means or foul. A state census taken in 1875 was the basis of the 1876 registration,[61] and it made the negro population 45,695 greater than the white population of the state. The city of New Orleans had 36,000 registered voters, of whom 11,000 were colored. The Democratic-Conservative party expected to poll 26,000 votes in New Orleans unless they were restrained from doing so.[62]

The people along Bayou Lafourche gave Nicholls a grand welcome on his return home from the Baton Rouge convention; Donaldsonville furnished a company of artillery and a brass band which was augmented by another band from Napoleonville; the sheriff of Assumption parish set up two cannon at the steamboat landing and fired a salute. The general was carried on the shoulders of admirers from the steamboat to his law office. At four o'clock in the afternoon, Nicholls addressed the throng of admirers from the steps of the court house. When the address was completed and the applause had subsided, a venerable colored man, who was a former family servant, mounted the rostrum "and with true native eloquence congratulated the general upon the honor of his nomination."[63]

Business men and Republican politicians admitted that the Democratic-Conservative ticket was the strongest that could have been made.[64] Unity had been attained by nominating a man from the country for governor, and one from the city for lieutenant-governor. The party was bound to-

---

[61] A. M. Gibson, **A Political Crime**, p. 114.

[62] Daily **Picayune**, October 30, 1878, commenting on the election of 1876.

[63] Assumption Chronicle (no date). Found in **Scrapbook** at Ridgefield, the Nicholls home.

[64] New Orleans **Times**, July 28, 1876.

gether by the single resolution to redeem the state, and great care was exercised to keep harmony.[65] Nicholls was the man to fuse conflicting sectional and personal interests into an effective unit. He made an excellent beginning with his acceptance speech and won the people of New Orleans at the Democratic rally in Lafayette Square on August 10. The *Picayune* spoke of it as an "immense mass meeting" that endorsed the action of the Baton Rouge convention with "unparalleled enthusiasm".[66] The *Times* stated 15,000 people met in council to ratify the Baton Rouge platform and nominations[67] while the *Republican* could see only 1,500 "very respectable looking people" at the meeting.[68]

The papers emphasized different happenings of the Lafayette Square meeting. The *Republican* made much of Nicholls' statement that, "We are not here, fellow citizens, to ascertain our wrongs or designate their authors, but we come here to rectify and remedy them."[69] The *Picayune* featured the advice Nicholls gave the people:

It is a first right step to that end that we who propose to enter upon this duty, should look upon and greet each other as we pass on to our respective missions. You by untiring work, strict vigilance, cool judgment, and correct conduct to place me in position for useful action and I to carry into practical enforcement the pledges which I here solemnly repeat.[70]

Nicholls again assured the colored citizens that he was their true friend and would protect them in all their legal rights. He repeated his plea for "peace and quiet, law and order, justice and right" in the conduct of the campaign.

---

[65] Louisiana Democrat, August 2, 1876.
[66] Daily Picayune, August 11, 1876.
[67] New Orleans Times, August 11, 1876. These were business men, voters, and 600 negroes.
[68] New Orleans Republican, August 11, 1876.
[69] Ibid., August 12, 1876.
[70] Daily Picayune, August 11, 1876.

THE CRITICAL ELECTION OF 1876   41

He warned the people of his helplessness unless they elected an honest legislature that would support him in all measures of reform. The mass meeting adopted resolutions saying the Democratic party was a party of reform and that "it deserves the support of the people because of its ability and readiness to administer the government with fidelity, honesty, and economy."[71] The ring of sincerity in Nicholls' oratory was convincing and many caught the inspiration of his crusading zeal. A Confederate veteran after listening to him address a political gathering greeted him as follows: "Giniral, all what's left of me is going to vote for all what's left of you."[72] As the campaign advanced, the old Whig associations and business men rose to action, many of whom had never taken an active part in politics before.[73] Merchants and planters even solicited the negro vote in order to win.[74] Although the campaign was exciting as predicted by the *Bossier Banner* and proved to be the climax of the Reconstruction struggle,[75] it was not as bitter and bloody as the *Times* anticipated.[76] The Democrats were determined to carry the election and succeeded in arousing the interest of the voters with great mass meetings, barbecues, and colorful parades.[77] The paraders sang stirring and emotional songs at these torch-light processions.[78]

[78] Illustrations of songs found in Nicholls' *Scrapbook* follow:

> Noble and brave as live oaks that wave
> In Southern fields of evergreen beauty,

---

[71] Daily Picayune, August 11, 1876.
[72] Chambers, History of Louisiana, I, p. 691.
[73] New Orleans Times, August 22, 1876.
[74] Ibid., August 25, 1876.
[75] Bossier Banner, October 1, 1876.
[76] New Orleans Times, May 7, 1876.
[77] Daily Picayune, August 30, 1876, reported 5,000 people at one meeting. The New Orleans Times, August 11, 1876, reported 15,000 present.

Conscious of right—as the planets that light
Heroic scenes of perilous duty
Of an arm bereft, only one leg left,
Laurel crowned where shot and shell rattle
Leading boldly today the blue and the gray,
Surely Nicholls must conquer November's battle.

* * * *

(1) O! bless de Lord, de day am here,
    De light am breaking fast;
    An' de Radicals dat wouldn't skeer,
    Is guine to de debbil at last.

Chorus
O hunt your holes, you scalawags,
An be gittin' out de way;
Fur de demicrat cock on top de fence
Is a crowin' loud fur day.

(2) Dey's takin' us niggers by de hand,
    An dey say, now Tom, you see,
    I'll swade de Congress to giv you land
    An' I want you to vote fur me.

Repeat Chorus

(3) But dey's run de machine too long,
    An' bin habbin dere own way;
    An' darkies sing de song dis year,
    O, Rads, you git out'n de way.

Repeat Chorus

(4) Dey gobbles offices, every one,
    An' dey promise dey'll tote fair;
    But whar's de darkey's chance wid dem?
    Dey don't do nuffin square. (It continued for eight verses and was sung to the tune of "Oh, Susanna").

The Democratic-Conservatives charged the Republicans with saying the Returning Board would count out the Democratic votes and take the election for the Republicans.[79] The

---

[79] **House Miscellaneous Documents, 45 Congress, 3 Session, No. 31,** p. 1054.

Republicans were accused of creating disturbances so as to provoke retaliation and bloodshed, thereby securing the aid of Federal troops,[80] and with making preparations to overthrow the election, should the returns show a Democratic victory.[81] The *Times* added:

> For some weeks a large number of clerks have been busy in upper rooms of the State House altering the registration books of 1874, so as to cover the fraudulent votes intended to be cast by the Radicals for the purpose of carrying the next election. In transcribing the register every third line is skipped to be filled in with negroes imported from Alabama.[82]

Packard wrote Nicholls, August 17, proposing a joint public discussion of the issues involved in the campaign,[83] but Nicholls was too shrewd to be caught in such an entanglement. Nicholls feared the excitement over joint debate would cause riots which would result in interference by Federal troops. He referred the matter to the Domocratic State Central Committee, and advised them that such a joint canvass might be productive of ill-feeling and disturbances.[84] The Republicans condemned the Democrats for refusing to speak from the same platform.[85] The Democrats felt no good could come from joint discussions, especially when they were exposing the frauds of the Republicans.

The Democrats had evidence that the Republicans intended to carry the election by dishonest means if necessary. Instructions to a supervisor stated:

> Your recognition by the next administration will depend upon your doing your full duty in the premises, and

---
[80] New Orleans **Times**, September 13, 1876.
[81] Lonn, **Reconstructon in Louisiana after 1868**, p. 415.
[82] New Orleans **Times**, August 26, 1876.
[83] Ibid., August 18, 1876.
[84] Ibid., August 28, 1876.
[85] New Orleans **Republican**, August 8, 1876.

you will not be held to have done your full duty unless the Republican registration in your parish reaches 2,200 and the Republican vote is at least 2,100 . . . Your recognition will be ample and generous.[86]

The 1876 census listed 24,300 adult male negroes in Orleans parish, although the entire negro population was only 57,647. It seems safe to assume that the adult males did not compose almost half the colored population;[87] furthermore, the colored vote of Orleans had never exceeded 13,000 with all the election machinery in their hands.[88] The Conservatives demanded that a Democrat be placed in each registration office to assure an honest vote. Antoine replied that all registrars had been appointed by August 23. Absolute strangers were named as supervisors of registration in some of the more important parishes,[89] and at least twenty such officers held positions in the Custom House, post-office, and police force.[90] The commissions of some supervisors had been issued in blank to the Republican candidate, or the representative of the district.[91]

The Republicans also launched the so-called Sewing Machine Swindle on the eve of the election. They sent 29,000 circulars by mail to the registered Democrats, and instructed the carriers to return all circulars that could not be delivered to the addressee in person. Thousands of voters were stricken from the rolls Saturday night before the election, giving them no opportunity to get re-instated before balloting time. Many of the oldest and most respectable citizens of the city

---
[86] House Reports, 44 Congress, 2 Session, No. 156, part 1, p. 5.
[87] Senate Executive Documents, 44 Congress, 2 Session, No. 156, part 1, p. 5.
[88] New Orleans Times, August 23, 1876.
[89] House Miscellaneous Documents, 44 Congress, 2 Session, No. 34, pp. 63-65.
[90] House Miscellaneous Documents, 45 Congress, 3 Session, No. 31, Washington, p. 1052.
[91] House Reports, 44 Congress, 2 Session, No. 156, part 1, p. 6.

were included in the black list and 8,000 Democrats were kept from the polls according to some reports.[92]

In spite of the white Republican claims, it was evident the negro leaders of that party were dissatisfied with the few political crumbs handed them;[93] nor were some of the state and parish Republican tickets popular with the negroes.[94] The Democratic-Conservatives were quick to sense this dissatisfaction and put forth their best efforts to break down the color line. The white Democratic-Conservative leaders promised a longer school term, better wages, and lower taxes. After they had won the confidence and good will of the local colored leaders, the colored vote was assured for the Democrats. The negro leaders were invited to the barbecues and were given a place in the parades, often carrying the banners.[95]

As early as mid-August, the Picayune reported the steady growth of Conservative colored clubs, and the organization of the colored voters for General Nicholls.[96] Planters told the negroes that the Republicans were dishonest and corrupt. They met the colored man on a friendly basis and reasoned with him in a manner that could be understood; when the negro was ill, he called a Democratic doctor; in litigation, he hired a Democratic lawyer; in domestic trouble, he sought the advice of his old Democratic master.[97] It was easy to show the colored man that his interests and those of the planters were identical and that one could not survive without the

---

[92] House Miscellaneous Documents, 45 Congress, 3 Session, No. 31, pp. 1054-1055. Congressman Ellis was one of them.

[93] New Orleans Republican, files from August 1 to October 15.

[94] House Reports, 44 Congress, 2 Session, No. 156, p. 33.

[95] Senate Reports, 44 Congress, 2 Session, No. 701, p. 393, and House Miscellaneous Documents, 45 Congress, 3 Session, Louisiana, p. 555.

[96] Daily Picayune, August 15 and 26, 1876.

[97] House Miscellaneous Documents, 45 Congress, 3 Session, No. 31, Louisiana, p. 555.

other. It was equally obvious that schools could not be maintained when the Republican officials stole the school funds and taxes were too high. One colored man said he had to pay a tax of twenty-two dollars on a horse worth sixty dollars; another paid seven dollars on a cow worth twenty-five dollars. A cow and a calf were taxed nine dollars and sixty-five cents, and a forty-dollar piano was taxed thirteen dollars.[98] Another argument used to win the colored voters was that the planters would be masters of the state and if the negroes did not stand by them now, they would regret it.[99]

A negro club of New Orleans inquired if General Nicholls favored race discrimination and received the following reply:

> The laws should be general in their operation and any law directed against a class or race in the community would meet my most determined opposition. No such attempt, however, will be made, for independently of the constitutional barriers which would stand in the way, the Democratic and Conservative sentiment of the whole State is united against such action. To disregard and go back upon the pledges which I have given on this subject would be to disgrace me before the country.[100]

Late in 1875, a colored conservative club resolved:

> The object of this meeting is in the interest of the Conservative party. When we say interest, we mean we are ready to take part with them in their interest. We intend to campaign with our party in the coming election. We intend to support the candidate that may be put in the field and intend to remain with them as long as they act square with us.[101]

---

[98] House Miscellaneous Documents, 45 Congress, 3 Session, No. 31, Louisiana, p. 550.
[99] Senate Reports, 44 Congress, 2 Session, No. 701, part 2, p. 347.
[100] Scrapbook found at Ridgefield, July, 1932.
[101] New Orleans Times, November 29, 1875.

THE CRITICAL ELECTION OF 1876   47

The Democrats in their campaign program showed in the end that they understood the colored man. There is no doubt that a large number joined the Democratic party. It was estimated that 5,000 to 17,000 negroes were won over.[102] Some claimed the negroes were in the majority in every club in the country, but not in the city of New Orleans;[103] the number in the Democratic clubs of East Feliciana parish was put at 863; the colored men testified that four hundred of their race joined the Democrats of New Orleans at one time; three hundred negroes were enrolled in and present at a fifth ward mass meeting; twelve hundred uniforms were sent to negro Democrats of Bayou Sara.[104] The negro was proud of his club membership and a bright uniform appealed to him. Mr. Palmer of the Congressional Committee that visited Louisiana December, 1876, said he talked with over three hundred negroes, and was convinced Nicholls had won the confidence and respect of the colored men in the state.[105]

When the Republicans realized they were losing their hold on the colored men, they claimed the negroes were driven into the Democratic party through fear.[106] The *Times* charged the Republicans with saying, "It is necessary to have twenty-five or thirty negroes killed occasionally in order to carry the election."[107] The white people of Morehouse parish were reported to have hanged four or five negro ringleaders.[108] In Lincoln parish the whipping of the negroes was condemned: "The promoters of these murderous principles are well known and well watched, and the halter for their necks

---
[102] House Reports, 44 Congress, 2 Session, No. 156, part 1, p. 147.
[103] House Miscellaneous Documents, 45 Congress, 3 Session, No. 31, Louisiana, p. 550.
[104] Ibid., No. 31, Louisiana, p. 307.
[105] Ibid., No. 31, Louisiana, p. 1037.
[106] New Orleans Republican, August 13, 1876.
[107] New Orleans Times, September 3, 1876.
[108] Senate Executive Documents, 44 Congress, 2 Session. Quoted the Morehouse Clarion, June 26, 1876.

is already greased."[109] The Republicans sent a notorious fellow named Anderson to East Feliciana as supervisor of registration. Anderson was shot at from ambush and was frightened out of the parish. The Democrats had worked hard to win the colored voters of the parish and knew that the votes of the entire parish would be thrown out if the registration was not completed. To prevent losing the votes they hired Anderson to return and complete his job.[110]

Other troubles occurred over the state before the election. In March the people of East Baton Rouge were so disgusted and aroused over the rascality of their officials that a public meeting of the citizens demanded the resignation of the sheriff, judge, and tax collector. The officials resigned, but the governor ordered the district attorney to prosecute the leaders of the lawless mob. The district attorney refused to obey the order on the grounds that the officials were induced to resign at a peaceful gathering.[111] A month later the same parish had a double murder; a Mr. Myers and son were killed under circumstances that were never fully explained; the evidence indicated they were murdered by the Democrats in order to frighten the Republican leaders.[112] Mr. Twitchell, a Republican leader, was shot on May 4, at Coushatta by a masked assassin. The Democrats attributed the shooting to Twitchell's refusal to make good the promise of a job to a supporter and predicted the Republicans would make political capital of the crime.[113] Meanwhile, a disturbance in which

---

[109] **Senate Reports, 44 Congress, 2 Session,** No. 701, part 12, quoted the **Vienna Sentinel** of August 19, 1876.

[110] **House Reports, 45 Congress, 3 Session,** No. 31, Washington, pp. 5-6.

[111] **Annual Cyclopedia,** 1876, p. 485.

[112] **Senate Executive Documents, 44 Congress, 2 Session,** part 2, pp. 278-279.

[113] New Orleans **Times,** May 10, 1876. The newspaper reported Twitchell was killed, but Mrs. D. E. Brown, a native of Coushatta, and now living at Arcadia, Louisiana, says he was only wounded.

THE CRITICAL ELECTION OF 1876   49

shots were fired occurred at Port Hudson on June 17, and afforded the Republicans more political propaganda.[114]

The worst outbreaks were in Ouachita where a radical leader, Dinkgrave, had organized Republican clubs all over the parish by July. The Democrats attempted to weaken his influence by attending the Republican meetings and heckling the speaker. Some of the negroes committed bold acts, and were accused of shooting into the homes of white people. Dinkgrave and a companion were walking on the levee at Monroe, August 30, when they were approached by a man on horseback who shot Dinkgrave dead at a distance of thirty yards. The murderer was unknown to Dinkgrave's companion. The sheriff, assisted by the Rifle Clubs, pursued the murderer but he made a successful escape. The Democrats denied the act was political and tried to show the murder was the sequel to an old quarrel with a Wimberly family of Texas, but the Republicans attributed it to his boldness in behalf of their party.[115] The Republican leaders sought to avenge Dinkgrave's death by summoning all negroes to Monroe and telling them "The war had begun". A number of negroes assembled in armed bands at various points in the parish and threatened to burn Monroe and kill the white people. The Rifle Clubs of the Democrats assembled and persuaded the negroes to disperse without firing a gun and the Republican leaders fled from Ouachita parish.[116] As the negroes outnumbered the white men ten to one in some sections of Ouachita parish, the whites, nervous and uneasy, patrolled those districts at night until calm returned.[117] With such tension prevailing, it is not surprising that Ouachita was the scene of whippings and murders on the eve of election.

---

[114] New Orleans Times, June 26, 1876.
[115] Senate Reports, 44 Congress, 2 Session, No. 701, pp. 854-864.
[116] Ibid., p. 788. See also House Reports, 44 Congress, 2 Session, No. 156, part 1, pp. 41-42.
[117] House Miscellaneous Documents, 44 Congress, 2 Session, No. 34, part 4, p. 183.

The Republicans made much of the murder in Ouachita of the negro, Henry Pinkston. They charged that a party of men rode up to Pinkston's cabin and broke into his house when he failed to obey their summons to appear, seized, gagged, and then shot him seven times. It was also reported that his baby was murdered; his wife, Eliza, assaulted, gashed on the neck and breast with an axe and left for dead.[118] The Democrats tried to show that Henry Pinkston was killed by another negro and that his baby was killed by his wife, Eliza. They claimed that Eliza's testimony was trumped up by the Republicans, and that she changed the names of those accused.[119] The Democrats thought the Republicans played up Eliza Pinkston as a Saint for dramatic effect,[120] and her employer believed she killed her own child.[121] It is rather hard to believe she killed her own child unless crazed by despair or fear. Undoubtedly the case was magnified and exaggerated for political purposes.

The Republicans distributed arms to the Ouachita negroes from Thursday until Saturday before the election, and many armed negroes came into Monroe. The whites were alarmed and the mayor issued a proclamation forbidding armed men to come into the town. The roads leading into Monroe were picketed on Sunday, November 5, to prevent the Republicans from coming into Monroe and polling all their votes in the four city boxes. If no Republican votes were cast in the rural precincts it would indicate fraud. The Democrats were strong in the rural sections of the parish and did not desire those boxes thrown out. All pickets were withdrawn

---

[118] Gibson, A Political Crime, p. 163. See also **Senate Reports, 44 Congress, 2 Session,** No. 701, pp. 517-536, and 909.

[119] **House Miscellaneous Documents, 45 Congress, 3 Session,** No. 31, p. 1085.

[120] Ibid., No. 31, p. 1085.

[121] **Senate Miscellaneous Documents, 44 Congress, 2 Session,** No. 14, pp. 116-118.

THE CRITICAL ELECTION OF 1876 51

before daybreak of election day to avoid the accusation that the colored voters were intimidated.[122]

The campaign was too tense for a few people to support either of the two main tickets. Even Warmoth did not use his influence to elect Packard.[123] An independent group held a political meeting at Mechanics' Institute and appointed a committee to nominate candidates, but the movement was not very strong and soon withered away.[124]

The Republicans tried to convince the rural people that the city dominated the Democratic party. They circulated a charge that the New Orleans Cotton Exchange had promised campaign funds if Nicholls should be nominated, [125] and another rumor that the general, if elected, would resign the governorship to Wiltz, and go to the United States Senate—a story which Nicholls publicly denied.[126]

As a final measure the Democrats sought a fair election. They demanded and finally were given one commissioner at each poll.[127] However, this concession was virtually annulled when Hahn, registrar of voters, ordered that the Democratic commissioner be assigned to checking the names from the poll list, while a Republican would receive the ballots. Each party was allowed an equal number of challengers at the polls.[128] The Republican assistant supervisors proceeded to appoint from ten to fifteen constables for every poll, and al-

---

[122] Senate Reports, 44 Congress, 2 Session, No. 701.
[123] Daily Picayune, September 15, 1876.
[124] Ibid., October 4 and also the New Orleans Times, October 4, 1876, gave an account of the meeting.
[125] New Orleans Republican, July 28, 1876.
[126] Scrapbook in Nicholl's home, no date or name of paper.
[127] Daily Picayune, October 25, 1876.
[128] House Miscellaneous Documents, 45 Congress, 3 Session, No. 31, Washington, p. 1075.

lowed the commissioners of election pay for five days, but registrar Hahn declared the law must be obeyed and that he would not pay for more than three days, nor for more than two constables at any one poll.[129]

Notwithstanding the charges of fraud and intimidation made later, both sides seemed to agree that the election was surprisingly quiet and orderly.[130] Less than a thousand soldiers were stationed in the five parishes reported as restless; but there were thirty-five hundred marshals over the state of whom eight hundred were paid by the Federal government. Various devices were used to prevent a man from voting more than once. In New Orleans, a man at each poll put a spot of red paint on the shoulder of each suspect when he voted; in other instances, a fish hook was attached to some part of the clothing of the suspect.[131]

The early returns indicated a Democratic victory and caused the supporters of that ticket to rejoice prematurely.[132] The Democrats of Monroe held a torchlight procession November 11. The returns came in slowly, but the Republican Central Committee had asked the supervisors for duplicate returns which enabled the Republicans to know the result by November 13. The Republicans claimed fraud in Louisiana[133] as soon as they saw how its vote affected the national election and Kellogg[134] telegraphed the New York *Herald*,

---

[129] New Orleans **Times**, October 14, 1876. The law allowed them five dollars per day.

[130] Daily **Picayune**, November 8, 1876. See also **House Miscellaneous Documents**, No. 31, p. 608.

[131] **House Miscellaneous Documents, 45 Congress, 3 Session**, No. 31, p. 801.

[132] Daily **Picayune**, November 8 and 9, 1876.

[133] New Orleans **Republican**, November 8 and 9, 1876.

[134] Daily **Picayune**, November 12, 1876.

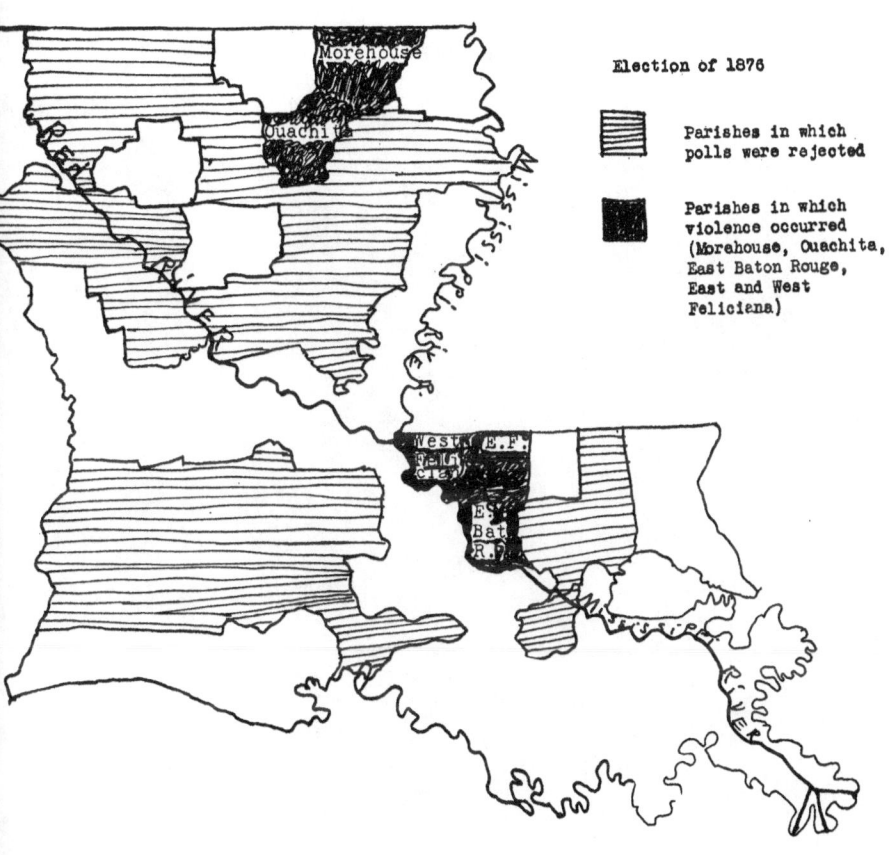

November 11, claiming proof of bulldozing in five parishes.[135] If this claim could be substantiated, the vote of these five parishes with their Democratic majority of six thousand would be thrown out. The five parishes had large negro populations which the Democrats claimed they had won over, but the Republicans charged that the White League patrol assisted by armed men from Arkansas and Mississippi drove off the white Republicans and murdered the negro leaders. Under such conditions both factions made extravagant claims. Kellogg claimed Louisiana went Republican by ten thousand votes and the Democrats claimed nine thousand majority.[136] The doubtful result was brought to the attention of President Grant and he telegraphed the following order to General Sherman on November 10:

> Instruct General Augur in Louisiana and Ruger in Florida to be vigilant with the forces at their command to preserve peace and good order, and to see that the proper and legal boards of canvassers are unmolested in the performance of their duties. Should there be any grounds of suspicion of a fraudulent count on either side it should be reported and denounced at once. No man worthy of the office of President should be willing to hold it if counted in or placed there by fraud. Either party can afford to be disappointed in the result. The country cannot afford to have the result tainted by the suspicion of illegal or false returns.[137]

---

[135] The five parishes were: Ouachita, East Baton Rouge, Morehouse, East and West Feliciana. The term "bulldozing" originated in this way: "a negro was about to be punished for some offense. A Dutchman who was a by-stander remarked, 'Ee shudt hab a bull dussen', meaning he should have a dozen lashes with a bull whip." See **Louisiana Historical Quarterly**, XV, p. 103.

[136] **Daily Picayune**, November 12, 1876. The official vote of New Orleans was published as 25,101 for Nicholls, and 14,909 for Packard. See New Orleans **Times**, November 13, 1876.

[137] Quoted in William C. Church, **Ulysses S. Grant**, p. 421.

President Grant requested several prominent republicans to go to New Orleans to witness the canvass of the votes by the Returning Board,[138] and the Democratic National Committee sent a delegation to witness the canvass, also.[139] The conservative papers trusted the fairness of the visiting gentlemen and believed their presence would assure a just count.[140]

---

[138] Sherman, Stoughton, Van Alen, Hale, Garfield, Parker, Kelly, Clark, and Wilson came at first. Others came later making 25 in all, scarcely a one of whom escaped criticism for their actions. They arrived in New Orleans, November 12, 1876.

[139] The Democrats were: Palmer, Trumbull, Randall, Bigler, Stevenson, Carroll, and others making more than twenty in all. They arrived November 13, 1876.

[140] New Orleans Times, November 11-12, 1876.

CHAPTER III.

THE RETURNING BOARD AND THE
ELECTORAL COUNT.

THE future of the Republican party in Louisiana and the choice of a President of the United States depended on whether the state went Democratic or Republican. This momentous question was solved by a partisan group. The Returning Board that canvassed the ballots of the election of November 7, 1876, was composed of four Republicans: T. C. Anderson, J. M. Wells, L. M. Kenner, and Gadane Casanave. The law provided for a bi-partisan board of five members, but the lone Democrat on the Board had resigned and no one was appointed to fill his place.[1] Wells, a native of Louisiana, who had been first a conservative and later a radical, had been governor from 1865 to June, 1867, when he had been removed by General Sheridan. He went over to the radicals and was now surveyor of the port of New Orleans.[2] Anderson, a poor man when the war ended, acquired considerable wealth through corrupt legislation as a senator.[3] Kenner (colored) held a job as servant in a gambling house and was discharged for stealing; he then opened a faro bank and a house of ill-fame near the State House.[4] Casanave (colored)

---

[1] Oscar Arroyo was the member who resigned, charging the Board with corruption. According to the law the other four members should have filled the vacancy. The New Orleans Times, November 21, 1876, gives a brief history of the Board.
[2] House Reports, 44 Congress, 2 Session, No. 156, part 1, p. 7. Also Rhodes, History of the United States, VII, p. 295.
[3] House Reports, 44 Congress, 2 Session, No. 156, part 1, p. 7. See also Annual Cyclopedia, 1876, p. 488.
[4] House Miscellaneous Documents, 44 Congress, 2 Session, No. 34, part 2, pp. 597-598.

was an undertaker who appeared too ignorant to understand
the obligation of an oath; his testimony before the Congressional committee showed he knew little of what went on, or
else he deliberately falsified as to his knowledge of the happenings.[5] On the partisan opinion of Senator John Sherman,
Wells was able and efficient, Anderson widely known and
very highly respected in Louisiana, Kenner intelligent and industrious, and Casanave a well educated citizen of excellent
character and good business judgment.[6]

The visiting Democrats, sent by the National Committee,
invited the visiting Republican delegation, sent by President
Grant, to confer with them November 15,

> in order that such influence as we possess may be exerted
> in behalf of such a canvass of the votes actually cast as
> by its fairness and impartiality shall command the respect and acquiescence of the American people of all
> parties.[7]

The Republicans replied that they were desirous of an honest
count, but they must decline to confer with the Democrats
because they were in New Orleans as private citizens and
could not supercede or alter any laws of the state. They
went on to say that any effort to influence any officer would
be condemned by every state as improper interference with
local administration.[8] Nevertheless, James A. Garfield and

---

[5] House Miscellaneous Documents, 44 Congress, 2 Session, No. 42, p. 189. Also, J. S. Black, "The Electoral Conspiracy," **North American Review**, July, 1877.

[6] Senate Executive Documents, 44 Congress, 2 Session, part 2, p. 6.

[7] Senate Executive Documents, 44 Congress, 2 Session, part 2, p. 31. Twenty-five Republicans came and included John Sherman, Stoughton, Van Alen, Hale, Garfield, Parker, Kelley, Clark, Wilson and Wallace. Twenty Democrats came and included Palmer, Trumbull, Randall, Bigler, Stevenson, and Carroll.

[8] New Orleans **Times**, November 17, 1876.

THE RETURNING BOARD 57

General Lew Wallace, members of the delegation, acted so as to exert considerable influence.[9]

The Returning Board formally organized on November 16, in their room at the State House in the presence of the distinguished visitors from the North, a committee of five representing the Louisiana Democrats, Judge Spofford representing state and parochial interests, and newspaper reporters from all parts of the country. The Democrats asked for open sessions and an opportunity to offer evidence against charges of violence. The Board met at noon Thursday and adjourned until Saturday, November 18; but it was on Monday, November 20, that real work began.[10]

Colonel Patton, speaking for the Democrats, asked that the Returning Board be reorganized so that its returns would be accepted by the people as just and impartial.[11] Chairman Wells of the Returning Board was in favor of excluding all except returning officers from the Board room,[12] but he was over-ruled and on November 18, the Returning Board invited a committee of five from each visiting delegation to attend its session, "in their capacity as private citizens of eminent reputation and high character" as spectators and witnesses.[13]

---

[9] House Miscellaneous Documents, **45 Congress, 3 Session**, No. 31, Washington, 417, pp. 790-792; 797; 1087. Garfield interviewed and helped examine negro witnesses. His questions were phrased so as to suggest the answer. Wallace showed unusual interest in some witnesses.

[10] **Proceedings of the Returning Board of the State of Louisiana— Election of 1876.** J. M. Wells was elected President, and Charles S. Abell, Secretary of the Board. An ample supply of clerks was on hand.

[11] New Orleans **Republican**, November 11, 1876. See New Orleans **Times**, November 11, 1876. Col. Patton represented the Democratic State Central Committee. He asked for two Democrats on the Board and half the clerks of the Board to be Democrats.

[12] Daily **Picayune**, November 17, 1876.

[13] Senate Miscellaneous Documents, **44 Congress, 2 Session**, No. 13 and 14.

The same day the candidates for electors on the Democratic ticket presented a protest against the Returning Board's jurisdiction over the subject, or its canvass of the votes relating to same.[14] The Board was in a questionable position because it had received returns from only thirty-seven of the fifty-six parishes.[15] Twenty of the supervisors took their returns in person to the Custom House rather than to the returning officers. The law required the returns to be sent by mail to the Returning Board and only seventeen complied with the law.[16]

The Returning Board adopted rules November 20, for canvassing the election as follows: (1) The returning officers shall meet at eleven a. m. daily, except Sunday. (2) The presiding officer shall have the roll called at each meeting. (3) The secretary shall keep daily an accurate account of the proceedings of the returning officers. (4) Returns from uncontested parishes will be taken up and considered first. (5) Contested cases must have all motions and arguments in writing. (6) No returns shall be inspected except under certain restrictions. (7) Neither party shall make or answer any objections to them. (8) No *exparte* affidavits shall be received as evidence except as a basis for investigation. (9) Returns by officers are to constitute *prima facie* evidence.[17] It was plain that all contested cases would be decided in secret session and the Democrats as well as the Federal supervisors protested against the rules. The conservative *Picayune* said the Board was engaged in solving the problem of how to elect the Republican candidates with a Democratic majority.[18]

---

[14] New Orleans **Times**, December 12, 1876.
[15] **Proceedings of the Returning Board of the State of Louisiana—Election of 1876.**
[16] Gibson, **A Political Crime**, p. 136.
[17] **Proceeding of the Returning Board of the State of Louisiana—Election of 1876.**
[18] Daily **Picayune**, November 21, 1876.

THE RETURNING BOARD

The Board was biased in its actions for it accepted approximately two hundred pages of *ex-parte* evidence from Kellogg and refused the testimony McEnery offered in opposition.[19] The returns from De Soto illustrate the fraudulent practices. George L. Smith, candidate for Congress on the Republican ticket in the Fourth District, brought down the returns of DeSoto with the returns of the other parishes in his district. The record showed the returns were sealed and sworn to November 10, notwithstanding protests were dated as late as November 25. The Returning Board attempted "to explain" but Senator Sherman said "the fact could not be disguised that the returns had been tampered with, so far as opening them and inserting documents was concerned.[20]

The canvass of the uncontested parishes was completed by November 27, and the Board heard testimony and argument until December 2, at which time secret sessions were held to complete the work. The testimony comprised 4,500 pages of manuscript which the Board could not have read between December 2 and 5, because three days of this time were spent listening to charges of intimidation in Ouachita parish.[21]

The Democrats[22] looked upon the proceedings of the Board as partisan and unfair, because the entire personnel including the clerical force was Republican. Moreover, two of the Republican nominees for electors were ineligible as both held offices at the time of the election.[23] The Democrats were not informed as to the order of investigation and the dates set for considering contests, and this handicapped them

---

[19] **Senate Miscellaneous Documents, 44 Congress, 2 Session, No. 2,** pp. 39-145.
[20] Daily Picayune, November 26, 1876.
[21] **Senate Executive Documents, 44 Congress, 2 Session, Nos. 2 and 14.**
[22] Burke, **Statement of Facts Relating to the Election of Louisiana,** November 6, 1876.
[23] New Orleans Times, November 21, 1876.

seriously because it required five or six days to get witnesses from the northern parishes to New Orleans.[24] When Democratic counsel reported on November 23, that certain returns were still in the possession of supervisors, the Board refused to order in the boxes. Chairman Wells asserted he knew of no law to compel the supervisors to hand in their returns,[25] and the returns of Franklin parish were refused even after the Democrats offered to pay the express charges.[26] The three hundred witnesses summoned to New Orleans by the Board were practically all Republicans, and they were summoned by the United States marshal at a cost of ten thousand dollars to the Federal government. The action of the Returning Board was based on the testimony of witnesses whose identity was never established by the officers administering the oath and their testimony and affidavits were prepared by Federal troops.[27] The witnesses were, for the most part, ignorant plantation negroes, dumbfounded by the sights of the city and their fears increased as they marched past policemen and faced stenographers. One hundred fifty-seven witnesses were examined after November 22, most of them from Ouachita.[28] The Republicans claimed the Democrats had concentrated their intimidation in Ouachita, Morehouse, East Baton Rouge, East and West Feliciana because of their huge negro population, and that the Democrats hoped to car-

---

[24] Senate Miscellaneous Documents, 44 Congress, 2 Session, No. 14, p. 30.

[25] Daily Picayune, November 24, 1876.

[26] Senate Miscellaneous Documents, 44 Congress, 2 Session, No. 14, p. 57.

[27] House Miscellaneous Documents, 45 Congress, 3 Session, No. 31, p. 1074 and No. 42, p. 316.

[28] Ibid., No. 31. Many of the witnesses denied their affidavits when read to them in 1878; one said he was drunk at the time he testified in 1876; while others said they signed false statements in order to get the mileage pay.

THE RETURNING BOARD 61

ry the remainder of the state if they could get the vote of these parishes thrown out.

The Democrats claimed that only one protest in the entire state was made within the time prescribed by law.[29] Mere protests of supervisors, unsupported by evidence, were accepted as valid; the vote of one parish was thrown out because marshal Packard made a protest.[30] The returns from Claiborne were not accompanied by any protest from the supervisor, but Chairman Wells ordered them held on the grounds of protests, and an affidavit sworn to on November 18, by parties unable to read and write, was filed with a subsequent report of November 24, charging that two hundred and fifty negroes were kept from voting at poll three by threats.[31] A large number of votes in many parishes were thrown out on mere technicalities, while others were counted as they suited the purpose of the Returning Board.[32] The *ex-parte* evidence accepted came from office seekers, disgruntled people, and even from fictitious persons.[33]

The Returning Board exercised its power in behalf of the Republican party and threw out enough carefully selected ballots to change a Democratic majority to a Republican ma-

---

[29] House Miscellaneous Documents, 45 Congress, 3 Session, No. 31, pp. 574 and 109.

[30] Ibid., p. 109. Kelly of Richland delivered his returns November 13, without protest. November 30, he filed a statement of alleged intimidation at certain polls. This protest was prepared by Kellogg.

[31] House Reports, 44 Congress, 2 Session, No. 156, part 1, pp. 23-24.

[32] House Reports, 44 Congress, 2 Session, No. 156, part 1, pp. 153-154. See Senate Miscellaneous Documents, 44 Congress, 2 Session, No. 14, p. 34.

[33] House Miscellaneous Documents, 45 Congress, 3 Session, No. 31, pp. 1463-1464.....See House Reports, 45 Congress, 3 Session, No. 140, p. 100.

jority.³⁴ The program as predetermined called for the Board to throw out the votes of the bulldozed parishes, and the count was suspended November 27, when it was discovered such an arrangement would elect Packard, but would defeat two of the Hayes electors. Messengers were dispatched to gather additional protests and all the affidavits brought in bore the date of November 27 or later.³⁵

Probably the most glaring case of fraud was in Vernon parish where Littlefield, a clerk, changed two polls with large Democratic majorities and counted the votes for the Republicans, by order of Wells. This act elected a Republican attorney and district judge, but the clerk made the error of not destroying the original tally sheet and the fraud was discovered. Wells found it extremely difficult to find a plausible explanation for his embarrassing situation and the best the Republicans could do was to say that Littlefield made out the sheet in order to cast doubt on the correctness of the returns.³⁶

---

³⁴ The writer found the statement of the number of votes thrown out varied. The writer consulted: The **Daily Picayune**, December 6-7, 1876; The **Republican**, December 6-7, 1876; The **Annual Cyclopedia**, 1876, p. 489; **Senate Executive Documents, 44 Congress, 2 Session**, part 2, p. 8; Fleming, **The Sequel of Appomattox**; Lonn, **Reconstruction in Louisiana After 1868**. Fleming says the Board threw out 19,436 ballots including all votes of East Feliciana and Grant parishes and 69 polls from 22 other parishes. No testimony was taken against Grant parish. It was thrown out on the ground that the election was not legally held. Miss Lonn concluded the Tilden electors won by 6,300 to 8,957, that the Returning Board cast out 13,311 votes for Tilden and 2,412 votes for Hayes electors, giving the Hayes electors majorities ranging from 3,437 to 4,800, that a Democratic majority of 7,639 was changed into a Republican majority of 3,437.
³⁵ **House Miscellaneous Documents, 45 Congress, 3 Session, No. 31**, pp. 591-592. Some of the ballots were lost and imperfect ones were substituted. The Republicans of Plaquemines parish improvised a ballot with the names of only three electors on it.
³⁶ **House Miscellaneous Documents, 44 Congress, 2 Session, No. 42**, p. 213.,See New Orleans **Times**, January 31, 1877.

THE RETURNING BOARD

The Board held secret sessions December 2 and 4, completed its labors the next day,[37] and published the official returns in the *Republican,* December 6.[38] Enough votes were thrown out to elect all Republican presidential electors, the entire Republican state ticket, and four Republican Congressmen out of six. The Board announced that the state senate would have 19 Republicans and 17 Democrats; the state house of representatives would have 71 Republicans, and 43 Democrats, and three Independents.[39] The announcement of the election returns included the Returning Board charges of intimidation, violence, and murder on a scale unheard of before in Louisiana.

The Democratic visitors reported their convictions on December 1:

> In view, however, of returns and the law and the facts which should control the Returning Board, with which we have made ourselves familiar, we have no hesitation in saying that the result shown by the votes actually cast cannot be changed without palpable abuse of the letter and spirit of the law governing the Returning Board, and a manifest perversion of the facts before it.[40]

They went on to say that irregularities existed on both sides, but not of such a character as to affect the general result; "An honest and fair canvass of the returns, even under Louisiana law, cannot materially reduce Tilden's majority, as shown on the face of the returns."[41]

---

[37] Daily Picayune, December 5, 1876.
[38] The afternoon edition of the Daily Picayune carried the returns also. See the New Orleans Times of the same date.
[39] For the number of votes received by each candidate see: The Daily Picayune, December 6-7, 1876; New Orleans Times, Annual Cyclopedia, 1876, p. 489; and Senate Executive Documents, 44 Congress, 2 Session, part 2, p. 8.
[40] New Orleans Times, December 3, 1876.
[41] Ibid. The signers of the report were: John M. Palmer, Lyman Trumbull, W. Bigler, George B. Smith, George W. Julian, and P. H. Watson.

The Republican report stressed the intimidation by the Democrats and argued that no grounds for complaint existed if an election won by illegal methods was upset by a duly appointed and lawful Board.

It is a tribunal from which there can be no appeal, and in view of the possible consequences of its judication, we have closely observed its proceedings, and have carefully weighed the force of a large mass of the testimony upon which that adjudication has been reached. Members of the board, acting under oath, were bound by the law, if convinced by the testimony that riot, tumults, acts of violence, or armed disturbance did materially interfere with the purity and freedom of election, . . . to reject the votes thus cast and exclude them from their final return.[42]

Anderson of the Returning Board gave out a statement in which he said that no publication would be made of the returns of polls not counted, but that the vote of each parish, as compiled, would be made public by the Board.[43] The Returning Board gave a statement to the Western Associated Press as follows:

---

[42] Senate Executive Documents, 44 Congress, 2 Session, No. 2, p. 8. See Annual Cyclopedia, 1876, pp. 491-492. The report was submitted to President Grant, December 6, who transmitted it to the House of Representatives the same day. The report was signed by John Sherman, E. W. Stoughton, J. H. Van Alen, Eugene Hale, J. A. Garfield, Courtland Parker, W. D. Kelly, Sidney Clark, and J. C. Wilson.

[43] New Orleans Times, December 9, 1876. This paper published on December 7, the Returning Board vote for state officers.

GOVERNOR:
    S. B. Packard (Republican) 74,626
    F. T. Nicholls (Democrat) 71,195

LT. GOVERNOR:
    C. C. Antoine (Republican) 74,669
    L. A. Wiltz (Democrat) 71,093

Secretary of State:
    E. Honore (Republican) 74,855
    W. A. Strong (Democrat) 70,393

(Footnotes continued on next page)

THE RETURNING BOARD   65

The votes purported to have been cast in the parishes of Grant and East Feliciana have been ignored entirely in the official canvass. In Grant Parish not one form of law was observed. There were no legal supervisors or commissioners of election and the vote taken was as informal as votes taken on a railroad train.

In East Feliciana the returning officers were unable to find one poll at which, from the evidence before them, they could certify that a full, free and fair election was had.[44]

During the uncertainty of the count, the pastors of the churches, the bank presidents, and leading citizens of the city of New Orleans met November 29, and issued an appeal to the nation setting forth the evil results of bad government in Louisiana. They regretted the impression produced on

---

Auditor:
    G. B. Johnson (Republican) 75,555
    A. Jumel   (Democrat)   70,391

Attorney-General:
    W. H. Hunt, (Republican) 75,036
    H. N. Ogden (Democrat)   70,836

Superintendent of Education:
    W. G. Brown (Republican) 74,445
    R. M. Lusher (Democrat)   71,105

The Board said the Republicans elected Congressmen from the 3rd, 4th, 5th, and 6th districts and all Republican Presidential Electors.

Republican:		Democrat:	
Kellogg	75,135	McEnery	70,508
Burch	75,127	Wickliffe	70,509
Joseph	74,014	Martin	70,553
Sheldon	74,027	Poche	70,335
Marks	74,418	DeBlanc	70,530
Levissee	74,003	Seay	70,525
Brewster	74,017	Cobb	70,423
Joffrion	74,736	Cross	70,566

The **Annual Cyclopedia, 1876,** pp. 488-489, gave the above data on electors.

---

[44] New Orleans **Times,** December 9, 1876.

their fellow citizens and the injury done to the business interests of the state by hasty military proclamations and the movement of troops.⁴⁵ In the minds of the people of Louisiana, the national canvass had been less important than that of the state, but the election was vitally linked with the choice of a President, for Tilden was elected if Louisiana went Democratic.⁴⁶

The Democrats of Louisiana had experienced the ruthless and illegal power of the Returning Board, and they had taken steps to canvass the vote in the state on their own account. The Democrats were in possession of a duplicate set of official returns as made out by the clerks in charge of the polls. On December 5, John McEnery, claiming to be the legal Governor of Louisiana, certified that he had, in the presence of H. N. Ogden, Attorney-General of Louisiana, and Judge A. L. Tissot of the 2nd District Court of Orleans, canvassed the votes cast in Louisiana November 7, as required by law, and found the vote to be in favor of the Democratic ticket, both state and national.⁴⁷ General Nicholls, on De-

---

⁴⁵ The New Orleans **Times**, November 30, 1876. Also New Orleans **Republican**, December 1, 1876, and the **Annual Cyclopedia, 1876**, p. 491.

⁴⁶ **Annual Cyclopedia, 1876**, p. 485.

⁴⁷ Ibid., p. 489. McEnery certified the following vote for electors and state officers. The Democratic Committee certified to the same results.

Democratic-Conservative Electors		Republican Electors	
McEnery	83,723	Kellogg	77,174
Wickliffe	83,859	Burch	77,162
Poche	83,474	Joseph	74,913
DeBlanc	83,633	Sheldon	74,902
Seay	83,812	Marks	75,240
Cobb	83,530	Levissee	75,395
Cross	83,603	Brewster	75,459
Martin	83,650	Joffrion	75,618

For Governor: Nicholls (Democrat), 84,487; Packard (Republican), 76,477. Lieutenant-Governor: Wiltz (Democrat), 84,242; Antoine (Footnotes continued on next page.)

cember 6, issued an appeal to the people of the state commending their orderly conduct and urged them to restrain their feelings, passion and resentment, and to refrain from violence as these were minor things compared to the great work of redemption which he believed was near at hand.[48] It was the duty of all to keep the peace and check others who might be tempted to violence as a way to deliverance.

Considerable excitement was created on December 6, by the report of a hole cut in the floor of the private office of Judge Alfred Shaw (Republican) of the Superior Court of New Orleans, and an underground passage way leading from it, in the direction of the clerk's office, where all the city ballot boxes were located. The boxes contained the ballots placed in them November 7. Attorney-General Steele gave a colored boy, whom he took to be Shaw's servant, a key to the office, but later he learned the colored boy was employed by Pitkin or Packard. It appeared that someone had attempted to tunnel into the clerk's office and steal the ballot boxes.[49]

The Democratic-Conservative electors met in the Chamber of the House of Representatives, December 6, and cast their ballots for Tilden and Hendricks.[50] The same day, the Republican electors met in the executive chamber of the State House to cast their votes. Two of the electors, Brewster and Levissee who were ineligible at the time of the election on account of holding Federal offices, had since resigned their

---

(Republican), 76,471. Those certified as elected to Congress were R. L. Gibson, E. J. Ellis, J. B. Elam, and F. W. Robertson, Democrats; C. B. Darrall and J. E. Leonard, Republicans.

[48] Annual Cyclopedia, 1876, p. 491. See The Opelousas Courier, December 16, 1876.
[49] New Orleans Times, December 6, 1876.
[50] Ibid., December 7, 1876. See Daily Picayune, December 7, 1876, and the Annual Cyclopedia, 1876, p. 491.

positions.⁵¹ These two gentlemen met with the other electors but their eligibility being questionable, they retired to a corner of the room, while the other six electors appointed them to fill the vacancies. They rejoined their colleagues and all cast their votes for Hayes and Wheeler.⁵² Tilden needed only one electoral vote to be President, and soon rumors spread that one of the Returning Board electors was for sale. It appears that a Democrat, named Kenner, asked Wells to name his price. Wells consulted Anderson and then named $200,000 cash for each of the Returning Board members. The negotiation was conducted by Maddox, a claim agent in the treasury department. Although Wells denied the negotiation, he entrusted to Maddox a letter addressed to Senator West, which was so damaging that Wells was never able to clear himself of its implications.⁵³

Two viewpoints arose among the members of the United States Senate as to the power of the Louisiana Returning Board. The Democratic senators believed it had no authority to inquire into and reject the returns from any voting place on account of intimidation, unless the foundation for such rejection was made at the time and in the manner pro-

---

⁵¹ Brewster was surveyor-general at a salary of $2,000 plus certain perquisites. He resigned this position November 14. Levissee was commissioner of a circuit court, which position he did not resign until November 19.

⁵² **Annual Cyclopedia, 1876,** p. 491. See **House Reports, 44 Congress, 2 Session,** No. 156, part 1, pp. 19-20. Mr. Levissee said he was offered $100,000 that day to vote for Samuel J. Tilden "but I consider the right to vote for Rutherford B. Hayes worth more than that."

⁵³ **House Miscellaneous Documents, 44 Congress, 2 Session,** No. 42, p. 144, p. 180, p. 377. The New Orleans **Times,** February 1 to 8, 1877, published the correspondence of Wells negotiating for the sale of the Louisiana electoral vote. February 1, 1877, the **Times** printed a letter of Wells to the National Democratic Committee, naming a price of $1,000,000 for him to "fix" the Louisiana vote for Tilden and Hendricks. The **Times** February 4, 1877, published Wells's letter to West dated November 21, 1876.

THE RETURNING BOARD 69

vided by law.[54] The Republicans held that if the commissioners had failed in their duty, the Board should not be prohibited from discharging their duty for them.[55]

The problem of the Republican leaders was made more difficult when the electors of Louisiana used but one ballot in voting for Hayes and Wheeler. The Constitution of the United States requires electors to use separate and distinct ballots for president and vice-president. After voting they signed in triplicate a certificate of the votes cast. One copy was deposited with Judge Billings of the United States District Court, one copy was mailed, and Anderson received one copy December 21, to carry to President Ferry of the Senate. Anderson reached Washington on Christmas eve and the following morning delivered the package to Mr. Ferry, who observed that the superscription on the envelope which stated the contents thereof was not signed by the electors as required by law. Ferry suggested that Anderson examine the law to ascertain if the certificate itself was made out in proper form. Anderson took the envelope to his room, opened it, and found the certificate did not conform to the law. He left that night for New Orleans with the opened envelope, and reached there on the morning of December 28. Kellogg was consulted and a decision was reached to substitute new certificates for the ones made out December 6. Time was a factor as one set had to be mailed and another set had to be in the hands of the messenger by five-twenty of the afternoon of December 29; both had to be on the train leaving at that hour, in order to reach Washington by January 3, 1877. Two of the electors were out of the city and could not be reached in time for the certificates to reach Washington. It was decided to forge their names and a clerk was called

---

[54] Senate Miscellaneous Documents, 44 Congress, 2 Session, No. 14, p. 9.
[55] Senate Reports, 44 Congress, 2 Session, No. 701, part 2.

in to do the deed.[56] Judge Billings of the United States District Court in New Orleans refused to let the forged certificate of December 29 be substituted for the one of December 6, so that the Republicans in Congress were forced to accept the first certificate, even if it did not conform to the law, or lose the vote of Louisiana.

All together there were seven reports made on the Louisiana election of 1876. Two of these reports have been considered; one by the visiting Democrats,[57] and one by the Republicans sent by President Grant.[58] As these partisan reports were conflicting, soon after Congress met in December, each House appointed a special committee to make an investigation. The House Committee arrived in New Orleans and held its session, on December 12, in Parlor "P" of the St.

---

[56] A. M. Gibson, **A Political Crime**, pp. 173-186. The New Orleans Times, December 27, 1876, gave the story to that date. The two absent electors were Levissee, who was in Shreveport, and Joffrion, who had gone to his home in Pointe Coupee. Shreveport was in Northwest Louisiana and was several days' journey from New Orleans.

[57] **Annual Cyclopedia, 1876**, p. 492. See **Senate Miscellaneous Documents, 44 Congress, 2 Session, No. 12.** The Democrats argued that the law of 1872 did not provide for the Returning Board to canvass the electoral vote and the law of 1870 applied. The law of 1870 provided for the canvass of the votes for electors by the governor in the presence of the secretary of state, attorney-general and a district judge and Governor McEnery obeyed these when he certified the election of Democratic electors. The Returning Board Act of 1868 had been revised in 1872. See Chambers, **History of Louisiana**, I, pp. 668-669.

[58] Senate Executive Documents, 44 Congress, 2 Session, No. 2, p. 8. See **Annual Cyclopedia**, 1876, p. 492. The report declared masked and armed men rode through the country at night, whipping, shooting, wounding, maiming, mutilating, and murdering women, children, and defenseless men, and forcibly entered houses at night.

Charles Hotel.[59] The Returning Board denied the power of the committee and refused to open its archives on the plea that the Board was a state tribunal; but it finally agreed to furnish the committee with a copy of its records provided the committee would pay the expense of preparing it.[60] The Returning Board never let the clerks of the House Committee see or examine its documents, which were read to the clerks.[61] The Western Union Telegraph Company also refused to deliver copies of messages to the Louisiana Congressional Committee.[62] Rumors were abroad that the Morrison Committee would report Wells of the Returning Board and President Orton of Western Union for contempt in refusing information requested.[63] At the first meeting of the committee there were one hundred and ten witnesses on hand to testify. The negroes were examined closely to ascertain if they were

---

[59] The Committee of the House of Representatives was composed of the following Democrats: Morrison, Jenks, McMahon, Lynde, Meade, Blackburn, House, Phelps, New, and Ross. Republicans: Townsend, Denford, Hurlburt, and Joyce, according to Daily Picayune, December 6, 1876. This committee divided into two sub-committees headed by Morrison and Blackburn and were later referred to as: Morrison committee and Blackburn committee.

[60] Daily Picayune, December 13, 1876. See New Orleans Times of same date, and Annual Cyclopedia, 1876, p. 492.

[61] Daily Picayune, December 13, 1876.

[62] New Orleans Times, December 16 and 26, 1876.

[63] New Orleans Times, January 28, 1877, recorded that the House of Representatives found Wells and the Returning Board in contempt of the House of Representatives, by the vote of 145 to 86, and ordered them to go before the Morrison committee. The same paper, January 17, 1877, contained the following telegram addressed to: Hon. S. B. Packard, New Orleans; D. H. Chamberlain, Columbia, S. C.; General Martin, Tallahassee:

> New York, November 8, 1876—We are now absolutely certain of 185 votes for Hayes, if your State is safe, and Tilden is sure of the rest. Can you defeat all Democrat attempts, by fraud, false counting, or bribery, to capture it? Answer when sure.
> Z. Chandler.

forced to vote either the Democratic or Republican ticket. Some testified one way, some the other, and many denied the use of pressure or force.[64] It is worth noting that Eliza Pinkston procured a certificate from the house physician of Charity Hospital that she was unable to be moved when she was summoned to appear before the committee.[65]

The Senate Committee[66] arrived in New Orleans and held an informal meeting[67] December 16, but did not begin examining witnesses until it established quarters on December 18, in the United States District Courtroom in the Custom House.[68]

The House and Senate Committees each had majority and minority reports with partisan views and conclusions. The Republicans of each Committee were convinced of the fairness and legality of the action of the Returning Board; the Democrats of each Committee were equally convinced of its fraud and prevarication.[69] The majority of the House Committee was Democratic and its report was adverse to the Returning Board:

> Taken altogether, the act and doings of said Board force upon your committee the conclusions that it entered upon the canvass and compilation of the votes cast at the re-

---

[64] Daily Picayune, December 29, 1876.
[65] New Orleans Republican, December 21, 1876. The House Committee met in New Orleans December 12 to 21 and December 26 to January 2, 1877. It met in Washington January 22-23 and 30-31, and February 9. The sub-committees took testimony in the parishes by journeying to the parish seat.
[66] The Senate Investigating Committee was composed of: Howe (chairman), Oglesby, McMillan, Wadleigh, McDonald, and Saulsbury. The last two were Democrats. The others were Republicans.
[67] New Orleans Times, December 17, 1876.
[68] Daily Picayune, December 19, 1876. The Senate Committee divided into sub-committees known as the Wadleigh Committee and Howe Committee.
[69] Senate Reports, 44 Congress, 2 Session, No. 701, p. 63.

cent election with a pre-arranged purpose to change the result, and fraudulently declare the result in favor of Hayes and Wheeler; that in the accomplishment of this unlawful purpose, the members of the Board did not hesitate to commit any act of official perfidy necessary to the end to be attained.[70]

It concluded that

The Democratic electors received a majority of the votes actually and legally cast at the recent election . . . and the vote of that State cannot be counted for Messrs. Hayes and Wheeler without the confirmation and approval of the illegal and fraudulent action of said Returning Board.[71]

The Senate Committee, with a Republican majority, reported:

That very gross intimidation was employed in the parishes examined there seems no room to doubt. And that such intimidation very materially and very surprisingly changed the result of the election, there seems no room to doubt.[72]

The minority report of the Senate Committee presented at great length a view similar to the majority report of the House Committee.

A year and a half later—in June, 1878—the 1876 election and the part played by the visiting statesmen on the

---

[70] House Reports, 44 Congress, 2 Session, No. 156, part 1, p. 9.

[71] Ibid., p. 20. The Morrison Committee of the House completed its work January 16, 1877. See New Orleans Republican and New Orleans Times, January 17, 1877.

[72] Senate Reports, 44 Congress, 2 Session, No. 701, pp. 41-42. The New Orleans Times, January 20, 1877, published its version of what the majority report of the Senate Committee would be. It was fairly accurate. The New Orleans Times, January 31, 1877, reported Senator Howe's speech of the previous night, before the Senate caucus. He thought there had been much fraud in Louisiana, and it was not all by the Democrats. Evidence showed the Returning Board altered the returns to produce the results desired. His speech was a surprise to his colleagues.

action of the Returning Board were again subjected to the spotlight of Congressional investigation. Over two hundred witnesses were examined and three hundred pages of testimony were taken, at the conclusion of which the (Democratic) majority said:

> Men who thought the welfare of the country depended upon the continuation in power of the Republican party would naturally have been disposed to consider almost anything justified to retain it there. To us it seems impossible that the flagrant and atrocious conduct of the Returning Board was not realized above all by the men of most political experience, or that the most dangerous and outrageous political fraud of the age was not assisted and advised by those who next proceeded to take possession of its best fruits.[73]

The Democrats said the marshals produced untruthful witnesses to prove their point, and that one could tell more lies in an hour than could be disproved in a day.[74] The army officers could hardly be accused of partiality towards the Democratic-Conservative party and they testified that there was no Democratic intimidation.[75]

It has been established that the Republicans controlled and abused the election machinery. They were determined to reject enough votes in certain parishes to carry the election and most of the witnesses who swore to intimidation voted the Republican ticket. On the other hand, the Democratic-Conservative party leaders desired to win the negroes, by peaceful means if possible, but they were determined to carry the election. If the Republicans really believed bulldozing occurred, the entire vote of Ouachita parish should have been thrown out. There was little justice in throwing out the Democratic polls and counting the Republican votes.

---

[73] House Reports, 45 Congress, 3 Session, No. 140, p. 47.
[74] House Reports, 44 Congress, 2 Session, No. 156, part 1, pp. 6-7.
[75] Ibid., pp. 76-77.

It is now in order to consider the dispute in Congress over the method of counting electoral votes from states sending more than one set of returns and the part Louisiana played in that dispute. The Republicans had made electoral returns signed by Governor Kellogg, and the Democrats had sent up a certificate signed by McEnery, who claimed to be governor. The question of how to count the electoral vote was raised. The Constitution stated: "The President of the Senate shall, in the presence of the Senate and House of Representatives, open all the certificates, and the votes shall then be counted." The Republicans took the position that it was the power and duty of the President of the Senate to determine the valid certificate, if a state had more than one certificate. The Republicans were influenced in their stand because the President of the Senate, Thomas W. Ferry, was a strong party man and would count the votes of Florida, Louisiana, South Carolina, and Oregon for Hayes. When it came to counting the electoral vote the position of each party was inconsistent with its previous principles. The Democrats abandoned states' rights doctrine and requested Congress to ignore the vote certified to by the state governors; the Republicans reversed themselves and argued that the action of a state was final, and its sovereignty must be respected.

The Twenty-second Joint Rule of 1865 might have solved the question of the electoral vote as in 1865, 1869, and 1873, but the first session of the Forty-fourth Congress had abolished the rule in January, 1876.[76] At least, President Ferry of the Senate said the Joint Rules were no longer in force, and his decision was upheld, December 8, 1876, by a vote of the Senate.[77] The Twenty-second Joint Rule gave either house the power of refusing to count the electoral vote of any

---

[76] Stanwood, **History of the Presidency**, I, p. 353. See Rhodes, **History of the United States**, VII, p. 305. The electoral vote of Louisiana was excluded in 1873 by the operation of the 22nd Joint Rule.
[77] Rhodes, **History of the United States**, VII, p. 329. The vote was overwhelming, 50-4.

state by its separate action. The House of Representatives had a Democratic majority whereas, the Republicans were in the majority in the Senate. If the Rule was in force the House could throw out the entire electoral vote of Florida and Louisiana, and Tilden would have a clear majority of the votes remaining. The Republicans needed every disputed vote in order to have a majority and could not afford to have the electoral vote of any state rejected. Tilden had an undisputed majority of the popular vote.[78]

The situation seemed desperate and civil war was not impossible. A joint Committee with equal numbers from the House[79] and Senate[80] met to wrestle with the problem, and the committee proposed the Electoral Count Bill.[81] The bill provided that when more than one certificate was received from a state (not duplicates) the valid certificate was to be decided by a commission composed of five Senators, five Representatives, and five Justices of the Supreme Court. The Commission was to render its decision in writing to the two Houses, and the decision was to be accepted unless at least five Senators and five Representatives presented written objections. Even then the decision was to stand unless the two Houses separately agreed otherwise. The committee agreed that the ten members of Congress serving on the commission should be five Republicans and five Democrats[82] and the bill provided for two Republican Justices and two Democratic Justices. The four Justices were to select the Fifth Justice,

---

[78] Stanwood, **History of the Presidency**, I, p. 383, listed the Republican count as giving Tilden 4,285,992 votes and Hayes 4,003,768. The Democratic count was, Tilden, 4,300,590, and Hayes, 4,036,298.

[79] **House Journal, 44 Congress, 2 Session,** pp. 44-45.

[80] **Senate Journal, 44 Congress, 2 Session,** p. 55.

[81] **House Journal, 44 Congress, 2 Session,** p. 306; Stanwood, **History of the Presidency,** I, pp. 382-387; New Orleans **Times,** January 18, 1877.

[82] Rhodes, **History of the United States,** VII, pp. 312-318; Stanwood, **History of the Presidency,** I, p. 382.

who by the very nature of the situation would be the key man.[83] The bill passed the Senate and House, and was signed by President Grant, January 29, 1877.[84] The next day the House[85] and Senate[86] chose the members from Congress to serve on the commission. On January 31, the House and Senate received a communication from the four Justices that Justice Joseph P. Bradley had been selected as the fifth member from the Supreme Court.[87]

The President of the Electoral Commission, Justice Clifford, notified both Houses February 1, that the Commission had met, taken the prescribed oath, organized, and was ready to proceed to the work for which it was chosen.[88] At one o'clock the two Houses met in joint session in the hall of the

---

[83] The Republican Justices were Miller and Strong, and the Democrats were Clifford and Field.

[84] House Journal, 44 Congress, 2 Session, pp. 305-310. The Daily Picayune, January 26, 1877, gave the Senate vote 47 for and 17 against. Daily Picayune, January 27, 1877, gave the House vote 190 to 86 for the bill.

[85] House Journal, 44 Congress, 2 Session, p. 338. The House members were: George F. Hoar, H. Payne, E. Hunton, J. Abbott, and James A. Garfield.

[86] Ibid., p. 341. The Senate members were: George F. Edmunds, F. T. Frelinghuysen, O. P. Morton, A. G. Thurmon, and Thomas F. Bayard. See Proceedings of the Electoral Commission for its complete personnel and the rules adopted to govern its action. It was in session from January 31 to March 2, 1877.

[87] Ibid., p. 344. Justice Bradley was a Republican and the Democrats were disappointed. The Joint Committee had virtually agreed upon Justice Davis as the fifteenth man of the commission. Davis was known as an Independent, but the very day the Electoral Bill was introduced in the House, the Illinois legislature elected Davis to the United States Senate from that state. This eliminated Davis from serving on the commission. It was now eight Republicans and seven Democrats.

[88] Ibid., p. 352, and Senate Journal, 44 Congress, 2 Session, p. 182.

House of Representatives.[89] President Ferry presided and the certificates of the electors of the several states were canvassed in alphabetical order. All was well until Florida was reached. There were three certificates from that state, each claiming to be the valid one. Objections were presented in due form and these with the certificates were turned over to the Electoral Commission for judgment. Ten days later, the Commission made known its decision of the Florida case to a joint session of Congress. The decision gave the Florida electoral vote to Hayes and Wheeler.[90]

The canvass then proceeded without interruption until Louisiana was reached. This state had three certificates, each purporting to be valid, just as in the Florida case. Objections were offered and all documents in the Louisiana case were turned over to the Commission. The Hayes electors were objected to on several grounds; invalid certificates, the action of the state Returning Board, and the eligibility of O. H. Brewster and A. B. Levissee. The Returning Board was charged with having offered to certify to the election of Tilden and Hendricks, if paid their price; William Pitt Kellogg was declared to have illegally usurped the office of governor.[91] The Commission required four days to decide that

[89] Senate Journal, 44 Congress, 2 Session, p. 182.
[90] House Journal, 44 Congress, 2 Session, p. 417; Stanwood, History of the Presidency, I, p. 389. The New Orleans Times, February 8-10, 1877, gives the Florida decision.
[91] House Journal, 44 Congress, 2 Session, pp. 425-429. New Orleans Times, February 13, 1877, gave the long objections. The argument of M. H. Carpenter before the Electoral Commission, p. 24, as to the Louisiana vote was: "If the Act of 1868 was in force, then there has been no canvass according to law of the votes cast for electors, and all the votes given by the Hayes Electors must be rejected, as they were four years ago by both Houses of Congress, for the same reason. If the Act of 1868 was not in force, then there was no law directing the manner of appointment of electors, and all the votes given by the Hayes electors must be rejected for that reason. Because it is evi-
(Footnotes Continued on Next Page)

the returns certified to by Governor Kellogg were valid. The decision recognized Kellogg as Governor and the Returning Board as a legally constituted body.[92]

The Democrats anticipated the decision and a caucus on February 17, decided that

> the count of the electoral vote should proceed, without dilatory opposition to the orderly execution of the Act of Congress creating the Electoral Commission, whose decisions shall be received and acted upon in accordance with the provisions of said law.[93]

The following Sunday morning E. A. Burke, agent for General Nicholls, called on Hewett, Chairman of the National Democratic Committee, to learn if the party had abandoned Louisiana and if so, why? Hewett pointed out the possibility of anarchy spreading over the country, and said the Democrats, not wishing to be the cause of such evil, were acting so as to place the responsibility on the Republicans. Burke was deeply disappointed and said Louisiana would endure her wrongs no longer; that Hewett and the Democratic leaders were wrong in believing peace and quiet were possible as long as carpet-bag governments remained in Louisiana and South Carolina. He went on to say that the Louisianians were in possession of the only government that could protect life and property and would try to avoid trouble with the Federal troops; but any attempt to destroy the Nicholls gov-

---

dent that if a State has omitted through its legislature to provide the manner in which electors shall be appointed, or, having made such provision, repeals it and makes no other, no constitutional appointment can be made by such State . . . And if this were otherwise, still the two votes given by the two persons elected by the Electoral College to fill the supposed vacancies must be excluded."

[92] House Journal, 44 Congress, 2 Session, p. 469.
[93] House Miscellaneous Documents, 45 Congress, 3 Session, No. 31, Washington, p. 970.

ernment would be resisted. He stated that members who had supported the electoral bill in order to save the country from anarchy could join a movement to demand guarantees for one state of the Union.[94] A man who had spent a month in Louisiana studying the situation wrote February 4, that he believed peace and prosperity could come to Louisiana only by the recognition of the Nicholls government, as nineteen-twentieths of the people of the state favored his government.[95]

Despite the caucus resolution, Burke and his friends began organizing a body of Democrats to filibuster. He organized a group of one hundred and sixteen which was large enough to defeat any action of the House[96] and when the Louisiana decision was read to the joint meeting of Congress February 19, objections were offered from eighteen senators and one hundred fifty representatives.[97] Despite the severe criticism heaped upon the commission, the Senate approved and the House disapproved the Louisiana decision the following day. At the joint session of the two Houses the same day, the President of the Senate announced the electoral vote of Louisiana for Hayes and Wheeler.[98]

Burke and his associates made it plain that they proposed to hold up proceedings and delay the count beyond

---

[94] **House Miscellaneous Documents, 45 Congress, 3 Session, No. 31,** Washington, p. 971. A similar sentiment was expressed in letters to President Hayes. See **micro-films,** Nos. 184 and 207 of the Hayes Memorial Library. The documents of this library have been photographed, and those bearing on the Louisiana question were sent to the writer for study.

[95] **Letter W. M. Garland to Rutherford B. Hayes,** South Haven, Michigan, February 24, 1877. **Micro-film** from Hayes Memorial Library.

[96] **House Miscellaneous Documents, 45 Congress, 3 Session, No. 31,** Louisiana, p. 601.

[97] **House Journal, 44 Congress, 2 Session,** p. 470.

[98] Ibid.; see also Rhodes, **History of the United States,** VII, pp. 339-340.

March 4; they especially desired to impress their intention on the Republicans in power and the President-elect, Hayes. The filibuster was helped by an article in the *Ohio State Journal,* February 22, whose editor, General Comely, was a friend of Hayes. The following statement was objectionable to the Southerners:

> The late civil war was termed in the South the 'Yankee Radical War', and when reconstruction was inaugurated it was, in the eyes of this Southern Democracy, the organization of a Radical party on the sacred soil of the South—in their very midst! It was commenced again, only in a different form, and has continued with gore but not glory for the Republicans in the South, until now our party in the States, though in some of them outnumbering the enemy, has gone down in defeat.[99]

Although Governor Young promptly repudiated the article for Hayes and the editor, and said it did not reflect Hayes's ideas, nevertheless, its publication probably strengthened the filibuster.[100]

In view of the rapidly moving events, the Southern Congressmen became anxious to know what would be the policy of Hayes with regard to the Southern States—would he support the carpet-bag governors with Federal troops, or would he withdraw the troops? An arrangement was worked out by the Democrats and representatives of Hayes and an understanding was reached which allowed the count to proceed.[101] The steps by which this understanding was reached were somewhat complicated. Congressman Charles Foster, a life long friend of Hayes, made a speech February 20, in which he indicated the policy Hayes might adopt toward the South. Congressman Lamar of Mississippi told Congressman Ellis

---

[99] **House Miscellaneous Documents, 45 Congress, 3 Session,** No. 31, Louisiana, pp. 598-601 (reprinted in this House Document from the original paper).
[100] **Ibid.,** p. 617.
[101] Fleming, **The Sequel of Appomattox,** p. 301.

of Louisiana that Foster had consulted Matthews, a brother-in-law of Hayes, before he made the speech and therefore revealed the true policy of Hayes toward Louisiana, namely, that Hayes would have nothing to do with Packard.[102] The Louisianians desired more tangible assurance, but could not agree to send Ellis to Hayes. A chance meeting of Matthews, Dennison, Sherman, Burke, and Ellis gave Sherman an opportunity to request an interview, which was granted. The conference took place behind locked doors in the Finance Committee Room. Burke, as spokesman for Louisiana Democrats, desired friends of Hayes to assure Grant that the removal of troops from Louisiana would not embarrass Hayes, but Sherman objected to this on the ground that Grant could not be influenced. Burke stated that Grant had, in conversation that very morning, suggested that it would be wise to let the Nicholls government prevail, as the sentiment of the country was clearly against further use of troops in Louisiana. Grant had continued that he would not interfere with the Nicholls government unless some violent act was committed, and further, that he had failed to remove the troops for fear of embarrassing his successor.[103] This was sufficient to convince the Republicans, and they agreed to see President Grant the next day and urge him to withdraw the troops from Louisiana. They assured the Louisianians that Nicholls would get Federal support when Hayes was inaugurated, and that Kellogg would not be installed. In return, Burke promised that the long-term Senator would not be chosen before March 10, thus allowing the cabinet of Hayes to be confirmed before the Louisiana Senator took office. The postponement

---

[102] **House Miscellaneous Documents, 45 Congress, 3 Session,** No. 31, Washington, p. 973.

[103] **House Miscellaneous Documents, 45 Congress, 3 Session,** No. 31, p. 618.

of the senatorial election would necessitate a special session of the state legislature.[104]

In order to prevent a misunderstanding, a meeting was arranged for the men representing Nicholls and those representing Hayes. This meeting known as the Wormley Conference, was held the same night. Messrs. Burke, Ellis, and Watterson went to Mr. Evart's room at the Wormley Hotel and found Messrs. Matthews, Garfield, Sherman, Dennison, and Foster. Burke explained that the filibuster holding up the electoral count was due to Hayes's failure to clarify his Southern policy. Whereupon, Matthews replied that Mr. Hayes was tired of the rule and plunder going on in the Southern states and had no use for the carpet-bag leaders, and their bayonet rule. He then produced a letter from Hayes to Foster thanking him for his speech of February 20. The statement of Mr. Matthews was concurred in by Messrs. Dennison, Foster, and Sherman.[105] The meeting ended after Matthews outlined a practical way of starving out Packard's government, and Burke read a statement embodying what he had told Matthews, February 18.

Burke telegraphed the terms of the agreement to General Nicholls and requested that same be ratified by legislative caucus; which was done the next day. Burke stated to the Associated Press:

> It is ascertained that satisfactory guarantees have been given assuring the permanent establishment of the Nicholls government.[106]

Congressman Levy of Louisiana made a speech in the House on March 1, advising his friends to end the filibuster:

> The people of Louisiana have solemn, earnest, and, I believe, truthful assurances from prominent members of

---

[104] House Miscellaneous Documents, 45 Congress, 3 Session, No. 31, pp. 619-620.
[105] Ibid., p. 596.
[106] Ibid., p. 623.

the Republican party high in Mr. Hayes's confidence that he will be guided by a policy of conciliation toward the Southern States and that he will not use Federal authority or the army to maintain government not desired by the people.[107]

Hayes displayed wisdom and discretion in making no public statement of his policy. It was believed Hayes had a high regard for Southern character, thought the most intelligent citizens should rule the country, and was sincere in what he said in his letter accepting the nomination.[108] Bishop Wilmer interviewed Hayes while the filibuster was delaying the electoral count and concluded that peace was not to be disturbed in Louisiana.[109]

Grant assured Burke, Levy, and Ellis on February 28, that he would withdraw the troops as soon as the electoral count was completed, and would so inform Darrell and Kellogg. They understood that the War Department would send immediately the military order to use the troops to protect life and property from mob violence only. Secretary of War Cameron was peeved that the agents had ignored him in going directly to President Grant, and the Republican loss of the two senators from Louisiana did not help his feelings. Hence, he caused the instructions embodied in the so-called Sniffen telegram to be held in the telegraph office at Washington.[110]

Around four o'clock on the morning of March 2, the electoral count was completed. President Ferry called for

---

[107] Record, 44 Congress, 2 Session, p. 2047.
[108] House Miscellaneous Documents, 45 Congress, 3 Session, No. 31 Washington, p. 880.
[109] House Reports, 45 Congress, 3 Session, No. 31, Louisiana, p. 617.
[110] House Miscellaneous Documents, 43 Congress, 3 Session, No. 31, Washington, p. 890. The Sniffen telegram dated March 1, was sent by Sherman to General Augur in Louisiana about noon, March 2, (Sniffen was secretary to President Grant and Sherman was the general of the army).

THE RETURNING BOARD 85

order and announced Hayes was elected President of the United States by the electoral vote of 185 to 184.[111]

Mr. Hayes was duly inaugurated President and was confronted with the vexing problem of what to do with the political situation in Louisiana. The President shifted to a commission the question of recognizing the government of Nicholls without jeopardizing the validity of his own election.[112] The commission was sent to Louisiana to find a way to get a legal government out of the two rival factions. The solution of the baffling problem will be told in the following chapter.

---

[111] House Journal, 44 Congress, 2 Session, p. 357.
[112] Annual Cyclopedia, 1877, p. 457. See Daily Picayune, March 22, 1877; and Rhodes, History of the United States, VII, p. 352. It is interesting to know that the Louisiana Republican electors received good political jobs after they delivered Louisiana to the Republican party; O. H. Brewster was appointed surveyor-general of the land office for Louisiana; M. Marks was made district-attorney for the 4th judicial district of Louisiana; J. H. Burch was appointed member of the Board of Control of the Deaf and Dumb Asylum; Oscar Joffrion was made supervisor of registration for Pointe Coupee; A. B. Levissee became a commissioner for the Circuit Court of the United States for the District of Louisiana on November 7, 1877. For this information see In the Matter of the Count of the Electoral Votes of Louisiana, 1877; and Rhodes, History of the United States, VII, pp. 353-354 (footnote).

CHAPTER IV.

DUAL GOVERNMENT

BY the latter part of December there were rumors in Louisiana that a compromise on the election was pending,[1] and the people became more excited as the time for the legislature to convene drew near. The members-elect of the senate and house reached New Orleans a week before the legal time for organization of the general assembly. The Democrats met from day to day to discuss the situation and agree upon a line of policy, but it was apparent that there were as many diverse and conflicting plans as there were speakers.[2] The Republicans, likewise, were arriving early. They began barricading the State House, in evidence of an expected conflict.[3] The populace, as well as the politicians, were watching and waiting to see what Monday, January 1, 1877, would bring to the troubled political situation.[4] Governor Kellogg ordered two hundred armed policemen and militia to occupy the State House and admit no one to the legislative hall, except those with certificates of election from the Returning Board. The result was that nineteen senators and sixty-eight representatives—all Republicans, were allowed to enter; eight of the senators were holdovers and the remaining eleven senators and all representatives held certificates of election from the Returning Board.[5] The constitution of Louisiana provided for a legislature of thirty-six senators and one hundred and twenty representatives. The Republican representatives

---

[1] New Orleans Times, December 28, 1876.
[2] Newspaper clipping in Scrapbook at Ridgefield, July, 1932.
[3] New Orleans Times, December 26, 1876.
[4] Ibid., December 31, 1876.
[5] Annual Cyclopedia, 1876, p. 492.

passed into the chamber through the speaker's room, since all other doors were barred, and the door to the speaker's room was locked as soon as all were in. The chief clerk, Mr. P. J. Trezevant, was the legally constituted person to call the roll of the house members, but he refused to call the roll unless the militia was withdrawn and the doors unbarred.[6]

Mr. Trezevant met with the Democratic-Conservative body at St. Patrick's Hall and reported his experience at the State House. He announced that he had come "in an endeavor to organize the house of representatives."[7] The assembly at St. Patrick's Hall consisted of twenty-one senators and sixty-two representatives. Nine of the senators had held over; eight had been declared elected by the Returning Board; and four claimed to have been elected and held certificates to that effect from the Democratic Committee on Returns. Forty of the representatives held official certificates, while the remaining twenty-two were without such credentials.[8] The St. Patrick's Hall body elected Louis Bush speaker of the house, and Louis A. Wiltz president of the senate.

Each of these assemblies claimed to be the legal legislature of the state, and to have a quorum of members lawfully elected, and each protested against the existence of the other. The State House assembly declared Packard and Antoine elected, whereas the St. Patrick's Hall body declared Nicholls and Wiltz elected.[9] The St. Patrick's Hall legislature created a Board of Canvassers to canvass and compile the vote for the other officers. This board was composed of the lieutenant-governor, speaker of the house, and three senators to be chosen by the senate from different political parties.[10]

---

[6] New Orleans Times, January 2, 1877.
[7] Ibid., January 2, 1877.
[8] Journal of the House of Representatives, 1877, pp. 4-13. See Annual Cyclopedia, 1876, p. 493.
[9] New Orleans Times, January 3-4, 1877. Daily Picayune, January 3-4, 1877. New Orleans Republican, January 3-4, 1877.
[10] New Orleans Times, January 8, 1877.

Before the Democratic legislature settled down to business, Speaker Bush led the representatives to the State House and demanded entrance thereto, and the removal of the police and militia from its vicinity. When these demands were refused, the representatives returned to St. Patrick's Hall where Speaker Bush read a formal protest against the executive usurping the rights of the legislature, and against United States troops and Metropolitan police occupying the State House.[11]

Governor Kellogg's message to the State House assembly gave an account of his stewardship of the past four years. He stated that the total state debt was $45,183,907 when he became governor, and he had reduced the interest-bearing debt to $11,855,922; and state taxes had been reduced from twenty-one and one-half mills to fourteen and one-half mills on the dollar.[12] He pointed out helpful financial amendments to the constitution during his administration and claimed the rural section was better off economically than New Orleans, attributing this condition to political manipulation in New Orleans by the Conservatives who occupied the official positions in the city.[13]

The Republican legislature desired protection and a bill appropriating $200,000 for paying the state militia was hastened through all three stages in one day. The governor was

---

[11] New Orleans *Times*, January 2, 1877. The Senate appointed Senators Boutner, Stephens, and Garland to call on Governor Kellogg for any message, and to protest against five companies of the United States troops near the State House. Boutner and Garland were arrested, and Antoine ordered Stephens to be kept in the Republican senate as he held a Returning Board certificate.

[12] New Orleans *Times*, January 2, 1877. Governor Kellogg failed to say the total state debt of $45,183,907 in 1873 was composed of a bonded and floating debt of $24,093,407 with contingent liabilities of $21,090,500. He gave the interest-bearing debt of 1877, as $11,855,922 and said nothing of contingent liabilities.

[13] New Orleans **Republican**, January 3, 1877.

empowered to take over all the state buildings and to maintain peace and order in their vicinity; all seats in the house of representatives not occupied by January 6 were to be declared vacant.

The Democratic-Conservative legislature moved to Odd Fellows Hall,[14] January 4, and proceeded to declare that Democratic government was destroyed by the Returning Board and Federal troops. The Democratic body proclaimed itself the legal government, and called on the people, both whites and negroes, to stand by and support it with their taxes and strength, and to wait patiently for a better day.[15] They knew they had the moral and material support of the people of the state, and wished to avoid any violence while they put their government into shape.[16] It was reported that the capitalists of New Orleans were backing Nicholls to the extent of $100,000 and that the financial committee of each branch of the People's legislature was ready to furnish another $100,000. This amount was judged to be sufficient to finance the People's government until the contest over the Presidency was settled at Washington.[17]

Each faction perfected plans for the inauguration of its governor. Some days previously Kellogg had barricaded every door to the State House except one, and at this door was stationed a staff officer and a detachment of police for the purpose of admitting only legislators with proper credentials.[18] Barricades with holes for the use of rifles were erected on the porch of the State House facing St. Louis and Royal

---

[14] Daily Picayune, January 5, 1877.
[15] Journal of the House of Representatives, 1877, pp. 11-12. Also Daily Picayune, January 4, 1877.
[16] Opelousas Courier, January 6, 1877. The New Orleans Republican, January 6, 1877, stated the New Orleans Exchange, the heads of the insurance companies, commercial organizations, and all great monopolies were for Nicholls.
[17] New Orleans Times, January 7, 1877.
[18] New Orleans Evening Democrat, January 6, 1877.

streets.[19] Packard and Antoine[20] were inaugurated governor and lieutenant-governor, respectively, behind closed doors at the State House January 8. The inaugural address of Packard contrasted the present with four years previously and dealt with Republican principles and progress, Federal protection, domestic policy, schools, immigration, and municipal affairs. Packard defended the legality of his election and promised peace and harmony through a wise enforcement of the laws.

Kellogg had telegraphed President Grant requesting Federal troops for the inauguration, but the President replied that he did not propose to interfere with the two inaugurations as he had no evidence to justify the recognition of either faction. He would await the reports of the Congressional Committees engaged in investigating all the facts of the late election.[21] A large crowd surrounded the State House on the day of Packard's inauguration; some glass was broken and other petty acts committed that annoyed the Republicans. The besieged Republicans became hungry and efforts were made to take baskets of food into the building, but some boys took possession of the baskets and the crowd applauded. The people did not disperse until nightfall after Nicholls had ordered them to retire to their homes.[22]

A committee arranged for the inauguration of Nicholls and Wiltz at St. Patrick's Hall, and the assembly adjourned at noon to witness the ceremony.[23] A delegation of citizens

---

[19] New Orleans Times, January 9, 1877.
[20] Daily Picayune; New Orleans Times; and New Orleans Republican, January 9, 1877, carry accounts of the inauguration. See also Annual Cyclopedia, 1876, p. 493. The State House was also known as the St. Louis Hotel. It had been used as the Capitol for a number of years. Packard had occupied it since the first of January.
[21] New Orleans Times, January 8, 1877.
[22] New Orleans Times, and Daily Picayune, January 9, 1877.
[23] Daily Picayune, and New Orleans Times, January 8, 1877.

called for Nicholls and Wiltz at their hotel to escort them to their carriage, but the enthusiasm of the people became so great that the horses were unhitched and the vehicle was drawn by human hands up Camp Street to St. Patrick's Hall, Ten thousand people were gathered in Lafayette Square when the band played "Hail to the Chief". The inauguration took place on the balcony of St. Patrick's Hall facing Lafayette Square. The balcony was draped in flags of all the liberal governments of the world, and surmounted by the United States flag. Senators Robertson and Penn, and General Beauregard escorted the governor and lieutenant-governor to their seats. Special seats were reserved for the members of the clergy and bar. Cannon in the square belched forth roaring congratulations; the Reverend Dr. Palmer offered prayer; the lieutenant-governor took the oath of office, and Mr. Ogden, president of the senate, introduced General Nicholls. Judge Tissot administered the oath of office,[24] and Governor Nicholls delivered an address composed of glittering generalities phrased to impress the nation with his righteousness:

> Self must be sunk, and the general good alone serve as the guide to the civil and political action of each citizen. Laws operating equally upon the whole people, without distinction to race, color, or condition, must alone be found on the statute books, and these laws should be thoroughly, fairly and impartially executed ... The first object of all government is to secure peace, plenty and prosperity, and to give the largest possible opportunity for development to the individual citizen. His interest should be its constant aim and the citizen should recognize and feel the government only through its beneficent and vivifying influence.

---

[24] New Orleans Times and Daily Picayune, January 9, 1877; Chambers, History of Louisiana, I, p. 693. Packard was inaugurated behind closed doors, hence there was little for the people to become excited over. They had an opportunity to display their pent-up feelings at the Nicholls inauguration.

> I shall devote every energy to the great work of restoration, and to securing an efficient administration of public affairs, with the least possible cost to those upon whom the burdens of state rest. Honesty and capacity will be required as absolute conditions to appointment, and every avenue by which the people can be injured will be carefully guarded to the extent of the legal power of the executive.[25]

Newspaper comment was laudatory. The *Times* characterized the speech as

> wise in its brevity, energy, and freedom from anger. Its freedom from mere party resentment combined with its strong and just declarations of right and duty and purpose have greatly strengthened his cause as the rightful Governor of the State.[26]

The *Republican* took note of the large crowd at Lafayette Square to see General Nicholls take an oath of office as governor and said the General

> had his address prepared and delivered it feelingly, after which his friends saluted him in the most friendly manner.[27]

The *Evening Democrat* said everybody was happy at the inauguration of Nicholls. Even an inebriated man was happy to be the first man arrested by the Nicholls police, and proclaimed his happiness over the honor of being the first incumbent of the Nicholls jail.[28] Nicholls issued a proclamation the next day cautioning against collecting in crowds and advising the people to be careful.[29]

---

[25] New Orleans **Times**, January 9, 1877, and Daily **Picayune** of the same date. The inaugural address was also printed in pamphlet form.
[26] New Orleans **Times**, editorial, January 9, 1877.
[27] New Orleans **Republican**, January 9, 1877.
[28] New Orleans **Evening Democrat**, January 9, 1877.
[29] **Messages and Proclamations of Governor Nicholls**, p. 2; Daily **Picayune**, January 10, 1877.

Executive Department,
New Orleans, January 9, 1877

To the People of Louisiana—

I would be most profoundly surprised and disappointed should any citizen of Louisiana, at this moment so far forget himself as to be guilty of any excess whatsoever. There is danger in collecting together in large bodies. I urge upon you, therefore, to retire at once peacefully to your homes.

The greater the wrongs to which you have been subjected, the greater to your credit should you recognize and recollect your own simple and plain duty, as citizens.

Let no one be injured, however obnoxious he may be and let the people of the whole country see that we are law abiding, just, and moderate.

Francis T. Nicholls,
Governor of the State of
Louisiana.

The day following his inauguration, Nicholls went to his office in Odd Fellows Hall at an early hour to set in motion his plan of action. The strategy of the plan was to get a *de facto* state government fully organized with all three branches in operation and at the same time to avoid doing anything offensive which would alarm the Republican leaders at Washington and cause them to interfere actively in behalf of Kellogg.[30] Governor Nicholls reached his decision after listening to many counselors, but he told few people of his proposed strategy. His reticence caused some newspaper criticism, because a few editors thought the public should know the policy of the administration. But secrecy was essential for success.[31]

---

[30] "An Autobiography of Francis T. Nicholls, 1834-1881," edited by Barnes F. Lathrop, **Louisiana Historical Quarterly**, XVII, pp. 254-255. The autobiography was a letter from Nicholls to his brother-in-law, William W. Pugh, October 8, 1881. The letter is important because Governor Nicholls gives his plans and motives.
[31] **Ibid.**, pp. 260-261.

Governor Nicholls appointed a new Supreme Court because the terms of the judges of the old court had expired and Packard had not reappointed them at that time. The failure to appoint a new court and get the judges confirmed by the senate might have been a capital blunder in the Republican programme.[32] Governor Nicholls regarded the installation of the Supreme Court as the pivot upon which his government would turn, for it was necessary to complete the three departments of government. He saw that the possession of the Supreme Court building and the records were essential to the success of the Democratic cause. Furthermore, he believed the National Republican party would not consider the court buildings essential to the Packard adherents.[33] Consequently, his first act was to nominate five Justices of the Supreme Court which the senate approved. He also appointed an Adjutant General and the Board of Commissioners of the Metropolitan Police.[34]

Upon instruction from Governor Nicholls, the Crescent City White League was ordered to report at dawn, January 9, by General Ogden, the commander. Accordingly, men of all ages, armed and determined, met at Masonic Hall and their plans were kept in secrecy—even from their wives. The marching of armed men gave the city a martial appearance by ten o'clock of the forenoon. The members of the White League were enrolled in the state militia, and were formally sworn in as they reached Lafayette Square.[35] The

---

[32] "An Autobiography of Francis T. Nicholls," **Louisiana Historical Quarterly**, XVII, p. 260.
[33] Ibid., p. 255.
[34] **Messages and Proclamations of Governor Nicholls**, January 8, 1877. The Supreme Court was: T. C. Manning, Chief Justice, and the following associate justices, R. H. Marr, W. B. Eagan, A. DeBlanc, W. B. Spencer. The Adjutant General was D. B. Penn; the Metropolitan Police Commissioners were H. C. Miller, E. Tobbe, G. Dupre, S. Chopin, and A. Brewster.
[35] New Orleans **Times**, January 10, 1877.

armed men were well disciplined and their intention to fight, if necessary, was so well known and appreciated that the force at the Supreme Court building surrendered without a blow. The Conservatives in a short time had possession of all the other court rooms in the parish, the police stations, and the state arsenal. The new Supreme Court judges took their places immediately and issued orders for the information of the bar, the very day it took office, as follows: (1) all cases heard and not determined by the late Supreme Court, prior to December 24, shall be called for trial and argument in regular order on the docket; (2) counsel for parties with interest in cases heretofore submitted to the previous court and which have been reassigned for trial under the order of January 9, 1877, will be required to file briefs as provided by the seventh rule of the court; (3) petitions for rehearing before the old court will be considered by the present court.[36] The judges of the lower courts were installed with little disturbance.

All movements were carried out with care and forethought in order to avoid, if possible, the precipitation of a conflict. The Peoples' Police (new Metropolitan Police) left Masonic Hall at 10:30 a. m. to patrol the city under the new Board of Metropolitan Police Commissioners. When the armed patrolmen moved toward the State House, much excitement was created, and the police within the building lined up in the corridors with Winchester rifles. A hundred or more colored militia formed in line over the St. Louis Street entrance. Not far away, troops of the United Staes army were ready for action on a moment's notice.[37] The Democrats meant to hold what they had, but did not desire a conflict, and therefore withdrew from the environs of the State House. All this was accomplished with a minimum of disturbance

---

[36] New Orleans Times, January 10, 1877.
[37] New Orleans Times; Daily Picayune; and New Orleans Republican, all of January 10, 1877, give a similar account of the movement.

and without bloodshed. The amazing fact was that all commercial houses continued their daily routine of business.[38] By nightfall Packard held only the State House (St. Louis Hotel). Many people, pleased with the success, began a clamor for Nicholls to seize the State House and disperse the Packard legislature by armed force. Nicholls refused this demand because he did not believe it was essential that he have possession of the State House but declared,

> I did believe that possession of that building by the Packardites would be deemed by the (Federal) government essential or very important for the National Republican Party .... I felt that it would be risky to attempt to take the building (State House) for the General Government would probably go to the rescue & if it once interfered *at all* it would interfere in the matter of the Court buildings also & *in the whole case*.[39]

This attitude of irresolution was condemned but Nicholls explained:

> I was resolved to take all risks *essential* to *our* success but to attempt nothing which being non essential to us would be or might be considered by the federal government as essential to the National Republican Party.[40]

The President had said he did not intend to recognize either government until all the facts were ascertained and had so instructed General Augur.[41]

---

[38] New Orleans Times, January 10, 1877.
[39] "An Autobiography of Francis T. Nicholls," **Louisiana Historical Quarterly**, XVII, pp. 255-256.
[40] Ibid., p. 255.
[41] Daily Picayune, and New Orleans Times, January 11, 1877. President Grant impressed Messrs. Levy, Gibson, and Ellis as unusually courteous and friendly. The telegram to Augur was:

        War Department, January 10, 1877.
Gen. C. C. Augur, New Orleans, La.

 It is reported that the State House in New Orleans is surrounded by a mob.

DUAL GOVERNMENT

The supporters of Packard weakened as soon as they realized they were besieged in the State House. One colored man said:

> I ain't fur Packard no more. He is too skeery. Ain't he just said he was gwine to execute de law and put down bull-dozers. Is dis de way he's gwine ter do it?[42]

The garrison, guarding the State House, said if their hard tack was the best food the Packard government could give them it was weak indeed, and a legislator commented that the government could not last on hard tack.[43] The garrison, weakened in morale, was ready to negotiate with agents of the Democratic government. The Radical press sought to strengthen the morale by condemning the Nicholls police. Such headlines as "Biennial Rising of the White League" and "The State House in a State of Siege" were found in the papers.[44] The Kellogg-Packard group used

---

If this is so, notify all persons to disperse and compel compliance with your order. It is the determination of the President to see that the Legislature is not molested. When he has full knowledge of all the facts in the premises he will decide which should be recognized.

J. D. Cameron, Secretary of War.

The Daily Picayune, January 16, 1877, says the Supreme Court room was legally in the possession and custody of the Civil Sheriff, T. C. Handy, of Orleans parish, and held by his deputies. Packard sent 75 armed men, January 6, to eject the deputy sheriffs from the building. Packard's force held the building until January 9, when the militia helped Sheriff Handy regain possession of the court building. The New Orleans Times, January 9, 1877, says Sheriff Handy refused to recognize the legality of the Packard Supreme Court headed by Ludeling and the court suspended him from office and appointed Alfred Bourges civil sheriff **pro tempore**.

[42] Scrapbook at Ridgefield. Article headed, "The Kellogg Government Mysteriously Disappears." The New Orleans Times, January 10, 1877, reported a number of the members of the Republican legislature wished to get out of the building to join the Democratic legislature.
[43] Ibid.
[44] New Orleans **Republican**, January 13, 1877.

every means to get President Grant to recognize it, for without the support of Federal authorities, the cause was lost, and it was feared Nicholls would possess New Orleans and the entire state within a short time.[45]

General Augur in an exchange of telegrams with Secretary of War Cameron on January 9 and 10, ascertained the exact intent of his instructions.[46] Governor Nicholls gave assurance that he had given strict orders to prevent any disturbance,[47] after which General Augur confined his efforts to preserving the *status quo* and to preventing disturbance. He requested a written statement from Packard that he would respect the President's wishes; Packard complied with the request, asserted the legality of his position, and stated that "the wrongs committed in the last eight days will be set right." Packard gave the letter to the press before it was received by Augur who gave him a stinging rebuke for this discourtesy.[48]

Although President Grant telegraphed General Augur, that his policy was to take no part in settling the question of the rightful governor of Louisiana, a later message added:

> But it is not proper to sit quietly by and see the state government gradually taken possession of by one of the Claimants for gubernatorial honors by legal means . . . Should there be a necessity for the recognition of either it must be Packard.[49]

The attitude of the President in this telegram was surprising and disappointing to the Democrats for it condemned

---

[45] House Miscellaneous Documents, 45 Congress, 3 Session, No. 31, Louisiana, pp. 603-604.
[46] See footnote 41 of this chapter for copy of one of these telegrams.
[47] New Orleans Times, January 11, 1877.
[48] Annual Cyclopedia, 1877, p. 456.
[49] House Miscellaneous Documents, 45 Congress, 3 Session, No. 31 Washington, p. 962, and New Orleans Times, January 14, 1877.

the Supreme Court set up by Nicholls. A special telegram from the Louisiana delegation in Washington was encouraging; it stated the President's instructions to Augur were believed to be for the purpose of preventing desertions from the Republican legislature as the collapse of the Republican government in Louisiana at that time would destroy the claim of Hayes to the presidency. Grant in an interview reiterated his determination not to favor either governor until the committees then in Louisiana made their report.[50]

The President's telegram of January 14 caused Packard to renew his demand for Nicholls to get out, the Democratic legislature to disband, the court buildings and police stations to be turned over to his agents. Packard wired the President that the Democrats not only refused his demand, but that the White League gathered in force "prepared to resist any attempt to compel obedience to state authorities."[51] The Packard lieutenants could not raise a force sufficient to combat the White Leaguers, but Zach Chandler advised Packard to create a disturbance so as to involve Federal troops, even if he had to die in the streets. General Augur threatened to use the troops against Packard if he ventured beyond his domain of the St. Louis Hotel.[52] Packard's position seemed to be weakening and a New England Republican senator was reported as saying:

> People were getting tired of backing governments that could not stand alone without bayonets.[53]

Every influence possible was brought to bear on President Grant to induce him to change his policy.[54] It was re-

---

[50] New Orleans Times, January 16, 1877, and Daily Picayune, January 15, 1877.
[51] New Orleans Republican and Daily Picayune, January 16 and 17, 1877.
[52] Daily Picayune, January 16, 1877.
[53] New Orleans Times, January 18, 1877.
[54] Ibid., January 13, 1877.

ported that Mr. Casey, a brother-in-law of the President, was influential in shaping the Louisiana policy.[55] Some thought General Weitzel, a classmate of Governor Nicholls, advised President Grant of the lofty character, truthfulness, and fearless courage of Nicholls, and that this advice helped to influence the *status quo* policy.[56] Miss Lonn says:

> a high officer of the United States army kept the Nicholls party informed of all that transpired in the Packard camp. Every night, at two o'clock, this officer visited the Nicholls headquarters at the City Hotel and supplied complete accounts of all that had transpired during the day at the opposite stronghold. It is not likely that this was done without the knowledge and approval of the authorities in Washington.[57]

Mr. R. L. Gibson informed Nicholls from Washington that Packard would not be recognized, but stressed the necessity of maintaining peace and order. He said if Hayes should become president, the Democratic legislature would have to elect two Hayes men to the United States Senate in order to obtain the recognition of Nicholls, and that he had made such a promise.[58]

Nicholls was especially anxious to hold his forces together and adopted a conciliatory policy. The adjournment

---

[55] New Orleans Times, January 18 and 26, 1877. Mr. Casey was disappointed because the carpet-bag legislature of Louisiana did not elect him to the United States Senate. It was said he took revenge on the Louisiana Republicans through an active interest in the affairs of the Nicholls administration.

[56] Scrapbook (no date on clipping) at Ridgefield. Article headed, "Nicholls". Read July, 1932.

[57] Lonn, Reconstruction in Louisiana after 1868, pp. 520-521; Chambers, History of Louisiana, I, p. 693, states there was an understanding between Nicholls and Grant and attributes it to their friendship of army days before 1857. Chambers believed that Grant promised not to disturb the Nicholls government, provided it would do nothing to hinder Hayes from becoming President of the United States.

[58] Telegram, Gibson to Nicholls, January 25, 1877.

of his legislature would have been disastrous and in order to hold it together concessions were made but no principles were violated. He offered the Republicans, who would join his legislature, the same consideration as that given the Democratic legislators. The Republicans who came over were allowed a minor amount of the patronage because Nicholls believed that,

> it is *better* to have *a few bad* appointments and to make them than by failing to make them to bring about or perpetuate a condition of things where the power of appointment would be lodged in hands where *all* the appointments would be bad.[59]

This action was further justified on the ground that it enured to the public good and was necessary.

The strength of Nicholls was steadily augmented; the City of New Orleans, January 16, formally recognized his government;[60] the clergy and business men of the city declared their sympathy for it; mass meetings endorsed it; even Republican office-holders and Republican parishes fell in line. The Democratic government of far away Indiana sent a message strongly endorsing Nicholls. The First District Court decided against a Returning Board Commission and in favor of the district attorney commissioned by Nicholls.[61] Mr. G. T. Ellis, who had been counted in as Judge of Catahoula parish, returned his commission to Kellogg stating the pay of the office was not great enough for him to accept a position to which he had not been elected.[62] Governor Nicholls, on January 11, issued commissions to eight officials of Ouachita

---

[59] "An Autobiography of Francis T. Nicholls," **Louisiana Historical Quarterly**, XVII, pp. 261-263.
[60] J. S. Kendall, **History of New Orleans**, I, p. 99. Mr. Kendall gives the ordinance number as 3816 A. S.
[61] **Annual Cyclopedia, 1877**, p. 455. Also New Orleans **Times**, January 13 and 19, 1877.
[62] New Orleans **Times**, January 10, 1877.

parish before President Grant requested that no further changes be made. The officials took office without disturbance and the President allowed them to retain their positions; but a short time later he reversed this attitude and decided against Democratic officials in Natchitoches parish.[63] Many Democrats in Washington thought it wise for the Conservative legislature to elect Casey to the United States Senate. They believed Casey, with the help of his wife and Mrs. Grant, could control the President and prevent Packard's recognition and probably secure that of Nicholls.[64] The Packard legislature, January 11, elected Kellogg to the long term of the United States Senate.[65] The senate lacked a quorum which caused some to doubt whether the United States Senate would seat Kellogg. Article 33 of the Constitution of Louisiana provided that

> not less than a majority of the members of each House of the General Assembly shall form a quorum to transact business, but a smaller number may adjourn from day to day, and shall have full power to compel the attendance of the absent members.[66]

The Packard legislature was divided into factions, and a number threatened to leave the body if it did not grant their desires. Pinchback desired to be elected to the short term of the United States Senate.[67] Two colored members, Demas and Wheeler, wrote to Governor Nicholls:

> will you maintain the equality of all men before the law, and use the influence of your administration to advance

---

[63] **House Miscellaneous Documents, 45 Congress, 3 Session, No. 31,** Louisiana, p. 609.
[64] **Special Telegram,** January 12, published in New Orleans **Times,** January 13, 1877.
[65] New Orleans **Republican,** January 11, 1877.
[66] New Orleans **Times,** January 26, 1877.
[67] **Ibid.,** January 13, 1877.

DUAL GOVERNMENT

the educational, political and material interests and rights of the colored people, and protect them in the exercise of the rights guaranteed them by the recent amendments to the Constitution of the United States, and the laws in pursuance thereof?[68]

They promised to join the Democratic legislature and to recognize Nicholls as governor if he answered in the affirmative. Nicholls replied favorably and the two came over to his legislature and were sworn in. They were accompanied by Pinchback who was permitted to address the Democratic senate. The previous day a Republican caucus decided to send General Badger and some Packard policemen to Pinchback's home to prevent him from joining the Democratic legislature. Pinchback drove them away with threats and appealed to the Metropolitan Police for protection, thereby recognizing the police under Boylan.[69] Other desertions occurred[70] until both houses of the Republican legislature were without a quorum,[71] and the dissatisfaction was more than political. Packard had promised his police $80.00 per month,[72] but it was reported that he paid them less than half this amount,[73] and the members of the legislature demanded pay when funds were not available.[74] Pinchback in his speech to the Democratic senate spoke of the Packard assembly in these words:

> For corruption and venality, for dishonesty, it has not its equal anywhere on the face of God's earth ... When

---

[68] Daily Picayune and New Orleans Times, January 14, 1877.
[69] Daily Picayune, January 13, 1877. Boylan was Chief of Police appointed by Nicholls.
[70] Daily Picayune and New Orleans Times, January 13 to 20, 1877.
[71] New Orleans Times, January 21, 1877.
[72] Ibid., January 12, 1877.
[73] Ibid., January 22, 1877. A news article stated they were paid $13.00 for a month's wages on January 21.
[74] Ibid., January 24, 1877.

I saw in the pretended House of the Representatives, two monster rings demanding prices for every vote, this thing is too corrupt for me to stand it any longer. I tell you that there can be passed in that body today, no bill, no law, and no measure without bribe.[75]

Pinchback had bribed Anderson and three other radical senators to desert the Packard body January 10, in order to break the quorum and void the election of Kellogg as United States Senator. In spite of this lack of a quorum Kellogg was eventually seated by the Senate. The Packard senate never had a quorum after January 10; therefore, no legislation could be enacted thereafter.[76] The Packard house of representatives at one time had sixty-eight members, all of whom held Returning Board certificates, and forty of them were negroes. The members were not allowed to leave the St. Louis Hotel after January 10, because Packard feared they would desert and join the Nicholls legislature.[77] The New Orleans *Republican* printed no journal of the Packard senate after January 14, and concentrated its efforts on propaganda for the house. However, both houses pretended to engage in legislative activities until March 1, when they adjourned *sine die*.

A reporter made his way into the St. Louis Hotel, past a file of unkempt and dispirited policemen, and described the scene as deplorable. The second floor was covered with rubbish and garbage; the air was filled with smoke and the odor of whiskey; groups of dirty and unkempt policemen were

---

[75] New Orleans **Republican**, January 15, 1877. Pinchback was making a revenge speech because the Packard legislature elected Kellogg to the United States Senate, instead of himself. It should not be taken too seriously. Yet, the charges of corruption and bribery are substantiated by other evidence.

[76] **House Miscellaneous Documents, 45 Congress, 3 Session, No. 31,** Louisiana, pp. 225-226.

[77] **Journal of the House of Representatives, 1877,** pp. 17-18.

playing cards or lounging on the floor of the upper rooms; and a small number were on guard immediately within the Royal Street entrance and at the head of the stairs.[78]

The legislature of Nicholls always had a quorum numerically, and announced its program in a "Declaration and Appeal" to the people of the United States. The program promised peace, free education, honesty, reduction of expenses of government and the public debt, and closed with an appeal in behalf of local self-government.[79] Nicholls knew that financial support was absolutely necessary for him to contest his election successfully. A scheme was worked out on January 2, and a large committee of citizens cooperated in collecting five per cent of the state taxes and licenses in advance for the support of the Nicholls government.[80] The taxpayers responded in a surprising manner paying 25 per cent and even 50 per cent of their taxes in advance. After two days the committee reported to the president of the senate and the speaker of the house that funds were available for their use.[81]

Reform was the order of the day, and the first bill reported proposed abolishing the Returning Board and the substitution of a Board of Canvassers, composed of the lieutenant-governor, speaker of the house, and three senators elected by the senate from different parties.[82] One measure was designed to reduce the cost of canceling bonds, and another attempted to secure better management of charitable institutions. Many of the undesirable laws of 1869 and 1870 were

---

[78] New Orleans Times, January 12, 1877, and New Orleans Picayune, January 13, 1877.
[79] **Annual Cyclopedia,** 1877, p. 458.
[80] Daily Picayune, January 3, 1877; New Orleans Times, January 3, 1877.
[81] **Journal of the House of Representatives, 1877,** p. 16.
[82] **Acts of the Legislature of the State of Louisiana, 1877.**

repealed; salaries were fixed on a reasonable scale; and penalties were remitted for delinquent taxes paid by December 1.[83]

Nicholls sent E. A. Burke to Washington as his personal agent to persuade the Federal government that his government was the legal one. Burke was to ascertain what demands would be made upon the governor and legislature, and to inform Nicholls of all occurrences that might affect the interests of his state government; his further duties were to present the condition and interests of Louisiana in the best way possible, and to confer and cooperate with the leaders of the National Democratic party in Washington.[84] Burke was to work with the Louisiana congressmen, Ellis, Gibson, and Levy, but they were not to barter away the National Democratic cause to save Louisiana.[85] Ellis had interviewed President Grant about fifty times from December to February, and perceived a decided change in the attitude of the President.[86] He was vague and non-committal at first, and then became so interested that he suggested the program for the Conservatives to follow in establishing the Nicholls government.

The policy of non-interference was certainly a definite break with the former attitude of the President, and the change was shown in the telegram of January 7, which refused Kellogg's request for troops. Burke believed Grant was convinced by the eighth of January the Packard government should not stand, but the President had to maintain the

---

[83] Acts of the Legislature of the State of Louisiana, 1877.
[84] House Miscellaneous Documents, 45 Congress, 3 Session, No. 31, Washington, p. 1009.
[85] "An Autobiography of Francis T. Nicholls," Louisiana Historical Quarterly, XVII, p. 256.
[86] The conciliatory attitude of the President was noted in the preceding chapter of this study. See footnote 103.

status quo in order to prevent the Republican government in Louisiana from collapsing before the inauguration of Hayes.[87]

Burke left for Washington, January 15, and had his first interview with Grant, January 20. He was in constant communication with Nicholls from that time, reporting every detail and giving advice. Nicholls was aware that the Republicans of Louisiana were misrepresenting affairs to the President.[88] He also knew that the President was peeved at them because they had not elected his brother-in-law, Casey, to the United States Senate. Nevertheless, Burke and his associates had little peace of mind during January and February because party considerations might come before personal feelings and cause a change of policy; so they made every effort to get the Federal troops withdrawn from Louisiana before President-elect Hayes sent his cabinet nominations to the Senate.[89]

Packard contended that the appointment of officials by Nicholls, even without disturbance, was contrary to the President's orders. This question and the right of appeal to the district courts were presented to President Grant who replied that there must be no change. The Louisiana delegation believed the Federal officials were determined to uphold Hayes and inaugurate him at all costs.[90] President Grant ruled January 24, that when both governors commissioned the same man he should assume office; when one commission was issued and no contest was raised by the incumbent and no charge of intimidation was made, that man should take office; when the governors commissioned different parties, the old

---

[87] House Miscellaneous Documents, 45 Congress, 3 Session, No. 31, Washington, pp. 1009-1013.
[88] Ibid., Washington, pp. 1009-1013.
[89] Ibid., p. 1016.
[90] Ibid., Louisiana, p. 605.

incumbent should hold over.[91] Grant was much concerned over the necessity of Louisiana's remaining peaceful and let Burke know how embarrassing it would be to the President if violence should occur. He even suggested how Nicholls might collect taxes without infringing on the *status quo* — that is, collect the taxes without the President's knowing about it.[92]

The college friendship of Congressman R. L. Gibson of Louisiana and Secretary of War Cameron made it easy for Gibson to present the facts concerning Louisiana which almost convinced Cameron that Nicholls should be allowed to remain as governor, and it also paved the way for Burke to show Cameron a legal way to sustain Nicholls, even though the electoral vote went for Hayes. Burke cited the law giving the legislature the sole right to count the vote for governor and lieutenant-governor, despite the fact the Returning Board could and did pass on the Presidential electors.[93] It was proposed that Nicholls and the legislature sign a memorial, embodying the facts and the law, whereby a bill or resolution of Congress could separate those questions, and at the same time be consistent in recognizing Nicholls. The leaders in Louisiana did not thoroughly understand the proposition, and believed it would appear that they were deserting the National Democratic party; hence the question was dropped. Burke showed his unwillingness to abandon Tilden early in February when he met Senator Matthews who was acting with Dennison as counsel for the Republicans. Matthews in the conversation with Burke hinted that Louisiana should understand the views of Hayes, and Burke casually replied that it might be necessary to confer on the subject.

---

[91] **House Miscellaneous Documents, 45 Congress, 3 Session,** No. 31, Louisiana, pp. 608-609.
[92] **Ibid.,** p. 599.
[93] Ibid., Washington, p. 1014.

DUAL GOVERNMENT 109

The Wormley Hotel Conference, described in the preceding chapter, resulted from this remark.

An incident occurred on February 15, which seems to have been planned to gain the sympathy of Northern Republicans, since Packard felt his fortunes were waning at Washington. A young man named Weldon made his way into Packard's office and attempted to assassinate him. It was reported that he fired point-blank at Packard's head at close range, yet the bullet grazed the skin on the kneecap. A guard shot Weldon in the left arm and captured him.[94] The Republicans charged the Democrats with responsibility for the attempted assassination.[95] The *Times* and *Picayune* pointed out that there was something strange about the shooting, since the coroner, representatives of the press and all outsiders were forbidden to see Weldon, and only Republicans in the St. Louis Hotel saw the purported wound of Packard until weeks later.[96] Packard not only attempted to make political capital of the shooting, but four months later, he made a trip North to receive sympathy for his lost cause by displaying his wound.[97]

Several incidents alarmed the city. The greatest of these occurred when two Italians were caught taking eight kegs, each containing twenty-five pounds of gunpowder, into a cabaret adjoining the State Supreme Court building. It was thought at first that this was an attempt to blow up the Supreme Court building.[98] There was some inclination to accuse the Republicans of being the instigators of the plot; but apparently the two men had bought their powder in small lots and rented a storage room for use until they had con-

---
[94] New Orleans **Republican**, February 15, 1877.
[95] Ibid., February 16, 1877.
[96] New Orleans **Times**, February 16, 17, and March 15, 1877; Daily **Picayune**, February 16, 1877.
[97] New Orleans **Times**, June 17, 1877.
[98] **Ibid.**, March 7, 1877.

centrated enough for a shipment to Mexico.[99] The populace appeared nervous and excitable when a soldier was found dead at the military stables, but all attempts to give it any political connection failed.[100]

During the early days of January, about four hundred people were shut up in the State House, but the number had dwindled to one hundred and fifty by March 4, and it was truly claimed the Nicholls government was recognized everywhere except the square of ground on which the State House stood. Packard had under his control and in the possession of his officers the great seal of the state, the archives and records of the offices of secretary of state, attorney-general, auditor, treasurer, superintendent of public education, and of the land office.[101] In April it was reported that only one hundred and sixty-eight appointive and two hundred thirty-four elective officers recognized Packard, while twelve hundred fifty-five of the thirteen hundred twenty-two elected officials outside Orleans parish recognized the legality of the Nicholls government.[102]

Packard telegraphed President Grant on March 1, requesting the recognition of his government, and asked the President not to withdraw the United States forces after the electoral vote had been announced. He asserted withdrawal of the troops would turn the state over to Nicholls and his armed White League. The President's secretary answered the same day saying:

> The President directs me to say that he feels it his duty to state frankly that he does not believe public sentiment will longer support the maintenance of State government in Louisiana by the use of the military, and that he must concur in this manifest feeling.

---

[99] New Orleans Times, March 8 and 9, 1877.
[100] Ibid., March 14, 1877.
[101] Ibid., March 5, 1877.
[102] Ibid., April 22, 1877.

DUAL GOVERNMENT 111

The telegram stated that the President would not recognize either claimant, and the troops would be used to protect life and property from mob violence.[103]

It appears that President Grant issued an order about noon, March 2, to withdraw the troops from Louisiana,[104] and the order was not submitted to Secretary of War Cameron but to General Sherman who sent it to the adjutant general for delivery. Cameron was angry because Grant ignored him, and had the order held in the telegraph office, which in turn incensed the President.[105]

Meanwhile the members of the Democratic-Conservative party in Louisiana were conducting themselves in a manner designed to win the favor of President Grant. A joint session was held each day after January 9, to ballot for a United States Senator, because the Louisiana delegation in Washington advised such action until Nicholls was recognized.[106] They induced the President to remove District Attorney Beckwith upon representations that no peace could exist in the state while Mr. Beckwith continued to hold office.[107] Governor Nicholls issued a proclamation to the people of Louisiana, March 2, enjoining them to maintain peace, observe the law, and respect the rights of all persons. He said the situation at the moment demanded, "more than ever, the

---

[103] **House Miscellaneous Documents, 45 Congress, 3 Session,** No. 31, Washington, 104; New Orleans **Times,** March 3, 1877; New Orleans **Republican,** March 4, 1877.
[104] New Orleans **Times,** August 3, 1877. Col. Levy said the President showed him a draft of the order.
[105] **Ibid.,** March 3, 1877. Cameron was quoted as saying, "Damn the President and Sherman, too. I am either Secretary of War or I am not. Grant, who is an old soldier, ought to have known better than to do a thing which is a deliberate insult to me."
[106] Files of the New Orleans papers for the period show a joint ballot was taken each day for United States Senator.
[107] New Orleans **Times,** March 3, 1877.

exercise of combined firmness, moderation, and devotion to principle."[108]

The regular session of the legislature expired on March 1, because of legal limitation, but Governor Nicholls thought the condition of public affairs required an extra session of the general assembly.[109] He, therefore, issued a proclamation, February 28, calling a special session to meet March 2; the session was limited to fifteen days and was to consider among other things the questions of: "education, revenue, appropriations, levees, elections, registration, city and parochial affairs, and election of United States Senators."[110] The understanding with Hayes had included the postponement of electing United States Senators until Hayes was well established in office, and the extra session was necessary for this, if nothing else. The choice of a Senator was more difficult than at first anticipated because it was not until April 24, that Judge Spofford was elected for the long term,[111] and the Honorable J. B. Eustis was chosen for the short term.[112] The time of the extra session was extended beyond the original fifteen-day limit and adjournment *sine die* did not come until April 26. The legislature had been in session since January 1, one of the longest legislative sessions in the history of the state up to that time.[113]

---

[108] **Messages and Proclamations of Governor Nicholls,** March 2, 1877; **Annual Cyclopedia, 1877,** p. 457. This proclamation was issued because Burke, Gibson, Ellis, and Levy telegraphed Nicholls, March 2, that President Grant desired Nicholls to issue such a proclamation at once urging "protection, amnesty, and peace." See **House Miscellaneous Documents, 45, Congress, 3 Session,** No. 31, p. 1041.

[109] **Messages and Proclamations of Governor Ncholls,** February 28, 1877.

[110] **Official Journal of the House of Representatives of Louisiana, Extra Session, 1877.** Packard issued a call for an extra session of his legislature also.

[111] Daily **Picayune,** April 26, 1877; New Orleans **Times,** April 25, 1877.

[112] Opelousas **Courier,** April 28, 1877.

[113] Daily **Picayune,** April 27, 1877; New Orleans **Times,** April 27, 1877.

DUAL GOVERNMENT 113

The people of Louisiana trusted their leaders and those leaders had such assurances "from prominent members of the Republican party, high in the confidence of Mr. Hayes," that they could afford to wait for results.[114] The Southern Congressmen were satisfied with the inaugural address of President Hayes, but the carpet-bag delegates were disappointed because it failed to endorse them. The editor of the *Times* said:

> Compared with the crude messages usually presented by his predecessor it is a creditable State paper and carries the impression of a broad and intelligent grasp of the subjects commented on.[115]

Hayes did not remove the troops from Louisiana immediately after taking office, which occasioned some uneasiness. Although the *Picayune* announced early that no compromise was desired, [116] the report spread that the President planned such a solution for the Louisiana situation.[117] During the weeks of waiting, many rumors were prevalent concerning the removal of troops.[118] To please the people, Attorney-General Ogden of the Nicholls government filed a petition for a writ of ejection against Packard, Johnson (auditor), Brown (superintendent of education), and others residing in the St. Louis Hotel.[119] About one hundred fifty citizens, including bankers, insurance men, cotton factors, merchants of all classes and representative men in general, sent a telegram to President Hayes on March 15, endorsing the legislature of Nicholls and approving the President's declared Southern

---

[114] New Orleans Times, March 27, 1877, quoted from a speech of Congressman Levy in the House of Representatives March 1; See New Orleans Times, March 21, 1877.
[115] Ibid., March 6, 1877.
[116] Daily Picayune, March 9, 1877.
[117] Ibid., March 26, 1877.
[118] New Orlean Times, March 18, 1877.
[119] Ibid., March 20, 1877.

policy. The dispatch stated that the only government in the state was the one headed by Nicholls; it urged the withdrawal of the military forces; and promised that the protection of life, liberty, and property would result if that government were recognized.[120] In reply to this appeal, President Hayes issued a statement that he understood why the people of Louisiana were anxious that their matters should be settled, but he was unable to give his attention until the necessary routine duties of his office were over, and that he would take up this question as soon as the Senate adjourned.[121] A few days later, the press announced the Cabinet unanimously approved the Southern policy of the President, and that a special session of the Cabinet would be held to devise means for putting the policy into effect.[122]

Numerous letters were written to the President by private individuals giving their views of the Louisiana question. A good example was the letter of Mr. Henry Ware who wrote that the Republicans were convinced Nicholls was elected and that they intended to sustain him in enforcing the law and protecting equally the rights of all citizens, for

> Mr. Packard could not as governor of this state protect the interest of all citizens without the aid of the United States forces in many places, and to keep the state government backed up by troops would result in trouble and confusion.[123]

A sugar planter wrote the President of the suffering in Louisiana and stated that extreme politicians on both sides had over-stated the issues between the factions.[124] The historian, Charles Gayarre, also approved the President's Louis-

---

[120] Daily Picayune, March 17, 1877.
[121] New Orleans Times, March 17, 1877.
[122] Ibid., March 21, 1877.
[123] Hayes Memorial Library, Film No. 259.
[124] Hayes Memorial Library, Film No. 258. The letter was dated March 31, 1877.

DUAL GOVERNMENT

iana policy.[125] The reports and appeals coming from various sources in Louisiana must have been confusing to the President, because the white Republicans of New Orleans issued an appeal March 15, to the people of the United States in which they charged the White League Democracy with intimidation, violence, outrages, and murders in the different parts of the state.[126]

Governor Nicholls issued a proclamation March 24, thanking the people for their loyalty and aid on January 9, and requesting financial support:

> The state government being now complete in all its branches, and in full performance of all its functions, it becomes the duty of the people of Louisiana to promptly discharge their pecuniary obligations to it, in order that all just claims against it may be punctually met . . . The people of Louisiana may rest confidently assured that the government of which they have chosen me the executive head will not be imperilled or impaired by any compromise of their rights.[127]

Packard issued a proclamation two days later in which he denied the allegations of Governor Nicholls, and claimed the legality of his authority was recognized and supported by a large part of the people and the local authorities outside New Orleans.[128] The members of the New Orleans Cotton Exchange sent a telegram to Washington in which they denied Packard's claim that merchants and business men of the city endorsed him. The message stated:

> that F. T. Nicholls is recognized and obeyed as the lawful governor of this state by nine-tenths of the honest, in-

---

[125] Hayes Memorial Library. Letter dated April 22, 1877.
[126] Annual Cyclopedia, 1877, p. 459.
[127] Ibid., p. 460; **Messages and Proclamations of Governor Nicholls,** March 24, 1877.
[128] Annual Cyclopedia, 1877. p. 460.

telligent, taxpaying classes of the state, and by a large numerical majority of its citizens without distinction of race or color.[129]

The citizens of New Orleans sent a petition to the President in which they professed loyalty to the Union but desired local self-government.[130] The people of New Orleans were aroused sufficiently to hold a great mass meeting at Lafayette Square, April 6.[131] The people of Shreveport thus stated their position:

> The rights of the people as expressed at the ballot box are too sacred for compromise, and we will have the government chosen by the people, or force a military government . . . Francis T. Nicholls has been elected governor of Louisiana and we pledge to his support our lives, our fortunes, and our sacred honor.[132]

The administration at Washington had been considering its course for some time.[133] The objective was a withdrawal of military interference without precipitating an outbreak of violence that would necessitate intervention again. Vice-President Wheeler was sent to the South to observe the result of the President's Southern policy, and his report[134] prompted the decision to send a commission to New Orleans which would represent the President unofficially, but which would nevertheless, endeavor to carry out his purposes. The Louisiana delegation in Washington opposed the appointment of the commission [135] as illegal, unconstitutional, and injurious to every interest of the state.[136] The Louisiana delegation,

---

[129] New Orleans Times, March 24, 1877.
[130] Ibid., March 28, 1877.
[131] Daily Picayune, April 6, 1877; New Orleans Times, April 6, 1877.
[132] Opelousas Courier, March 21, 1877, quoted from New Orleans Democrat, which in turn had quoted from the Shreveport Times.
[133] New Orleans Times, March 8, 1877.
[134] Ibid., March 14, 1877.
[135] Daily Picayune, March 22, 1877.
[136] Ibid., March 24, 1877.

however, gave up the idea of protesting to the President against the commission and were well pleased with its personnel when it was appointed.[137]

The instructions for the guidance of the commission were drawn up by the Secretary of State on April 2. They mentioned the military intervention under Grant, but stated the only present duty of the President was

> to examine and determine the real extent, form, and effect, to which such intervention actually exists, and to decide as to the time, manner, and conditions, which should be observed in putting an end to it.[138]

The commission was not to examine, or report upon the facts of the recent election, or of the canvass of votes at that election, but to ascertain the

> real impediments to the regular, legal, peaceful procedures under the laws and Constitution of the State of Louisiana, by which the anomalies in the Government there presented may be put in the course of settlement, without involving the element of military power as either an agent or a make weight in such a solution.

The instructions went on to say that the President desired the commission to devote its main attention to a removal of the obstacles to an acknowledgment of one government for purposes of an exercise of authority within the state in its relations to the Federal government, leaving to the judicial or other constitutional arbitrament within the state the question of ultimate right. If it was impossible to set up a single government in all its departments, then the commission

---

[137] New Orleans Times, March 28, 1877; Daily Picayune, March 28, 1877. It was appointed March 28, and consisted of: J. R. Hawley, (Conn.), C. B. Lawrence, (Ill.), J. M. Harlan, (Ky.), Ex-Governor J. C. Brown, Tenn.), Wayne McVeigh, (Penn.). Brown was the only Democrat on the Commission.
[138] Annual Cyclopedia, 1877, p. 460.

should secure the recognition of a single legislature representing the will of the people.

The commission reached New Orleans, April 5,; the next day it visited the Cotton Exchange, saw the twenty thousand Democratic voters in mass meeting at Lafayette Square, and held conferences with Nicholls and Packard.[139] Each of the two gentlemen claiming to be the governor was asked, "What do you demand of the National Government? What are your reasons for making this demand?"[140] The mass meeting welcomed the commission, protested loyalty to the Federal government, denounced Packard, praised Nicholls, and gave warning that no compromise infringing the rights of the people would be accepted.[141]

President Hayes was faced with the difficult problem of recognizing Nicholls without repudiating the electoral vote that made himself President, and the commission was devised to act as a shock absorber. Packard wrote the President asking if the inquiry would be limited to, "How Nicholls can be sustained and Packard stoned to death."[142] and later, in an open letter, he protested against the instructions to the commission for omitting the following questions:

(1) Which is the legal government entitled to recognition?
(2) Which is the legal judiciary?
(3) Do domestic violence and insurrection prevail within the meaning of section 4, article 4, of the Constitution of the United States?[143]

The Republicans accused the Democrats of taking and holding their position with a standing army, and such a policy was reported to have convinced the commission "That the

---

[139] New Orleans Times, April 7, 1877.
[140] Ibid., April 8, 1877.
[141] Annual Cyclopedia, 1877, p. 461.
[142] New Orleans Times, April 5, 1877.
[143] New Orleans Republican, April 7, 1877.

law and facts of the case are with Packard, but the actual possession and the power to maintain it are with Nicholls."[144]

The legislature endorsed the policy of the President on April 16, and believed it would bring the people of Louisiana harmony, happiness, and prosperity. It pledged the government headed by Francis T. Nicholls to accept in good faith the Thirteenth, Fourteenth, and Fifteenth Amendments to the Constitution of the United States; the rigid and impartial enforcement of the law; the promotion of kindly feelings between the white and colored citizens of the state; a free and equal school system; and promised not to persecute individuals for past political conduct.[145] The legislative resolutions were handed to the commission accompanied by a letter from Governor Nicholls in which he endorsed the resolutions and pledged his government to carry them into effect. He also stated that the withdrawal of the United States troops to their barracks would be the source of profound gratification to the people, and would be accepted as proof of the confidence of the President in their capacity for orderly self-government.[146] This letter created a good impression over the nation.[147]

The commission in its report to the President, April 21, gave the following picture of affairs on its arrival in New Orleans:

> Governor Packard was at the State House with his legislature and friends, and an armed police force. As there

---
[144] New Orleans Republican, April 14, 1877.
[145] Annual Cyclopedia, 1877, p. 461; Daily Picayune, April 17, 1877.
[146] Messages and Proclamations of Governor Nicholls, April 18, 1877; Annual Cyclopedia, 1877, p. 461; Senate Reports, 45 Congress, 3 Session, No. 855, p. 606; New Orleans Republican, April 21, 1877.
[147] New Orleans Times, April 20, 1877. Governor Nicholls said he made no bargains and that President Hayes recognized him because the President feared the consequences if the Louisiana question was not settled. See "An Autobiography of Francis T. Nicholls," Louisiana Historical Quarterly, XVII, pp. 263-264.

was no quorum in the Senate even upon his own theory of law, his legislature was necessarily inactive. The Supreme Court, which recognized his authority, had not attempted to transact any business since it was dispossessed of its courtroom and custody of its records, on the 9th day of January, 1877. He had no organized militia, alleging that his deficiency in that respect was owing to his obedience to the orders of President Grant to take no steps to change the relative position of himself and Governor Nicholls.

Governor Nicholls was occupying the Odd Fellows Hall as a State House. His legislature met there, and was actively engaged in the business of legislation. All the departments of the city government of New Orleans recognized his authority. The Supreme Court nominated by him and confirmed by his Senate was holding daily sessions, and had heard about two hundred cases. The time for the collection of taxes had not arrived, but a considerable sum of money in the form of taxes had been voluntarily paid into his treasury, out of which he was defraying the ordinary expenses of the State Government.[148]

The report proceeded to give the legal basis upon which each faction claimed authority. No attempt was made to say who was the lawful governor. The commission, as previously stated, exerted itself to procure a legislature with a constitutional quorum in both senate and house of representatives

---

[148] Daily **Picayune**, April 21, 1877; **Annual Cyclopedia, 1877**, pp. 463-464. The new legislature of Nicholls had 62 Democrats and 57 Republicans in the House of Representatives, and 20 Democrats and 16 Republicans in the Senate, giving the Democrats a majority of 9 on a joint ballot. The New Orleans **Times**, April 22, 1877, stated the commission reported 1,225 of the 1,322 elected officials outside the parish of Orleans recognized Nicholls. This included 16 of the 18 district judges and 47 of the 56 parish judges who were for Nicholls. 46 parish clerks out of 51; 48 parish recorders out of 51; and 46 parish surveyors were for Nicholls. All the 56 district attorneys and the 56 tax collectors; 205 of the 249 police jurors; 323 of the 396 justices of the peace; 301 of the 387 constables supported Nicholls.

whose title to their seats was valid. It recommended the withdrawal of Federal troops, leaving the legislature of the people to work out a solution of the legal entanglement.

Hayes was criticised before he withdrew the troops because many of his friends had grown impatient. Congressman Brown of Kentucky published in the Louisville *Courier-Journal* on March 28, the written guarantees of Foster and Matthews to him, and asked President Hayes to carry out his promises and the assurances of his friends. The same day Congressman Ellis, of Louisiana, published his recollections of the agreement. Mr. E. A. Burke of Louisiana came to the aid of the President with a published statement that the original agreement was to be kept a secret, unless the terms were violated, and he declared President Hayes had not yet violated his agreement.[149]

The object of the commission had been effected by April 20, as the legislature of Nicholls had an undisputed quorum for many members of the Packard legislature had joined it.[150] The same day President Hayes directed Secretary of War, George W. McCrary, to see that proper orders were issued for the removal of Federal troops to their regular barracks by noon April 24. The next day General Sherman ordered General Sheridan to remove the troops, and Sheridan transmitted the order to General Augur, commanding the troops at New Orleans.[151]

---

[149] House Reports, 45 Congress, 3 Session, No. 140, p. 114.

[150] **Annual Cyclopedia, 1877**, p. 462; New Orleans **Times**, April 20-21, 1877. The Nicholls legislature now contained sixty-five Returning Board members in the house and twenty-two in the senate.

[151] General Sherman was commanding the army and General Sheridan was in command of the Division with headquarters at St. Louis. April 24 was the fifteenth anniversary of the taking of New Orleans by Federal troops.

The President's instructions were carried out and the Federal troops were withdrawn to their barracks April 24, and Packard evacuated the State House. The next day officials of the Nicholls government took formal possession of the St. Louis Hotel.[152] The people in rural Louisiana expressed their joy by ringing bells, making music, and firing salutes,[153] while the Democrats of New Orleans proposed a torchlight procession as a form of celebration.[154]

---

[152] Daily **Picayune,** April 26, 1877.
[153] New Orleans **Times,** April 24, 1877; Daily **Picayune,** April 25, 1877.
[154] New Orleans **Times, April 27, 1877.**

CHAPTER V.

THE TRIUMPH OF NICHOLLS

THE withdrawal of the troops left Packard as meek as a lamb, because his handful of so-called legislators had disbanded three days previously. When Mr. Matthews wrote Packard on February 27, that as soon as the Federal troops were removed Nicholls would be governor, but that Packard "should receive consideration and position in some appreciable way," Packard replied that he would remain as governor though the effort cost him his life. He considered that devotion would be a better heritage to leave his children than the plaudits of the White League of the state, when gained by a surrender of both manhood and duty.[1] The most energy that Packard put forth at the crucial moment was to issue an address to the Republicans of Louisiana in which he reviewed the events since January 1, advised them to maintain the party organization, and criticised the work of the President's commission.[2]

Money was used to get the Packard legislators to go over to Nicholls. It was said that when they transferred to Nicholls they received eight dollars per day dating from January 1, and it was alleged $15,000 was used to bribe the

---

[1] New Orleans **Times**, March 16, 1877. Packard's letter of reply was dated March 14, 1877. Packard was taken care of as promised and he chose the Consulate at Liverpool in preference to the collectorship of the port of New Orleans. The Packard Supreme Court was destroyed by offering one of the judges a collectorship, and another was given hope of a judgeship in an international court in Egypt. These offers destroyed the quorum of the court.
[2] Daily **Picayune**, April 26, 1877; **Annual Cyclopedia, 1877**, p. 465; New Orleans **Times**, April 26, 1877.

leaders. The new legislature at the request of the commission appropriated $50,000 to pay the Packard legislators and policemen,[3] and allowed Packard to have a voice in apportioning the funds among his force.[4] A few Democrats did not favor the measure but their leaders had agreed to it when refusal would have been detrimental to their cause.

When the Packard group evacuated the State House, they left the building in the most filthy condition imaginable; it required several days to prepare the building for occupation. They also left about two hundred stands of arms stacked in good order, in addition to many guns scattered over the building with locks missing, stocks sawed off, and other forms of mutilation.[5]

Governor Nicholls was a very devout man and it was fitting that he should set May 10 as a day of "solemn thanksgiving to Almighty God for the political redemption of the state and for all the blessings consequent upon that consumation."[6] In his proclamation he invited all the good people of the state to abstain from labor and to repair to their accustomed places of worship for thanksgiving, and to ask for Divine guidance. Governor Nicholls desired to forget past dissension and bitterness in order for all to unite in the fulfillment of a common and happy destiny.[7] The day was generally observed over the state, and the *Times,* said it was Louisiana's Jubilee of Deliverance.[8] The people in rural sec-

---

[3] Daily **Picayune**, April 25, 1877; New Orleans **Times**, April 22 and 23, 1877.
[4] New Orleans **Times**, April 29, and May 3, 1877. The settlement gave $23,000 to 592 suppporters of Packard. Employees of the house and senate of Packard were to receive from $20.00 to $70.00. Each policeman was to receive $34.85, and the police officers $90.00 each.
[5] New Orleans **Times**, April 26, 1877.
[6] Daily **Picayune**, May 10, 1877.
[7] Thanksgivng Proclamation of Governor Nicholls, issued April 28, 1877, see **Messages and Proclamations of Governor Nicholls, 1877.**
[8] New Orleans **Times**, May 11, 1877.

tions were reported to have observed the day with much rejoicing.⁹

The demand for political jobs caused Governor Nicholls much concern and it was reported in March that he had on file 9,000 applications for office. No less than three hundred forty-six lobbyists were seeking the office of harbor master at New Orleans.¹⁰ This scramble for office indicated that many of the Democrats were more interested in the spoils of office than in freeing Louisiana of bad government. The editor of the *Times* appeared much concerned, as he believed the demand for office would destroy all the benefits derived from the government of the people. He wrote:

> Things are known to those who keep up with the progress of the inside negotiations which would hardly be believed. Propositions are made by patriots, who shout their loyalty to Conservatism, as the Pharisee did his prayers on the corners of the streets, that make us wonder if Judas Iscariot was not after all a rather good sort of citizen.¹¹

The success of the administration of Nicholls would depend in a large measure upon its ability to correct known abuses. The same editor philosophized that the curse of all great cities was organized political rings that managed to have a powerful voice in public affairs. Half the seven hundred men on the New Orleans police force were to be dismissed, yet twenty-five hundred people were applying for jobs as policemen.¹² No person could have pleased all political rings and job seekers for the simple reason that there were not enough jobs to go around. The facts indicate that Nicholls intended to carry out the pledge he made in accepting the

---

⁹ The Opelousas Courier, May 19, 1877. A detailed description was given of the rejoicing in St. Landry parish.
¹⁰ New Orleans Times, March 15, 1877.
¹¹ Ibid., April 24, 1877.
¹² Ibid., April 28, May 5, and May 11, 1877.

nomination, when he said honesty and ability to perform the duties of the office would be the qualifications for appointment to office. The city friends of Lieutenant-Governor Wiltz claimed he was the one responsible for establishing Governor Nicholls in office, and were indignant that he received no recognition. This feeling of resentment over failure to receive political favors drove a wedge between the governor and lieutenant-governor and led to a break between them before their term of office was ended. Clubs were already formed that would develop into straightout political organizations later. The Native Americans claimed six hundred members at the time, and a combination of the "straightout Democrats" and colored men was being talked.[13]

In addition to the state and city job seekers, there was a host of aspirants to the Federal jobs which were expected to go to Republicans.[14] President Hayes, however, had decided to appoint no one to a Federal office of importance in Louisiana who came to the state after the war. For instance, although Casey claimed that Hayes promised him the collectorship at New Orleans for another four years, King, of Packard's supreme court, received the position and took over the duties May 16.[15] President Hayes asked for the resignation of the United States Marshall, Pitkin, and when he refused the President replaced him.[16]

King, the new collector of customs at New Orleans, had his own ideas of how to perform his duties, and they did not coincide with those of Anderson who got him appointed.[17] King was appointed, but was never confirmed by the Senate.

---

[13] New Orleans Times, May 2, 1877. The writer believes Nicholls was too honest and too good an Episcopalian to please the gambling politicians, who when they learned of this, decided to break with the governor.
[14] New Orleans Times, April 27, 1877.
[15] Ibid., May 1 and 17, 1877.
[16] Ibid., May 15, 22, and 30, 1877.
[17] Ibid., July 2, 1877.

THE TRIUMPH OF NICHOLLS

By August, the Louisiana Republican leaders were in Washington endeavoring to have King removed, because no fewer than four of them desired the job themselves.[18] The President did not propose another man for the collectorship at New Orleans until January, 1878, at which time he nominated George Williamson.[19] The Senate rejected Williamson and left President Hayes in a quandary over the appointment. Eventually an agreement was reached between the Senate and President Hayes, and George L. Smith was made collector at New Orleans.[20]

Likewise, all was not harmony among the Democratic leaders, some of whom could see little value in the victory of Democracy if they were not to monopolize its laurels and its spoils. On the other hand, supporters of Governor Nicholls believed that he was free from that restless egotism and small personal ambition which made Louisiana politics a hotbed of intrigue for the advancement of little men. One paper expressed it thus:

> There can be no fear of a personal government under a man who has throughout his life subordinated his own interests to those of the public and who has never once sought leadership except at the call of duty.[21]

The opposition to Nicholls was due in some instances to envious politicians who thought more of themselves than they did the promotion of the prosperity of the state or the preservation of their party.[22] It must be remembered that a number of Republicans had joined the Democratic party in 1872. Because Nicholls objected to these men assuming leadership and sought to keep them in the rear, he was accused

---
[18] New Orleans Times, August 21, October 3, 16, 23, and November 9, 1877.
[19] Ibid., January 17, 1878.
[20] Ibid., January 26, February 22, May 3 and 7, 1878.
[21] Scrapbook at Ridgefield, the Nicholls home, read July, 1932.
[22] Ibid.

of disrupting the Democratic party. The breach, which was visible early in the spring, had become wider by July. The rural press was proclaiming that there was no Nicholls or anti-Nicholls party, but that a clique of schemers without political theories or principles was trying to tell Governor Nicholls what to do. These schemers had found the governor resolute, conscientious, and incorruptible, striving to protect the public interest and preserve the honor of the commonwealth.[23] The city press declared the opposition was the work of a New Orleans political ring which had extended its influence through both branches of the legislature, but that the popularity of Nicholls was as strong in the country as it was January 9.[24]

In analyzing Louisiana Democracy, it was pointed out that many young men had never voted until after the war, and to them Democracy meant resistance to Federal aggressiveness and Returning Board despotism. They never perceived that an era of justice and reform would begin with the overthrow of the Republican party in the state.[25] They were trained in opposition technique but were not prepared for constructive cooperation in government.

The grand jury of Orleans parish June 27, recommended that the court instruct the district attorney to file information against the members of the Returning Board "for perjury, forgery, and altering returns of the parish of Vernon and other parishes of the state." The information was filed July 5, and the accused, when arraigned, pleaded not guilty. They were arrested and brought to trial in January, 1878.[26] Governor Nicholls denounced the indictment of the Return-

---

[23] Opelousas **Courier**, July 21, 1877.
[24] New Orleans Times, July 8, 1877.
[25] Daily **Picayune**, July 3, 1878.
[26] Annual Cyclopedia, 1877, p. 466; New Orleans **Times**, June 28, July 1, and 17, 1877; Daily **Picayune**, July 6, 1877.

ing Board as a violation of the spirit and intention of the solemn compact of the general assembly, which read in part:

> Desirous of healing the dissensions that have disturbed the state for years past, and anxious that the citizens of all political parties may be free from the feverish anxieties of political strife and join hands in honestly restoring the prosperity of Louisiana, the Nicholls government will discountenance any attempted persecution, from any quarter, of individuals for past political conduct. [27]

It was obvious that the ring was trying to trap the governor as he felt himself honor bound to pardon the Returning Board if they were convicted. The pardon could be made an impeachment issue. Three state officials had gone so far as to urge the governor to write a letter to the grand jury requesting it to cease further investigation of the Returning Board. Happily, the governor had no desire to go on record as attempting to usurp the power of the judiciary.[28] Some thought this move was to set the stage for the next campaign.[29]

The indictment of the Louisiana Returning Board for perjury irritated President Hayes because he regarded the Matthews-Foster bargain as covering such matters, just as did Governor Nicholls. Mr. Wells wrote the President asking him to interfere in the matter of his indictment, and the letter was presented at a cabinet meeting. The cabinet felt the Federal government should not interfere, and was of the opinion that Nicholls realized the indictments were contrary to the spirit of the agreement by which matters in Louisiana were settled and that he would bring about an abandonment of the prosecution.[30] A few Republicans were really jubilant

---

[27] Daily Picayune, July 11, 1877.
[28] New Orleans Times, July 8, and 18, 1877. Judge Whitaker denied having any designs against the Governor and knew of no political plot.
[29] Ibid., July 9, 1877.
[30] Ibid., July 4, 5, and 8, 1877.

over the indictment of the Returning Board. Blaine thought the action proved that the Southern people could not be trusted, and friends of Kellogg thought it would enable Blaine to influence enough Senators to reject Spofford and seat Kellogg.[31] After a lengthy contest between these two men, the Senate seated Kellogg.[32]

The four members of the Returning Board—Anderson, Casanave, Kenner, and Wells—filed into the Superior Criminal Court at New Orleans on January 18, 1878, to answer the charge that they feloniously forged and altered the returns of the election of 1876; they pleaded not guilty, and were released on bond.[33] When the time came for trial, they defied the law and the sheriff by hiding in the United States Custom House in New Orleans. The United States Marshal arrested the sheriff when he attempted to enter the Custom House to get them. The Custom House was guarded by United States Marines, and Sheriff Houston created considerable excitement when he showed his determination to take the Returning Board by force, before a truce was called pend-

---

[31] New Orleans Times, July 11 and 12, 1877.

[32] Ouachita Telegraph, November 2, 1877; New Orleans Times, October 19, 21, 25, November 2, December 2 and 11, 1877; Daily Picayune, December 1 and 11, 1877. Kellogg was seated by the vote of 30 to 28. Eustis, Democrat, was admitted to the United States Senate for the short term by the vote of 49 to 8. His term expired March 4, 1879. Kellogg's term was to run until March 4, 1883.

[33] Ouachita Telegraph, January 25, 1878; New Orleans Times, January 19, 1878. The specific charge was that after the election of November 7, 1876, they "feloniously forged the returns from Vernon Parish by adding 178 votes to those received by Wm. P. Kellogg and the seven other Hayes electors and deducting 395 votes from those received by Robert M. Wickliffe and the other seven Tilden electors, and then uttered as true said forged returns." See, State vs. Anderson, **30 Louisiana Annual Repports, p. 557.**

ing advice from Washington.³⁴ It was reported the President was going to investigate the action of the United States District Attorney in advising the United States Marshal not to allow the sheriff to serve the process of the state court on the Returning Board, and the President desired to know who ordered the United States Marines to the Custom House.³⁵ Anderson, Casanave, and Kenner were soon taken into custody and appeared in court with their counsel, but Wells escaped and was not taken until February 3.³⁶ In the meantime, it was erroneously reported that Wells was in Washington demanding protection at home, or a position abroad.³⁷

The jury selected to try the Returning Board was composed of ten whites and two negroes, all Democrats, and the prosecution decided to try Anderson first.³⁸ Anderson applied for a change of venue and when it was denied, the Board applied to the United States Supreme Court for a writ of prohibition upon the Louisiana state court, but it was refused also.³⁹ President Hayes decided it did not behoove him to interfere in the trial of the Returning Board, but he was disturbed over the report that the employees of the New Orleans Custom House were assessed to pay the attorneys for the Returning Board trial.⁴⁰ The jury deliberated forty minutes before it returned a verdict of "guilty" against Anderson⁴¹

---

³⁴ New Orleans Times, January 27, 1878. The United States Custom House officials were adjudged in contempt of court and were not released from the charge until February 15, 1878. See New Orleans Times, February 16, 1878.
³⁵ Ibid., January 31, 1878.
³⁶ Ibid., January 29, 1878.
³⁷ Ibid., February 2 and 4, 1878. J. M. Wells was arrested at Rigolets, Louisiana, and the report that he was in Washington was incorrect.
³⁸ Ibid., January 30 and 31, 1878.
³⁹ Ibid., February 2, 1878.
⁴⁰ Ibid., February 5, 1878.
⁴¹ Daily Picayune, February 8, 1878; New Orleans Times, February 8, 1878; Ouachita Telegraph, February 15, 1878.

"and recommended him to the mercy of the court." Whereupon, his attorneys filed a motion for a new trial on the grounds that the verdict was against the evidence and contrary to law as specifically set forth in the bills of exception taken during the trial and these were made a part of the motion for a new trial.[42] The charge was made that James Prince, one of the jurors, was under twenty-one years of age despite his oath to the contrary, and therefore, Anderson was tried by only eleven qualified jurors. The bill of information was attacked also on the ground that it was filed by an officer of the White League, and that Judge Whitaker, the trial judge, was a public defaulter for over six hundred thousand dollars.[43] The application for a new trial was denied and then Anderson's attorneys filed a motion for arrest of judgment.[44] The case was eventually taken to the State Supreme Court,[45] and it was rumored Governor Nicholls was waiting for the Supreme Court to pass on the appeal. Reports were to the effect that great pressure was being brought from Washington by both Democrats and Republicans to procure a pardon for Anderson.[46] Senator Sherman was enraged at the severe sentence Judge Whitaker gave Anderson which was two years at hard labor and cost of court.[47]

Much concern was evinced over the conviction of Anderson. A petition was circulated in the Louisiana house of representatives, and most of the Republicans signed it, asking Governor Nicholls to pardon Anderson on the grounds that by his conviction,

> the law had been vindicated and that the granting of a pardon to him now would be in harmony with the spirit

---

[42] New Orleans Times, February 10, 1878.
[43] Ibid., February 12, 1878.
[44] Ibid., February 24, 1878.
[45] The Daily Picayune, January 28, 1878, estimated it would cost the city of New Orleans $10,000 to $12,000 to try the Returning Board.
[46] Ouachita Telegraph, March 1, 1878.
[47] New Orleans Times, February 26, 1878; Daily Picayune, February 15, 1878.

of the joint resolution adopted last winter by the legislature as the basis of settlement of the then existing political troubles.[48]

Even one of the jury, W. F. Converse, wrote to Governor Nicholls asking him to pardon Anderson.[49]

The conviction of Anderson attracted national attention for Anderson wrote to President Hayes and Senator John Sherman that the only way for him to get a pardon was to give up his office, and he preferred going to jail.[50] The President was sufficiently interested to write Attorney-General Devers in reference to the Returning Board prosecutions and mentioned his meeting on April 16, 1877, with three Louisiana Congressmen, and one or two others. At this meeting it was agreed that no political prosecutions would be instituted and this agreement was telegraphed to Governor Nicholls, who also approved it; the Returning Board came within the scope of the agreement.[51] The President soon realized he had made a mistake in writing the letter to Devers, and this was emphasized even more when the Attorney-General of the United States advised him that the general government could not interfere with the process of law in Louisiana.[52] The Returning Board prosecution was discussed in cabinet meetings, but no action was taken.[53] The press reported President Hayes sent General W. S. Hancock, a friend and classmate at West Point of Nicholls, to Louisiana. General Hancock reached New Orleans, February 15, and was feted. The subject of Anderson's conviction was presented to Nicholls the evening of February 19, but it was March 1 before the governor agreed to pardon Anderson, provided the

---

[48] New Orleans Times, February 9, 1878.
[49] Ibid., March 10, 1878.
[50] Ibid., March 14, 1878.
[51] Ibid., February 11, 1878.
[52] Ibid., February 18 and 20, 1878.
[53] Ibid., February 14, March 7 and 9, 1878.

Supreme Court did not liberate him. General Hancock left New Orleans two days later.[54]

John Sherman, Stanley Matthews, J. A. Garfield, Eugene Hale, and Harry White sent Anderson a telegram February 4, saying:

> The undersigned feel it due you under present circumstances, to assure you of unhesitating belief that in the matter wherein you stand charged, you are altogether guiltless of any offense against law, that you are falsely accused and maliciously persecuted, that the proceeding against you, though in the form of law, is without the substance of justice, that we hereby tender our earnest sympathies and express our hope that the sense of justice, and love of peace of the people of Louisiana will protect you and not permit the best interests of the whole country to be disturbed by a revival of sectional animosities. In any event, we are confident the American people will redress any injustice of which you may be made the victim.[55]

The Anderson case was argued in due time before the State Supreme Court and resulted in a reversal of the lower court on an error in the indictment. The Court held there was no such crime known to the law of Louisiana as "uttering and publishing" as true, an altered, false and counterfeited instrument.[56] Whereupon, the attorney-general filed an application for a rehearing which was denied.[57] Anderson thus gained his liberty.[58]

---

[54] New Orleans **Times**, March 27, 1878. The State Supreme Court was composed of men Nicholls had appointed and it is not altogether improbable that they were conscious of relieving the governor of an embarrassing situation when they freed Anderson.

[55] **Ibid.**, February 12, 1878.

[56] Anderson vs State, **30 Louisiana Annual Reports**, p. 557; New Orleans **Times**, March 13 and 19, 1878; Daily **Picayune**, March 18, 1878; Ouachita **Telegraph**, March 22, 1878.

[57] Anderson vs State, **30 Louisiana Annual Reports**, pp. 565-575; New Orleans **Times**, March 23, 1878.

[58] New Orleans **Times**, April 1, 1878.

A number of radical Democrats were disappointed at the end of the Anderson case as they wished to keep it before the country and force Governor Nicholls to act on the question of pardoning Anderson.[59] They thought a pardon would have enabled them to break down his administration, which would have given them the control they desired.[60] The Supreme Court was attacked and charged with failure to function for the best interest of society.[61]

Ex-Auditor, George B. Johnson, sought an injunction restraining Allen Jumel from acting as auditor, but failed to procure the injunction.[62] Johnson refused to answer questions of the grand jury and declined to produce the books belonging to the auditor's office. For this refusal, he was found guilty of contempt and was sentenced to ten days in jail and fined fifty dollars.[63]

Louisiana was in great need of economy and reform in 1877. The state debt was complicated and confusing because of the numerous bond and credit issues, and the financial chaos was made worse by inadequate bookkeeping. It is difficult, if not impossible, for one not a trained accountant to reach an accurate conclusion as to the finances of the state through an examination of the annual reports of the state auditor and treasurer. The tax burden bore heavily upon the people and in February the Real Estate and Taxpayers' Union

---

[59] New Orleans Times, February 16 and March 23, 1878.

[60] Ibid., March 20, 1878.

[61] Ouachita Telegraph, March 29, 1878.

[62] New Orleans Times, June 8, 1877; Daily Picayune, June 8, 1877. The State Supreme Court was composed of Chief Justice T. C. Manning and the following Associate Justices: R. H. Marr, A. DeBlanc, W. B. Egan, and W. B. Spencer.

[63] Daily Picayune, June 21, 1877; New Orleans Times, July 1, 1877.

asked the Nicholls legislature to lower taxes on real estate.[64] A country editor claimed that Louisiana had the heaviest state tax of any state in the Union and that St. Landry paid the heaviest parish tax of any parish in Louisiana. He proposed a Board of Equalization to equalize the taxes within the state.[65] The need for relief was great if the report was true that fifty thousand people were delinquent in their taxes at the end of 1877.[66]

Governor Nicholls desired to equalize the tax burden and sent a circular letter to all parish assessors inquiring about the ratio of assessment to cash value of property. A city editor claimed that if agricultural property was assessed at full value as city property was the revenues of the state would be doubled.[67] The property in the state was valued at approximately $175,000,000 and a levy of five and one-half mills was to pay the interest on the consolidated bonds, while a levy of four mills went into the general fund.[68]

---

[64] New Orleans Times, February 23, 1877.
[65] Opelousas Courier, January 22 and November 24, 1877.
[66] Ibid., December 29, 1877.
[67] New Orleans Times, September 3, 1877.
[68] Auditor's Report, Year ending December 31, 1877, p. 114.

Items	Assessment 1876	Assessment 1877
Real estate of non-residents	$ 8,419,454	$ 8,613,956.22
Real estate of residents	130,775,661	129,550,891.20
Horses, Mares, geldings	10,227,059	10,556,832.25
Carriages, vehicles, etc.	1,501,156	1,747,763.00
Stock, and interest in ships	284,910	571,356.00
Money loaned or in possession	359,406	488,665.00
Capital stock of banks and other corporations	11,583,405	11,454,878.00
Household goods, jewelry, etc.	1,007,225	840,325.00
Total Assessment	174,601,524	174,633,682.67
Amount of tax on the Assessment	$ 2,531,721	$ 2,532,188.15

The New Orleans Times, February 14, 1877, pointed out that the total assessment of the state was $174,000,000 plus, and that New Orleans
(Footnote continued on next page.)

THE TRIUMPH OF NICHOLLS

The legislature appointed a joint committee to investigate the accounts of the auditor, treasurer, and superintendent of education, and it reported the "most palpable frauds," but failed to give evidence to support the charge.[69] The records showed a cash balance of $529,936.33 on January 1, 1877, from total receipts of $3,021,083.29 less total disbursements of $2,491,146.96 for the calendar year of 1876.[70] The records for the following year showed a cash balance of $416,875.61 January 1, 1878. The Nicholls legislature spent $113,060 more than it collected in 1877, for the receipts were given as $2,719,412.25.[71] The total state debt of Louisiana after the funding operations were completed was estimated to be $11,785,293.21. This did not include unpaid interest coupons past due, or outstanding interest warrants, or the "property bank bonds." The state warrants advanced in value from fifty-five cents in March to par at the end of the year. The city of New Orleans was in greater financial straits than the state, for the bonded and floating debt of the city amounted to $21,894,714.74.[72] The state on January 1, 1878, owed $110,000 of the $250,000 purchase price of the St. Louis Hotel. Furthermore, the first of the year found the

---

was assessed for $100,000,000 of this amount, which left approximately $74,000,000 for the entire state except New Orleans. By way of comparison the total assessment of the state in 1872 was given as $280,000,000.

[69] **Report Joint Committee of Auditors Investigation**, 188, p. 9.

[70] **Report of State Treasurer**, January 1 to December 31, 1877. The report stated nothing of interest due and unpaid.

[71] **Ibid.** The auditor's report for 1877 gave the actual total yearly expenditures as $2,450,534.25. The auditor's expenditures are less than those given by the treasurer. This discrepancy in the two reports is no doubt due to the treasurer reporting as expenditures all money appropriated by the legislature and the auditor reporting only the money actually paid out.

[72] **Annual Cyclopedia, 1877**, p. 466.

state unable to pay the $50,000 interest due on the state bonds.[73] The governor regarded the debt as a sacred contract between the people and the creditors, and was anxious for it to be properly funded. His convictions were so profound that the report spread he had resolved to resign if the debt was repudiated.[74] The legislature of 1877 pretended to economize by reducing the salaries and expenses of state officials and of the city officials of New Orleans, yet it spent more money than was collected.[75]

The confusion existing in the records left by the Radical regime was stated by Secretary Strong in these terms:

> On taking possession of the records of this office I found them in such confusion and loose condition that I deemed it prudent, and a security for future contingencies, in as much as there was no one to turn over these records and archives to me, to cause an inventory to be taken by a notary public, and I herewith annex a duly certified copy of said inventory. . . .
> I may also add that confusion existed in the State Library. A large number of valuable and important books have been withdrawn from the State Library by unknown and irresponsible persons; in many instances works of great value are rendered useless by the absence of some of their volumes.[76]

---

[73] New Orleans **Times**, December 29, 1877.
[74] **Scrapbook** at Ridgefield, the Nicholls home.
[75] New Orleans **Times**, April 2, 1877, placed the reduction for the state at $490,000 and for New Orleans at $200,000 annually; the Opelousas **Courier**, April 21, 1877, estimated the annual saving between $700,000 and $900,000. These estimated savings were to be effective in 1878. It has been shown that the legislature in 1877 appropriated $2,719,-412.25, whereas, the carpet-bag legislature of 1876 only appropriated $2,491,146.96.
[76] **Report of Secretary of State** for the year ending December 31, 1877, pp. 3-9. The report, pp. 32-33, gave the state officials as F. T. Nicholls, governor; L. A. Wiltz, lieutenant-governor; W. A. Strong, secretary of state; H. N. Ogden, attorney-general; A. Jumel, auditor; A. Dubuclet, treasurer; R. M. Lusher, superintendent of education.

THE TRIUMPH OF NICHOLLS

The legislature began its regular session of 1878, January 7, with thirty-six members of the senate and one hundred eighteen members of the house. The senate had twenty Democrats and sixteen Republicans, with one of the Republican seats contested. The house had sixty-four Democrats, fifty-two Republicans, and two Independents, with the returns from two parishes uncounted. The right of six Republicans to their seats was contested.[77] The legislature did not have the confidence of all the people and some were pessimistic enough to predict a session of log-rolling, dishonest scheming, bargains and corruptions, in fact, a session for the benefit of individuals and rings. The *Picayune* stated:

> Let us hope that they will rise above petty schemes for benefitting individuals, or rings and monopolies, at the expense of the state.[78]

The editor went on to say that the Democrats should prove their devotion to the state, and that the Republicans in the legislature had an opportunity to make their party respectable.

Governor Nicholls in his message to the legislature January 9, mentioned the conditions under which the body met the year before and said that:

> Today peace and quiet prevail throughout the state, political resentment has ended; the voice of the people is every where respected; the rights of all are fully guaranteed; the laws, through the instrumentality of the courts are properly and impartially administered and enforced and in spite of the unpropitious season, which has disappointed the expectations of our agriculturists

---

[77] New Orleans Times, January 7, 1878; Journal of House of Representatives, 1878; Daily Picayune, January 8, 1878; **Annual Cyclopedia**, 1877, p. 496. The **Annual Cyclopedia** inaccurately gives the date of meeting January 8.

[78] Daily Picayune, January 8, 1878.

and marred to some extent the bright material prospects of 1877, there exists a strong feeling of hope, relief, and content among all classes in Louisiana.[79]

The message was rather lengthy and presented the needs of each department of government, with many suggestions and recommendations offered to guide the legislature in its action. The work of the attorney-general's office was praised and the annual report and recommendations of the attorney-general were given to the legislature. The reports of the auditor and treasurer were not complete at the time, but the governor commented on the rise of state warrants from fifty-five cents to one dollar, or par, during the year just closed. He estimated the interest-bearing debt at $11,785,293.21, excluding warrants, which amounted to about $100,000 and certain interest bearing coupons and bonds known as Property Bank Bonds. It was suggested that the surplus in the general fund for the year should be applied: (1) to any deficiency in the current interest fund, (2) payment of any advancement heretofore made by the fiscal agent to the interest fund, (3) the matured and unpaid coupons of past years. It was necessary to keep expenses at the lowest figure possible according to the program of economy. The message dealt with such other subjects as, public education, the Board of State Engineers, public lands, public buildings, militia, criminal law, revised statutes, election law, vacancies, official bonds, Board of Health, Charity Hospital, immigration, Parish Exposition, the Institute for the Deaf, Dumb, and Blind, Asylum for the Insane, the Printing Board, and the penitentiary. In each case worthwhile and needed changes were suggested. The lessees of the penitentiary were in arrears to the state, and a suit had been filed in East Baton Rouge

---

[79] **Journal of House of Representatives, 1878**, Message of the Governor; Daily **Picayune**, January 11, 1878; **St. Lan|dry Democrat**, January 19, 1878; Ouachita **Telegraph**, January 18, 1878; **Journal of the Senate, 1878**, p. 6.

parish to dissolve the contract because the rent had not been paid. The legislature was called on to provide for the possibility or probability of the convict labor being thrown back on the hands of the state authorities. The support of the convicts cost the state nothing under the system then in force, which the governor thought should be continued unless the state adopted the system of building levees with the convicts.[80] The closing paragraph of the message protested against the failure of the United States Senate to seat Henry M. Spofford.[81]

The message was well received. The *Picayune* praised it as having "no shout of victory, no display of personal vanity, no denunciation of a fallen and flying foe."[82] The editor went on to say:

> The object of the governor seems to have been the reconciliation of all good elements, with sincere reform of all abuses by whomsoever perpetrated. . . The message evinces a conscientious and logical determination to carry out, in good faith, the great work of pacification and reform to which the movement that placed the government in power has been so solemnly pledged by a legislative resolve and executive indorsement. The burdens are to be lifted from the people; the costs of the government are to be reduced; the laws are to be enforced; and Louisiana is to be made again an attractive home to all who desire peace, prosperity, and social harmony.[83]

The St. Landry *Democrat* thought as well of the message as did the *Picayune* and praised almost the same points, saying, "Its whole tone is marked with moderation, with firmness,

---

[80] The convicts were being used at the time to construct the New Orleans Pacific Railroad.
[81] **Journal of the House of Representatives, 1878**, Message of the Governor; **Journal of the Senate, 1878**, pp. 6-13.
[82] Daily Picayune, January 11, 1878.
[83] **Ibid.**

and with exclusive devotion to the interests of Louisiana."[84] The governor seemed to have struck a popular chord in discussing the needed changes in assessing and taxing property when he said, "There ought to be no more privileged property than there ought to be privileged classes."[85]

The legislature began its work under more pleasant and comfortable circumstances than prevailed the year before. Both the senate and house chambers had been entirely refitted, and the new black walnut desks were described as an incentive for the members to do their best[86]—although such luxuries were not in harmony with the professed program of economy.

The legislature proceeded to the business before it, but all was not harmony. A few were ready to condemn Governor Nicholls for his conciliatory and conservative course since he assumed the reins of government.[87] Soon bills were in the legislative hopper designed to remedy the defects pointed out in the governor's message, and many of these reform measures were in the form of constitutional amendments. There was a faction which raised the question of a constitutional convention to completely change the fundamental law of the state and this divided the legislature and the voters. The Nicholls supporters believed it the part of wisdom as well as the part of expediency not to open a new struggle until time had cured many of the evils under which the people suffered. Moreover, it would be far more economical to amend the existing constitution than to frame a new one.

One amendment after another was proposed to the constitution to bring about the desired reforms.[88] Seventeen

---

[84] St. Landry Democrat, January 19, 1878.
[85] Ibid.
[86] New Orleans Times, January 5, 1878.
[87] St. Landry Democrat, January 26, 1878.
[88] New Orleans Times, February 6, 1878.

THE TRIUMPH OF NICHOLLS   143

of these amendments passed the senate without opposition
and were sent to the house,[89] but the attitude of that body
was such that a joint committee of the senate and house was
appointed.[90] This committee worked out twenty-one amendments to report to the two houses, estimating that the amendments if adopted would effect an annual saving to the state
of approximately $250,000. The legislators had learned the
wisdom of putting a label of economy[91] on their measures.
The amendments were passed by large majorities in each
house, and it was provided that they should be submitted to
a vote of the people, for approval or rejection, at the next
election of legislators.[92]

The proposed amendments dealt with the following subjects:

(1) Submitted the question of moving the state capital
from New Orleans to Baton Rouge.

(2) Provided for the election of the general assembly
and fixed the time of the meetings.

(3) Placed a limit on the amount of taxes that could be
levied by the general assembly, the city of New Orleans, and the parishes.

(4) Fixed salaries of the members of the general assembly at $500.00 each, per session of ninety days.

---

[89] New Orleans Times February 9, 1878; **Journal of the Senate of Louisiana, 1878**, pp. 101-106.
[90] St. Landry Democrat, February 23, 1878; **Journal of the Senate of Louisiana, 1878, Regular Session**, p. 89. The members of the committee were: E. D. White, Chairman, C. J. Boatner, F. C. Zacharie, F. P. Stubbs, H. L. Garland, F. S. Goode, A. Dumont, C. B. Wheeler, T. B. Stamps of the senate, and T. B. Lyons, R. J. Walker, J. B. Mc-Gehee, John Young, W. M. Washburn, D. A. Breard, B. F. Jonas, and A. Voorhies of the house.
[91] See footnote number 75 of this chapter for a previous claim of cutting the cost of government.
[92] **Annual Cyclopedia, 1878**, p. 498; **Journal of the Senate of Louisiana, 1878**, pp. 179-189.

(5) Prohibited the general assembly from passing local or special laws changing venue in criminal cases, etc.

(6) Fixed the salary of the lieutenant-governor at double that of an assemblyman.

(7) Fixed the salary of the governor at $7,000 annually.

(8) Revised the veto power and authorized the governor to veto one or more items in appropriation bills without invalidating the remainder of the bill.

(9) Abolished all fees to salaried officers.

(10) Revised the judiciary and provided for a supreme court, district courts, and justices of the peace.

(11) Fixed the salary of the chief justice at $7,000 and the associates at $6,500 per year.

(12) Authorized the general assembly to divide the state into not less than thirty and not more than forty-five judicial districts, with a judge elected by a plurality of the votes to preside over each district.

(13) Fixed salaries of the district judges at not over $5,000 per annum in New Orleans and not less than $2,000 nor more than $3,000 in the remainder of the state.

(14) Replaced the office of district attorney with a state's attorney.

(15) Excused the judge in certain cases, and when he was not personally interested in matters in contestation, he could select the judge to try the case.

(16) Fixed the time when the new system would take effect so as to prevent interregnum.

(17) Abrogated article 132 of the constitution of 1868. (Article 132 had required that all lands sold in pursuance of decrees of courts should be divided into tracts of from ten to fifty acres).

(18) Fixed the salary of the superintendent of public education at $3,500.

(19) Prohibited a license tax by the state, parish, or municipality on any mechanical trade, manufactory, or factory, except such as may require police regulation in towns and cities.

(20) Authorized the legislature to exempt from taxation household goods not exceeding $500.00 in value.

(21) Located the university departments of law and medicine in New Orleans, and the academic department elsewhere in the state. Provided also, for maintaining the institution.[93]

The legislature expired by limitation March 7, and the governor the same day called an extra session to last not longer than fifteen days. The subjects to be legislated upon were: "revenue, appropriations, registration and election, levees, penitentiary, floating debt, city charter and militia";[94] the variety of subjects indicated the dearth of essential legislation enacted at the regular session. The St. Landry *Democrat,* in analyzing the causes of the extra session, said the house had delayed action on the important measures until the last days of the session and did not get them to the senate in time for that body to give them proper consideration. The Democrats lacked organization and harmony was impossible with half the party aspiring to be leaders.[95] Two groups that worked for the extra session were those who favored a constitutional convention, and those who deemed the apportionment bill a party necessity. One paper thought the majority of the Democrats were opposed to the extra session, which was estimated to cost twenty-five thousand dollars.[96]

---

[93] **Journal of the Senate of Louisiana,** 1878, pp. 100-237; **Annual Cyclopedia,** 1878, pp. 498-499.
[94] **Journal of the Senate of Louisiana, 1878,** pp. 234; Daily Picayune, March 8, 1878.
[95] **St. Landry Democrat,** March 16, 1878.
[96] Ibid. The editor said, "They have left undone those things which they ought to have done; and they have done those things which they ought not to have done; and there is no health in them."

The special session only lasted ten days; thus the general assembly closed its labors after being in continuous session from January 7 to March 19. Extravagant claims were made that the laws enacted would lower the expenditures in every department of government. [97]

The people were talking economy but the scramble to get on the public pay roll was still prevalent. One paper observed that two hundred men were on hand asking for political jobs when the legislature convened on January 9, 1878.[98] The demand for jobs led to considerable "log rolling" among the legislators.[99]

The state legislature passed concurrent resolutions instructing the Senators and Representatives in Congress from Louisiana to cast their vote in favor of any resolution that might be presented in either branch of Congress looking toward the investigation of any charges of corruption and fraud in procuring the electoral vote of Louisiana for the President of the United States in 1876. The policy of President Hayes was endorsed as one of peace, conciliation, and justice, but another concurrent resolution protested against the seating of W. P. Kellogg by the United States senate.[100] The resolutions were provoked by an open letter of W. D. Chandler of the Republican National Committee in which he alleged that Mr. Hayes knew the price he was to pay for the

---

[97] Journal of the Senate of Louisiana, Extra Session, 1878; Annual Cyclopedia, 1878, p. 499. Senator White made a speech March 18, in which he estimated the savings and itemized each department. The total reached $3,365,475.18. The Annual Cyclopedia put the saving at $2,048,412.00. Such claims were absurd when the total expenditure for the state government (excluding local governmental units) was less than $3,000,000, annually.

[98] New Orleans Times, January 7, 1878.

[99] Daily Picayune, February 28, 1878.

[100] Journal of Senate of Louisiana, 1878, Regular Session; Journal of House of Representatives of Louisiana, 1878, Regular Session; Annual Cyclopedia, 1878, pp. 496-498.

Presidency was the betrayal of Packard and Chamberlain, and the sacrifice of his own honor, and that President Hayes deliberately paid the price.[101]

Ex-Governor Hahn reported that the Republican party was practically disbanded in Louisiana,[102] but the Democratic-Conservative party showed such lack of unity and agreement in the legislature that the Republican politicians were astute enough to take courage and hope. Pinchback summoned the Republican Executive Committee to meet in the office of H. C. Warmoth, March 27, to consider the course to pursue in the state election of 1878.[103] The Committee called the Republican State Convention to convene September 16, and proposed to put forth a full ticket, but the response was so weak that the Republican convention decided to abandon the idea of putting out a ticket.[104] The Republican State Central Committee sent a sub-committee to the governor to ascertain whether the law and the administration of the law could be relied on to allow free expression of political principles. The address assumed violence which the governor denied existed, and he made his usual promise of an impartial execution of the law.[105]

The Republican party was so weak that the New Orleans *Republican*, a weekly newspaper, ceased to be published after November 10, and the last issue contained a valedictory editorial ending with these words:

> Thus it appears that if the Republican party of Louisiana is dead as a political organization, its spirit still lives and the New Orleans Republican which has always fos-

---

[101] New Orleans Times, February 23, 1878.
[102] Daily Picayune, January 25, 1878.
[103] Ouachita Telegraph, March 1, 1878.
[104] New Orleans Times, September 17, 1878.
[105] Ibid., September 27, 1878.

tered this spirit, in its last moments, had the proud consciousness that its life work has not been wholly in vain.[106]

The chairman of the Democratic State Central Committee called a meeting of that body for the first of May.[107] It met and decided to hold the Democratic State Convention in Baton Rouge the first Monday in August.[108] The convention was for the purpose of nominating the Democratic candidates for Congress, state treasurer, state legislature, and all parish and local offices. Three candidates sought the Democratic nomination for state treasurer, and after a spirited contest E. A. Burke was nominated.[109] Mr. Burke was stronger in New Orleans than any other man who aspired to the nomination, because his work in organizing the Democratic party in the city for the elections of 1872, 1874, and 1876 had been outstanding. In the latter campaign, he worked diligently for Nicholls and represented him in Washington.[110] The candidates for Congress were nominated,[111] and a platform endorsing the administration of Nicholls was adopted by the convention. The platform endorsed the position previously voiced on the currency question and called for the abolition of the Federal tax on state banks.[112] Although one editor was partisan enough to say

---

[106] New Orleans **Republican**, November 10, 1878. It had been published every Saturday as a weekly since September, 1878, and preceding that date it was published daily for a short time.
[107] Ouachita **Telegraph**, March 22, 1878.
[108] New Orleans **Times**, May 2, 1878.
[109] Daily **Picayune**, August 8, 1878; New Orleans **Times**, August 8, 1878. Fifty-eight ballots were taken.
[110] Ouachita **Telegraph**, August 23, 1878.
[111] New Orleans **Times**, August 7 and 8, 1878. The nominees for Congress were: R. L. Gibson, E. W. Robertson, J. H. Acklen, J. B. Elam, E. J. Ellis, and J. F. King.
[112] Opelousas **Courier**, August 17, 1878; Ouachita **Telegraph**, August 23, 1878; New Orleans Times, August 7, 1878.

that the next United States Senator from Louisiana should be from the northern part of the state,[113] the Democrats of the state were fairly successful in uniting for the November election. The *Times* in an editorial praised the results of two years of Democratic-Conservative government.[114]

The Democratic political rallies were usually accompanied with a barbecue in order to get the people to come out. The following notice reveals the spirit of such gatherings:

There will be a grand rousing Democratic meeting in the Island tomorrow. Preparations have been made for an old-fashioned barbecue at the same time, and provisions collected to feed two thousand people. As the Island Democratic Club has a membership of only four hundred fifty members, it will be seen that preparations are made to entertain fifteen hundred fifty guests.[115]

The people of St. Landry held a great Democratic mass meeting and barbecue at Opelousas, Saturday, October 26, with all harmoniously satisfied.[116] The people of New Orleans held a "grand Democratic rally" at Odd Fellows Hall, the second of November.[117]

The election of November 5 was for the purpose of voting on the twenty-one amendments; choosing all members of the house of representatives of the general assembly and eighteen state senators, a state treasurer, six United States Representatives to Congress, parish judges, sheriffs, coroners, constables, justices of peace, and police jurors, as well as electing the mayor and other officials in New Orleans.[118] A fair election was promised,[119] and the election itself was described as orderly, peaceful, and quiet.[120] The success of

---

[113] Ouachita Telegraph, November 1, 1878.
[114] New Orleans Times, November 2, 1878.
[115] Ouachita Telegraph, October 18, 1878.
[116] St. Landry Democrat, November 2, 1878.
[117] New Orleans Times, November 3, 1878.
[118] **Messages and Proclamations of Governor Nicholls, 1878,** p. 407.
[119] Daily Picayune, November 5, 1878.
[120] New Orleans Times, November 6, 1878.

the Democratic ticket exceeded expectation as the party elected all its candidates for Congress.[121] and won a big majority of the next state legislature.[122] All the amendments were defeated, except the one to move the capital to Baton Rouge, which carried by a fair majority.[123] The papers seemed to take little note of the fact that twenty of the twenty-one proposed amendments were defeated, and one paper found room to speculate on the new general assembly electing Governor Nicholls to the United States Senate.[124]

The two problems of the state which needed immediate attention, according to one editor, were:

(1) A permanent establishment of our state credit and the adjustment of our finances on a sound basis.
(2) The occasional lawlessness over the state must stop.[125]

The other political parties, however, were not as well pleased with the results of the election as were the Democrats. The Citizens' Conservative Association announced its intention to protest the result of the election on the ground of fraud in registration and interference with Federal officers in the discharge of their duties at a Congressional election.[126] The report went out that at least sixty people in Louisiana would be arrested for intimidation at a Congressional election.[127]

---

[121] Ouachita **Telegraph,** November 8, 1878; New Orleans **Times,** November 7, 9, 1878. The regular Democratic ticket averaged 14,000 votes against 6,000 for the Citizens ticket and 7,000 for the National ticket.

[122] The senate would have 25 Democrats and 11 Republicans. The house of representatives would have 72 Democrats, 18 Republicans, 2 Nationals, and 2 Independents, as given in the Ouachita **Telegraph,** November 22, 1878.

[123] The vote was 27,957 for, and 21,628 against.

[124] Opelousas **Courier,** December 14, 1878.

[125] New Orleans **Times,** December 25, 1878.

[126] Ibid., November 8, 1878.

[127] **Ibid.,** November 14, 1878.

The United States Senate took note of the charges of irregularities and appointed a select committee to make sweeping inquiries into all phases of the recent election such as voting, intimidation, assessment of Federal office-holders or employees for election purposes, the conduct of United States supervisors of elections, and to report whether Congress should provide additional legislation to procure the right of suffrage to all citizens of the United States and resolved:

> That in prosecuting these inquiries the committee shall have the right, by itself or by any sub-committee, to send for persons and papers, to take testimony, to administer oaths, and to visit any portion of the country when such a visit may in their judgment facilitate the object of the inquiry.[128]

Three political parties were active in New Orleans during September, but on election day two months later, five tickets were presented for the electorate to choose from.[129] No less than 36,000 voters were registered and qualified to participate in the city election. Of this number, 11,000 were colored, and it was predicted the Democratic-Conservative party had 26,000 votes unless there was dissatisfaction over the way the nominations were made or with the character of the delegates to the nominating convention.[130] The only important opposition to the Democratic party in the city, however, was that of Republicans, since the Property Holders' Union and the Citizens' Conservative Association were not political in composition and purpose.[131]

---

[128] **Senate Report, 45 Congress, 3 Session,** No. 855.
[129] New Orleans **Times,** September 8, 1878; Daily **Picayune,** November 5, 1878. The **Times** named Democrats, Republicans, and Nationals in September. The five tickets presented in November were: Democratic-Conservative, Workingmen's, Citizens' Conservative Association, the Republican, and Property Holders' Union.
[130] Daily **Picayune,** October 30, 1878.
[131] **Ibid.,** November 1, 1878.

CHAPTER VI

A NEW CONSTITUTION AND A NEW ADMINISTRATION

VERY few men possessed sufficient political astuteness to foresee a break between Governor Nicholls and some of the leaders of the party, but the more discerning probably detected certain elements in the temperament and character of Nicholls that made party harmony impossible. One reason for this was Nicholls expected to render more than lip service to the program of economy and it has been shown that many party men desired the spoils of office. The religious question never came to the political surface, yet the fact that he was a devout Episcopalian seems to have been a factor in the opposition of the gambling element of the city.[1] Furthermore, Nicholls desired to remedy the defects of the fundamental law through amendments to the constitution, but certain party leaders thought the constitution of 1868 beyond repair and they proposed a constitutional convention to rewrite the fundamental law of the state. Nicholls believed a constitutional convention should be postponed until the return of better economic conditions.

As early as September, 1877, the Opelousas *Courier* came out for a new constitution arguing that amendments would not remedy the defects. It declared that the old system could not be amended and adjusted to present circumstances by piecemeal, that many reform schemes were disappointing, that a convention would be a means of bringing

---

[1] The opposition of the city gamblers developed after Nicholls displayed his strong religious convictions. The religious question appeared to be involved in the political alignments but the writer was unable to find tangible proof. The evidence seemed elusive.

about economy and retrenchment in the government, and that a convention would not arouse the fear of the negro voters. A week later the editor listed twenty-four changes needed in the constitution, and said the only argument against a convention was its expense.[2] The Shreveport papers, as well as a mass meeting in Jackson, were reported as favoring a convention.[3] The Ouachita *Telegraph* was strongly in favor of it, and Honorable F. P. Stubbs of Monroe favored it if held at a later date, but he thought the time inopportune. The Bossier *Banner* was quoted as desiring three things before it could be happy, "a railroad, immigration, and a constitutional convention."[4] The *Picayune* approached the subject by noting that the discussion had been confined almost entirely to the rural press, and two months later this paper boldly declared:

> The time is at hand when the representatives of the people of this State, convened in General Assembly, will be called upon to consider the necessity or propriety of authorizing and providing for a Constitutional Convention or otherwise amending the existing fundamental law.[5]

The *Times* said the ward politicians of the city looked upon the convention as a good way for the outs to oust the ins, hence, those in office opposed and those desiring office favored it. The people of New Orleans were divided but the rural section was thought unanimously in favor of the proposition.[6]

---

[2] Opelousas **Courier**, September 1 and 8, 1877. The **Courier** placed the cost of a constitutional convention at about $100,000.
[3] Ibid., September 29 and October 13, 1877. The Shreveport **Times** was quoted as saying the people and press of the state universally endorsed it. Capt. Kidd was the speaker quoted at the Jackson parish meeting.
[4] Ouachita **Telegraph,** October 5, November 2, and December 14, 1877.
[5] Daily **Picayune,** September 2, and November 9, 1877.
[6] New Orleans Times, September 23, and December 4, 1877.

The Pointe Coupee *Pelican* early in 1878 endorsed a constitutional convention.[7] The Baton Rouge *Advocate* predicted a "war in camp," if the legislature refused to call one because the Democratic party desired it and was demanding thorough reform.[8] The Opelousas *Courier* went so far as to name nine papers in New Orleans and eighteen rural papers representing every section of the state that favored a convention to change the fundamental law.[9] It was reported that a petition was being circulated and extensively signed in North Louisiana requesting the legislature to call a constitutional convention.[10] The rumors relative to the possibility of a convention disturbed financial circles in New Orleans,[11] because the commercial interests opposed holding one.[12] The question provoked so much concern that the business men of the city sent a petition to the legislature opposing the summoning of a convention. The petition set forth the argument that the legislature could pass such measures and propose such amendments as would meet the needs of the people, without incurring the expense of a constitutional convention.[13]

A few members of the legislature took a leading part in agitating the question of a constitutional convention to the

---

[7] Ouachita **Telegraph**, January 11, 1878, quoted the **Pelican** as endorsing a convention.
[8] Ouachita **Telegraph**, January 18, 1878, quoted from the **Advocate**.
[9] Opelousas **Courier**, January 18, 1878. The rural papers named were: Ouachita **Telegraph**, Ouachita **Observer**, Abbeville **Meridional**, Morehouse **Clarion**, Baton Rouge **Advocate**, Clinton **Patriot-Democrat**, Franklin **Enterprise**, Natchitoches **Vindicator**, Pointe Coupee **Pelican**, Colfax **Chronicle**, St. James **Louisianais**, St. John Meschacebe, Mansfield **Reporter**, Marksville **Bulletin**, Marksville **Villager**, Franklin **Sun**, and the Shreveport **Times**.
[10] New Orleans **Times**, February 3, 1878, quoted the Shreveport **Times**.
[11] Ibid., February 4, 1878.
[12] Daily **Picayune**, February 6, 1878.
[13] Ouachita **Telegraph**, February 8, 1878.

people of New Orleans,[14] and the citizens of Ouachita parish were interested to the extent of sending a petition to the general assembly requesting one.[15] The rural press believed that Charles Howard, president of the Louisiana Lottery Company, opposed the holding of a constitutional convention and reported that Howard's hired ruffians rotten-egged the speakers at a mass meeting on the streets of New Orleans favoring the convention idea.[16] It was shrewd politics for the lottery company to spread the impression that it opposed the convention, for that was an effective way to make the rural people favor it. Mr. Wade R. Young of Vidalia published a letter stating that:

> the influence of the numerous and varied monied rings, which seem to be one of the evils attending our civilization, and the fears and apprehensions of the so-called conservative politicians, have caused the members of the General Assembly to ignore the wishes of the people as expressed by the almost unanimous sentiment of the country press, and to adjourn without having made any adequate provision for the call of a constitutional convention.[17]

Early in March the *Picayune* indicated it hoped the constitutional convention bill would not pass the legislature,[18] but by the latter part of July this paper had become convinced that a new constitution was the only way permanently to satisfy the people.

If every amendment proposed was the perfection of legislative wisdom, if they all came from undisputed au-

---

[14] New Orleans Times, February 7, and March 3, 1878. Kidd of Jackson and Lee of St. Helena were two legislators who played a leading role in the agitation.
[15] The Ouachita Telegraph, February 7, and March 8, 1878.
[16] Opelousas Courier, February 23, 1878.
[17] Ouachita Telegraph, March 22, 1878. Letter of Wade R. Young of Vidalia to the editor.
[18] Daily Picayune, March 4, 1878.

thority, and if they would by their operation divest the old instrument of its objectionable features, there would still cling to the fabric constructed by fraud and usurpation the odor of despotism and humiliation.[19]

The *Times* thought the *Picayune*'s argument assumed the people could not understand the amendments proposed by the legislature, and that they would accept with satisfaction anything proposed by a convention, on the presumption the members of the convention would know what was needed and would only propose what was right and good.[20] The supporters of the movement sought the endorsement of the State Democratic Convention in Baton Rouge.[21] Although the delegates seemed to agree that the constitution needed revision, they did not believe the time had arrived for such action.[22] The question continued to be agitated, and a Democratic mass meeting in Monroe, August 19, wanted a constitutional convention called within ten days after the first Monday in January, 1879.[23] The defeat, in November, of all the proposed amendments except the one to move the capital to Baton Rouge, strengthened the demand for a new constitution and brought forth suggestions that a convention assemble in May of the following year.[24]

The division of the Democratic party over the question was such that the representatives of the people were accused of having been "recreant to their duty, false to their constituents, and failures as political reformers."[25] Senator White,

---

[19] Daily Picayune, July 25, 1878.
[20] New Orleans Times, July 28, 1878.
[21] Ibid., July 21, 1878.
[22] Daily Picayune, August 6, 1878; Ouachita Telegraph, August 2, 1878.
[23] Ouachita Telegraph, August 23, 1878.
[24] New Orleans Times, November 10, 1878.
[25] New Orleans Delta, March 29, 1878.

anticipating such an attack, in a speech in the senate, March 18, defended the legislature, claiming that even if the legislators had not brought to their work the highest intelligence, they had at least brought to it pure hearts and good intentions.[26]

The regular session of the legislature began January 6, 1879, and the question of a constitutional convention dominated the proceedings. The house of representatives chose J. C. Monsour speaker, because he was outspoken in favoring a short session and the calling of a constitutional convention immediately. Even the governor's message stated that since the amendments were defeated, the only way left to give the complete relief needed was by rewriting the state's fundamental law, and challenged the legislature in these words:

> Upon you devolves the grave duty of carrying on the work of relieving the people of the state from all the burdens consequent upon so many years of misgovernment, of preserving the public faith, of the lifting up of the standard of this great commonwealth to its former condition of prosperity and happiness. I am assured that you bring to the discharge of your constitutional duties a high sense of the great responsibility which they entail.[27]

The message contained a lengthy discussion of state finances, the keynote of which was, "I urge upon you as a sacred duty the most absolute economy in appropriations." It contained, also, a suggestion that the law be changed so as to give the executive less power when vacancies occurred in municipal offices.

---

[26] Journal of the Senate of Louisiana, Extra Session, 1878.
[27] **Messages and Proclamations of Governor Francis T. Nicholls, 1879; Journal of the Senate of Louisiana, Regular Session, 1879, pp. 7-20;** Daily Picayune, January 9, 1879; Weekly Advocate, January 10, 1879; New Orleans Times, January 9, 1879.

The atmosphere was well charged with politics, as was demonstrated by the difficulty encountered in trying to elect a United States Senator.[28] A number of joint meetings were held before B. F. Jonas was elected,[29] and the accusation was made that the deadlock on a Senator was planned, in order to send Governor Nicholls to the United States Senate.[30]

The *Times* still maintained that a constitutional convention should not be held because it was inadvisable and there was no special emergency making one indispensable for peace and prosperity.[31] A Democratic caucus of the legislature favored a convention;[32] the question was when to hold it; some desired it to meet in November to write a constitution to be ratified by two-thirds vote of the existing legislature when it met in January, 1880, while others wished to call a convention within the next thirty days.[33] The people were warned that a new constitution would mean an entire change in personnel of government and [34] "that any opposition to a convention would prove extremely damaging to the welfare of the city of New Orleans."[35] This warning was directed at the Chamber of Commerce, Cotton Exchange, and Stock Exchange, which were deliberating whether a constitutional convention was needed. They believed it would cost $400,000 instead of $40,000 as proposed by the legislature.[36] The New Orleans Chamber of Commerce finally joined the ranks opposing the movement and prepared a memorial of protest.[37]

---

[28] New Orleans Times, January 15, 1879.
[29] Daily Picayune, January 31, 1879. Mr. Jonas received 98 votes and H. C. Warmoth 28.
[30] Ibid., January 18, 1879. Nicholls declined to allow his name to be proposed for the United States Senate.
[31] New Orleans Times, January 1, 5, and 6, 1879.
[32] Ibid., January 7, 1879.
[33] Ibid., January 9, 1879.
[34] Ibid., January 11, 1879.
[35] New Orleans Democrat, January 12, 1879.
[36] Daily Picayune, January 13, 1879.
[37] Ibid., January 14, 1879.

A NEW CONSTITUTION   159

The outcome of the discussion was a legislative act which provided for a constitutional convention to convene April 21, and the selection of delegates on the eighteenth of March.[38] The legislature adjourned February 1, and the state immediately occupied itself with thoughts of the approaching convention. The people were urged to nominate men who would ably and competently represent the great interests of the city and the state.[39] The influential merchants lost little time in arranging the preliminaries for an active campaign to elect proper delegates to the convention,[40] and long before it met, charges were made that money was being used to influence it.

> The boys say there is money in it, money from the Gas Company, from the New City Government, from the slaughterhouse, or the water works.[41]

The election of delegates proceeded quietly on March 18, as scheduled, and the convention met at noon, April 21, in the State House at New Orleans. The delegates were described as "men of mature years and identified with the interests of their constituents." There were lawyers, doctors, merchants, planters, and a few professional politicians among the 98 Democrats, 32 Republicans, 2 Nationals, and 2 Independents composing the convention.[42] An attempted Democratic caucus on April 19, was adjourned for lack of a sufficient number to hold one, and it was postponed until two hours before the opening of the convention proper.[43]

---

[38] Daily Picayune, January 16, 1879; New Orleans Times, January 17, 1879.
[39] Daily Picayune, February 5, 1879.
[40] New Orleans Times, February 4, 1879.
[41] Ibid., February 11, 1879.
[42] Daily Picayune, April 21, 1879.
[43] New Orleans Times, April 21, 1879. Mr. Cosgrove was chosen printer for the convention by the caucus and this was ratified by the convention.

The convention was called to order by Governor Nicholls, and the secretary of state, W. A. Strong, called the roll with one hundred thirty-one delegates responding.[44] The governor made a brief charge to it as follows:

> No convention has ever had more serious and difficult questions to dispose of than will be presented for your consideration, and certainly no state ever more needed cool and judicious counsel in the formation of its organic law.
>
> I need scarcely say that I shall take the deepest interest in the proceedings upon which so much depends for good or evil. God grant that your earnest efforts will inure to the honor, welfare, happiness and prosperity of our people. Nominations for the presidency of this convention are now in order.[45]

The convention elected L. A. Wiltz, president, and he made a short address on taking the chair; Mr. W. H. Harris of Pointe Coupee was elected secretary.[46] It was soon observed that forty members were strictly Democratic and thirty strictly Republican in their views, with the remaining sixty-four conservatively holding the balance of power that represented the agricultural and business interests of the state.[47]

The second day of the convention a Republican delegate from Iberville parish offered the following preamble and resolution:

> Whereas, There is today a feeling of apprehension and alarm on the part of the colored citizens of the state with regard to the intended action of this convention, it is deemed proper, in advance of any official action of this body to disabuse their minds of any such apprehen-

---

[44] Three of the delegates were not present for roll call.
[45] **Official Journal of Proceedings of the Constitutional Convention,** April 21, 1879.
[46] New Orleans Times, April 22, 1879.
[47] Ibid., April 25, 1879.

A NEW CONSTITUTION 161

sions; therefore, be it, Resolved, That there is no intention whatever entertained by this body of impairing or restricting the political, civil, or religious rights of any class of the citizens of this state, but on the contrary the intention is to defend and perpetuate every and all rights now guaranteed them by this state and by the Constitution of the United States.[48]

An effort was made to get the resolution adopted by a suspension of the rules, but the motion was lost, and the resolution was never passed. Pinchback introduced an ordinance calling the convention's attention to the mayor's order to the chief of police. This order required the police of New Orleans to serve notice on the preachers of the colored churches that services whenever held must terminate at ten o'clock in the evening; under no circumstances could services be prolonged after that hour and all preachers violating same must be charged with disturbing the peace.[49] The convention refused to take any action on Pinchback's resolution.

A quarrel arose in the convention between the delegates from the upland and river parishes, because the hill people could not agree that they should be taxed for building levees to protect the people living along the rivers. A Democratic caucus reached an agreement whereby the entire state would be taxed five mills, and the river parishes ten mills for levee purposes;[50] the agreement was approved by the convention.

The Republicans were accused of spreading the false impression that the constitutional convention intended to repudiate the state debt. Such an impression was thought to be a malicious attempt to injure Louisiana and the South in the eyes of the nation.[51] Later events proved that the rumor

---

[48] Official Journal of the Constitutional Convention, 1879, p. 13.
[49] Ibid., p. 54
[50] New Orleans Times, May 26, 1879.
[51] Weekly Advocate, May 23, 1879.

of repudiation of the state debt was well founded. An amusing proposal was that the convention borrow $6,000,000 and buy the state debt at its "present market value."[52]

The Committee on the Public Debt disagreed and majority and minority reports were made.[53] The majority report declared the debt of Louisiana, January 1, 1879, to be $4,082,358. About $12,000,000 of outstanding state bonds were to be repudiated by the following provision:

> Any and all other evidences of debt now outstanding against the state are hereby declared to be illegal and fraudulent, and the legislature shall never make any provision, either directly or indirectly, for the acknowledgment or payment of the same in whole or in part. Nor shall the legislature enact any law, or the governor or any other official of the state enter into any contract or agreement whereby the state shall be made a party in any court of the state, or of the United States with the intent to test the validity of any such evidence of debt.[54]

The report stated that the legislature at its first session after the adoption must provide for the issuance of such bonds to take care of the recognized debt.

The minority report was a lengthy objection to repudiating the state bonds, and it presented a strong attack on the

---

[52] New Orleans Times, April 25, 1879.

[53] The majority report was signed by E. E. Kidd, (Chairman), H. R. Lott, M. M. Moore, J. C. Vance, B. F. Jenkins, H. M. Favrot, M. E. Girard, Joseph Henry, B. F. Forman, D. J. Reid, R. D. Bridger, and the minority report was signed by T. J. Semmes, D. Caffery, H. Breen, H. C. Warmoth, M. Cohen, and G. Le Gardner, Jr. The majority report made an arbitrary distinction in what part of the debt was to be acknowledged and the part to be repudiated. There seemed to be little logic or law for agreeing to pay part and repudiating the remainder.

[54] Official Journal, Constitutional Convention of Louisiana, 1879; Majority Report of Committee on Public Debt; New Orleans Times, June 1, 1879.

logic used by the majority in reaching the decision to nullify them.

What strikes the mind in contemplating the plan of the committee is, that the state is held bound to pay bonds when purchased by itself, as an investment of the school funds, while the state is considered discharged from responsibility for the same kind of bonds when purchased by individuals.[55]

The *Picayune* pointed out that the gentlemen who made the majority report came from a section of the state that had real property assessed at $25,295,750. Those who prepared the minority report represented an area with property assessed at $102,075,769, or more than seventy-five per cent of property taxed in the state. Thus, the tax-paying element was ready to acknowledge and pay the debt.[56]

The convention rejected both the majority and minority reports of the Committee on the Public Debt.[57] The difference of opinion on the debt question was strong enough to threaten to split the Democratic party, and some thought those differences would excite great suspicion throughout the country.[58] The feeling in the convention was such that a discussion of the debt was postponed for several days.[59] The threat of repudiation prompted the meeting of some foreign bond holders in London, July 24, to cable Governor Nicholls of the danger that would follow to the credit of Louisiana if the bonds were repudiated. The feeling upon the subject of

---

[55] **Official Journal, Constitutional Convention of Louisiana, 1879. Minority Report of Committee on Public Debt.**
[56] Daily **Picayune,** June 5, 1879.
[57] New Orleans **Times,** July 4, 1879; Daily **Picayune,** July 4, 1879; **Annual Cyclopedia, 1879,** p. 568. The majority report was rejected 90 to 39 and the minority rejected 80 to 49.
[58] New Orleans **Times,** July 11, 1879.
[59] Ibid., July 19, 1879.

threatened repudiation was not confined to the bondholders, but was quite generally shared in the financial and commercial community at large.[60]

The debt question was referred back to the committee, or rather a sub-committee, and finally a compromise was reached. The plan the convention approved provided for payment of 2 per cent interest for five years, 3 per cent for fifteen years and 4 per cent thereafter, but the bondholders were given an option of taking a new bond equal to 75 per cent of the old bond and bearing 4 per cent per annum. The plan levied a tax of three mills to pay the interest, and limited the state tax to six mills. This ordinance was to be voted on separately by the people and would become a part of the constitution, only when passed by a majority of the voters.[61] This plan amounted to about the same as scaling the entire debt 25 per cent and letting it bear 4 per cent interest, while the old debt bore 7 per cent interest. It was therefore partial repudiation.

The *Times* was pleased with the solution of the debt question, and urged the people to "Adopt the Constitution and reject repudiation."[62] It also observed that the "repudiators" no longer denounced the debt as fraudulent, but said the state had exhausted its resources and the convention adjusted the debt to meet the ability of the people to pay.[63] The *Picayune* was satisfied the debt ordinance was as just and equitable as could be agreed on, and as favorable as the resources of the people warranted at the time."[64]

---

[60] New Orleans **Times**, July 27, 1879.
[61] Ibid., July 22, 1879; Daily **Picayune**, July 21, 1879; Opelousas **Courier**, July 26, 1879; **Official Journal, Constitutional Convention, 1879.** The plan was adopted by a vote of 72 to 41. The Republicans as a body voted against the debt ordinance.
[62] New Orleans **Times**, July 25, 1879. The **Times** failed to realize that the debt ordinance was partial repudiation.
[63] Ibid., August 15, 1879.
[64] Daily **Picayune**, August 16, 1879.

A NEW CONSTITUTION

The debt question was among the most important that the convention had to solve and probably consumed more time than any other. In addition to this question there were the questions of the franchise, control of monopolies, reform of the judiciary, and the levees, looming as major problems.[65]

The Committee on the Franchise presented majority and minority reports. The majority desired to restrict the franchise to male citizens twenty-one years of age, actual residents of the state one year, of the parish six months, of a precinct thirty days, who had at least ten days before election, paid all taxes for the preceding years, and the poll tax for the present year. The minority report vigorously protested against these provisions as undemocratic, and discriminatory.[66] The efforts to limit the franchise showed that a small minority of the Democrats were desirous of disfranchising the greater part of the negroes even if a large number of poor and illiterate whites had to be excluded to avoid violating the Constitution of the United States and the Amendments thereto.[67]

A number of the women of the state felt that they were better qualified to vote than the vast majority of the negroes and many of the illiterate white men, and they presented a petition to the convention requesting the franchise. In addition to the women the petition was signed by a number of prominent men, including doctors, lawyers, and merchants.[68] The convention gave the women a special hearing, on June

---

[65] **Official Journal, Constitutional Convention, 1879;** New Orleans Times, June 23, 1879.

[66] New Orleans **Times,** June 23, 1879. The negroes and white Republicans voted against limitation of suffrage.

[67] **Official Journal, Constitutional Convention, of Louisiana, 1879,** pp. 309-310.

[68] New Orleans **Times,** May 5, 1879.

16.[69] Probably the majority of the women of Louisiana did not desire the suffrage and agreed with the *Times* that

> Politics is bad enough for men, without drawing ladies into such an atmosphere of corruption and publicity.[70]

The discussion of the franchise brought forth an interesting proposal similar to the Grandfather clause written into the constitution of 1898.

> No person shall have the right to vote or be eligible to vote under the constitution of this state who is not able to read the constitution in the English language and write his name; provided, however, that the provisions of this article shall not apply to any person who owns property, real or personal, assessed for taxes in his own name to the amount of at least three dollars to the state, and assessed within the twelve months next preceding the election at which he offers to vote, nor to any person prevented by physical disabilities from reading and writing the English language.[71]

Only four members were willing to consider the proposal, and the final draft of the constitution showed no trace of the attempts to limit the suffrage. Every male citizen of the United States and every male person of foreign birth who had been naturalized and had been a resident of the state for at least one year, of the parish six months, and of the ward or precinct thirty days preceding the election, was declared an eligible voter, provided he was twenty-one years of age. No qualification of any kind for suffrage or office should be made on account of race, color, or previous condition. The general assembly was given authority to levy an

---

[69] New Orleans *Times*, June 19, 1879.

[70] Opelousas *Courier*, June 21, 1879.

[71] **Official Journal, Constitutional Convention of Louisiana, 1879**, p. 256.

annual poll tax for public school purposes upon every male inhabitant of the state over twenty-one years of age.[72]

There was quite a contest in the convention between New Orleans and Baton Rouge for the capital of the state. Those who favored Baton Rouge argued that it already had a capitol building, and living was cheaper there than in New Orleans.[73] The arguments advanced for New Orleans were its importance as a great traffic center, the expense of removing to Baton Rouge, and less likely to expose the legislature to corrupting influences. Moreover, New Orleans had a vigilant press, whereas, Baton Rouge had only two minor papers.[74]

The Capitol at Baton Rouge had cost $365,000, the grounds $25,000, and the iron fence around the square was valued at $4,000. The building could be repaired for $100,000, according to estimates. The convention made Baton Rouge the permanent capital because that was thought to be the wish of the people of the state. It was nearer the center of the state and the rural section feared the evil influences of New Orleans. The City of Baton Rouge was to pay $35,000 of the repair bill on the Capitol, and it was thought this sum, plus the proceeds from the sale of the St. Louis Hotel, would be sufficient to pay for all the reconditioning of the structure.[75]

The convention took note of the rumors of corruption by appointing an investigating committee to seek out the evidence.[76] The salaries of state officials under the old constitution totaled $70,350, and under the new they amounted to $24,000, a clear saving of $46,350. The elections were to

---

[72] **Official Journal of the Constitutional Convention of Louisiana, 1879.**
[73] Daily **Picayune,** July 1, 1879.
[74] New Orleans **Times,** July 11, 1879.
[75] **Ibid.**
[76] Daily **Picayune,** July 2, 1879; New Orleans **Times,** July 2, 1879.

be held at four year intervals and the legislature was to meet every two years.[77] The total annual savings by the new constitution were estimated at $1,003,680.[78] Mr. M. D. Logan presented a plan to the constitutional convention for the legislature to meet once every six years and thereby effect an annual saving of $450,000.[79] The constitution was unusually lenient toward those whose property had been forfeited to the state for taxes, because the property could be redeemed by paying the tax itself without any interest, penalties, cost, or charges. Payment could be made in depreciated warrants, which were again selling for fifty cents on the dollar.[80] The disastrous yellow fever of the preceding year and the uncertainty concerning the action of the constitutional convention toward the finances of the state had driven down the price of state warrants.

The appropriation of $40,000 made by the last legislature for the expenses of the convention was exhausted, and the finance committee reported an ordinance to appropriate $25,000 from the state treasury to pay the further expenses of the body.[81] The convention voted 67 to 41 in favor of the ordinance, and thereby assumed the power to legislate. Auditor Jumel refused to honor the voucher of the convention

---

[77] **Constitution of Louisiana, 1879**; Opelousas **Courier**, June 14, 1879. The salary schedule was governor, $4,000; secretary of state, $1,800 plus $1,500 expenses, plus fees; attorney-general, $3,000; superintendent of education, $2,000 plus $1,000 expenses; auditor, $2,500, plus $4,000 expenses; treasurer, $2,000, plus $2,000 expenses. The clerical expenses of the house were limited to $70.00 per day and the senate to $60.00.

[78] Opelousas **Courier**, August 16, 1879.

[79] New Orleans Times, April 26, 1879. The expense of the annual meeting of the legislature was figured at $300,000 and the election expenses for same at $15,000.

[80] **Ibid.**, July 27, 1879.

[81] **Ibid.**, July 2, 1879.

A NEW CONSTITUTION

for $25,000 on the ground that it had no power to appropriate money.[82] The convention reconsidered, and then postponed indefinitely the ordinance appropriating $25,000 for expenses. Later an ordinance was adopted authorizing the fiscal agent of the state to negotiate a loan of $25,000 in the name of the convention.[83]

One or two other acts of the convention need to be mentioned. To safeguard economy the legislature was forbidden to fix any salary above $3,500, and the salary of judges in the country parishes was fixed at $3,000. The salary of the district attorney for each district was $1,000, and he was to be elected every four years; the same length of term was given the justices of peace and the constables.[84] The convention before adjourning, abandoned its program of economy and gave its employees increased pay.[85]

The new document provided for an election of state officers; the constitution of 1868 was abrogated; and the people were given a chance to approve or disapprove the new constitution.[86] One of the last acts of the convention was to order 20,000 copies of the constitution printed and apportioned to the delegates for distribution, before adjourning the eighty-one day session on July 23.[87] The constitution provided that the election to approve the new fundamental law should be held on the first Tuesday in December and at the same election all the state officers and members of the

---

[82] New Orleans Times, July 4 and 6, 1879.
[83] Ibid., July 9, 1879; **Official Journal, Constitutional Convention of Louisiana, 1879.**
[84] Ouachita Telegraph, July 25, 1879; **Constitution of Louisiana, 1879.**
[85] **Official Journal, Constitutional Convention of Louisiana, 1879.** The secretary was paid $8.00, and the assistant secretary, reading clerk, minute clerk and sergeant at arms, $6.00 per day, pages $1.00 and the others from $3.00 to $5.00 per day.
[86] **Official Journal, Constitutional Convention of Louisiana, 1879.**
[87] Ibid. The convention met April 21 to July 23, 1879.

legislature should be chosen. The term of all the officers would commence the second Monday in January, 1880.

The press generally was pleased with the results, and few complaints against the constitution were noted. The Old Bourbons had redeemed all their pledges and "elevated the white man to the level of the darkey." Moreover, such Republicans as Pinchback, Allain, Demas, and Stamps, were pleased with the document, and thought that the constitution of no state in the Union did more to guarantee the civil and political rights of all classes.[88] The *Democrat* thought the guarantees given the colored people ought to satisfy the people of the North as well as the Republican leaders,[89] and the *Item* thought the document a compromise between two extremes in which the rural parishes fared better than New Orleans.[90] The rural press generally approved the constitution because it reduced taxation, reformed the judiciary, reduced the cost of government, substituted biennial for annual sessions of the legislature, and made provision for funding and scaling the state debt.[91]

It was noticeable that Governor Nicholls left the state immediately after the adjournment of the convention for the purpose of spending some time in Virginia, and officially notified Lieutenant-Governor Wiltz that he would be acting governor beginning July 24.[92] It was said the governor was going to Virginia in search of health, but some thought his absence had political significance. At any rate, his absence gave Wiltz the privilege of issuing the proclamation setting

---

[88] New Orleans Times, July 24, 1879.
[89] New Orleans, Democrat, October 19, 1879.
[90] Ouachita Telegraph, August 8, 1879, quoted from New Orleans Item.
[91] Opelousas Courier, August 9, 1879, listed the following papers as endorsing the constitution; Avoyelles Bulletin, Assumption Pioneer, Iberville Southerner, Tangipahoa Independent, West Baton Rouge Sugar Sun, West Feliciana Sentinel.
[92] New Orleans Times, July 24, 1879.

A NEW CONSTITUTION

Tuesday, December 2, as the day for voting on the new constitution and electing the various state, district, and parish officers.[93] It was reported that the executive office was thronged with visitors the first morning Wiltz was acting governor, and each visitor had important business to discuss concerning the state.[94]

Various political alignments had begun forming when the legislature passed the ordinance calling the constitutional convention. Soon a rumor spread that Governor Nicholls was contemplating resigning. Those who favored the convention thought it was because of his inability to administer his office in the manner and with the effect he had intended. They hastened to say they had never heard of any dissatisfaction with Nicholl's administration, except among disappointed and ambitious politicians.[95] The staunch supporters of Nicholls assured him the people were not dissatisfied with his personal conduct in office, nor did the people charge him, or even suspect him of having willfully neglected any means within his power of promoting their interests and securing their welfare. Nevertheless, Governor Nicholls believed the state debt a sacred contract between the people and the creditors and it was an obligation which the state could not escape. He believed it inexpedient and unbecoming to try to trace the state bonds in their present form back to their source to establish legality, and that the people could not honorably default or repudiate the financial obligation.[96] It is entirely possible that the friends of Nicholls spread the rumor of his intended resignation for political effect to give

---

[93] Proclamation, dated July 31, 1879, and found in the **Messages and Proclamations of Governor Francis T. Nicholls, 1879**. L. A. Wiltz signed documents, numbering 37 in all, and dated July 26 to September 2, 1879.
[94] New Orleans **Times**, July 25, 1879.
[95] Daily **Picayune**, February 28, 1879.
[96] New Orleans **Times**, March 1, 1879.

the governor an opportunity to learn how the people felt toward him. Furthermore, it would reveal his strength in the approaching convention, for powerful political alignments were being formed against the governor[97] and these politicians were sure to try to gain the upper hand in the convention.

The political conversations on the caucus for considering the solution of the state debt showed concern over the unity of the Democratic party.[98] The mass meeting at Lafayette Square of admirers of Captain Kidd and the forty who held out for the majority report of the state debt committee increased the uneasiness.[99] The Democratic machine feared the people of the country parishes would ignore party organization and discipline, and go into the approaching election divided into innumerable personal followings. The argument was used that the Republicans would offer no candidates, therefore, each aspirant should be privileged to make the race on his own merits.[100] The *Times* in its dislike for machine politics, hoped the people would rise up in the majesty of their indignation and relegate the machine managers to private life, and put men in office who were more interested in the welfare of the state than in the spoils and perquisites of office.[101] Later, the *Times* drew a sharper line between political parties and machine politics when it pointed out that party organization was essential to the advancement of political ideas and principles, but machine politics was a disgrace and curse to political parties, because professional politicians were exalted above statesmen and the true lead-

---

[97] "An Autobiography of Francis T. Nicholls," **Louisiana Historical Quarterly**, XVII, p. 259.
[98] New Orleans **Times**, July 10, 1879.
[99] **Ibid.**, July 16, 1879.
[100] New Orleans **Democrat**, July 18, 1879.
[101] New Orleans **Times**, August 1, 1879.

ers of the people.[102] The *Picayune* came out denouncing machine politics,[103] and the *Times* continued its denunciation of ring politics, by charging that the state treasury was in the hands of the editor of the New Orleans *Democrat*, the machine organ. One of the owners of the *Democrat* was to run for state auditor, and it seemed to be settled that a governor was to be elected from the machine clique.[104] The probable motive for the attack was that the *Democrat* supported the dominant faction in the constitutional convention and managed to retain the job of state printer. This faction was labeled the "machine" and it supported Louis A. Wiltz for governor.

The *Picayune* endorsed General Fred N. Ogden for governor as the man who could unite the party,

> enthuse it with his own spirit, and wield it as a unit in the coming days of intense political excitement now everywhere anticipated. He can place the party on higher ground, break the clasp of its rings, and lead it to victory in the pending struggle.[105]

On August 27, 1879, John McEnery, E. J. Ellis, D. B. Penn, and one hundred and twenty-two others asked General Ogden for permission to place his name before the Baton Rouge convention in October. They wrote General Ogden that the governor

> should be brave, honest, true, resolute in executing the laws, of unclouded judgment, unselfish in his patriotism, and entirely disconnected with and wholly independent of all combinations, cliques, and rings. In you do we find all of these qualifications united.[106]

---

[102] New Orleans Times, August 19, 1879.
[103] Daily Picayune, August 20, 1879.
[104] New Orleans Times, August 28, 29, and 30, 1879.
[105] Daily Picayune, August 20, 1879.
[106] New Orleans Times, September 5, 1879.

General Ogden considered for a week and then refused to be a candidate for nomination as governor at the Democratic state convention. He gave as his reasons, "sense of duty and honor."[107] His friends urged him to reconsider, and on September 19, he agreed to allow them to place his name before the convention, but he still refused to engage in any canvass for the governorship.[108] The anti-machine politicians organized an Ogden Campaign Committee and sought delegates to the state convention in an effort to defeat the nomination of the machine candidate, Louis A. Wiltz.[109] Ogden clubs were organized in New Orleans and claims were made that North Louisiana was for Ogden.[110] The *Picayune* said the purpose which animated the Ogden movement was to check the growing power of machine politics. The activities of the lottery clique and the professional politicians against Nicholls were held responsible for recent events. The key of the machine was the ward club, since the presidents of the ward clubs appointed the judges and commissioners of election. The judges and commissioners manipulated the primaries so as to win the delegates to the nominating convention.[111] The anti-ring Democratic-Conservative Association was formed for the sole purpose of securing for the Democratic-Conservative voters of Orleans parish a fair election of delegates for the state and parish conventions which nominated candidates for the various state offices.[112] It was reported that the country parishes had resolved to concede to New Orleans the governorship of the state for the first time in fifty years. This concession was to strengthen the Democratic-Conservatives in the city, and in a short time they were claiming two-

---

[107] Daily **Picayune**, September 5, 1879.
[108] **Ibid.**, September 19, 1879.
[109] New Orleans **Times**, September 24, 1879.
[110] **Ibid.**, September 25, 1879.
[111] Daily **Picayune**, September 25, 1879.
[112] New Orleans **Times**, September 18, 1879.

A NEW CONSTITUTION

thirds of the city of New Orleans for Ogden.[113] When the city delegates were finally selected, eighty-eight were for Wiltz and only forty for Ogden.[114]

On the eve of the Democratic convention it was reported that the Committee on Credentials was composed of five Wiltz and four Ogden men;[115] that the supporters of Wiltz were not only offering political trades with the country delegates, but had bought certain city delegates.[116] The convention met at Pike's Hall, Baton Rouge, and after organizing, W. M. Levy placed L. A. Wiltz and Don Caffery placed F. N. Ogden in nomination as candidates for governor. Both candidates made short addresses, and on the first ballot, Wiltz received 276, and Ogden 173½ votes. The nomination of Wiltz was then made unanimous. The nomination of the remaining candidates was mere routine.[117] The partisan platform ended with a tribute to Nicholls:

> Resolved, That Francis T. Nicholls now Governor of Louisiana is entitled to the grateful acknowledgments of his fellow-citizens for his patriotism and public services, his devotion to Louisiana and his success in effecting the redemption of her liberties.[118]

The machine politicians could afford to pay the governor this compliment after their success in the constitutional convention wherein they cut his four-year term to three.

---

[113] Daily Picayune, September 25, 1879; New Orleans Times, September 25, and October 1, 1879.
[114] New Orleans Times, October 5, 1879.
[115] Ibid.
[116] Daily Picayune, October 6, 1879.
[117] New Orleans Times, October 8, 1879. S. B. Poche was selected president pro tem, and Armant, secretary of the convention. The other nominations were: S. D. McEnery, lieutenant-governor; E. H. Fay, superintendent of education; A. Jumel, auditor; J. E. Egan, attorney-general; W. A. Strong, secretary of state.
[118] Opelousas Courier, October 18, 1879.

The Democratic campaign opened October 21, with a torchlight parade,[119] and gained strength when the Anti-ring Association endorsed the ticket.[120] Nevertheless, a few papers could not forget the fight Nicholls had made, and one announced:

> We bow with reverential tenderness to the true man, who without a pang of regret or of self-reproach, lays down the splendid burden of unsought power. . . . A man of antique mold, he accepted the great trust with no ambition and with no joy.[121]

A large crowd met at the St. Charles Theater to consider the new constitution and the issues to be met in the canvass.[122] The campaign proved to be comparatively dull with a few barbecues and political rallies.[123]

The Republican party was rather slow in getting organized for the campaign, for its state convention met in New Orleans, October 21, and nominated Taylor Beattie for governor and James M. Gillespie for lieutenant-governor, neither of whom had been outstanding. The caliber of these Republican nominees was partly responsible for the small number of votes cast in the election.[124] A number of resolu-

---

[119] Louisiana Capitolian, October 25, 1879.
[120] New Orleans Times, October 23, 1879.
[121] Daily Picayune, November 5, 1879, quoted from Louisianais of St. James. For the attitude of Nicholls on running for governor see "An Autobiography of Francis T. Nicholls," Louisiana Historical Quarterly, XVII, pp. 254-259.
[122] New Orleans Times, November 9, 1879.
[123] Opelousas Courier, November 15, 1879.
[124] Annual Cyclopedia, 1879, p. 571; New Orleans Times, October 20, 1879; Daily Picayune, October 21, 1879; Opelousas Courier, November 1, 1879. The other nominees of the Republican party were: Don A. Pardee, attorney general; C. Mayo, auditor; James D. Kennedy (colored), secretary of state; F. M. Bonzano, superintendent of education.

tions were passed one of which declared General Grant to be their unalterable choice for president in 1880. Another resolution declared the colored people would remain in Louisiana if they were allowed to vote and have their votes counted; otherwise, they would be forced to leave the state.[125]

On the eve of the election, another Democratic mass meeting was held in the St. Charles Theater to arouse interest.[126] But the people of New Orleans were not over-concerned, for less than 20,000 voted in New Orleans out of more than 40,000 qualified voters, although 35,000 had voted in the 1876 election.[127] The election was reported as quiet and orderly,[128] and the entire Democratic ticket was elected. The constitution was adopted, and the ordinance relative to the state debt was approved.[129] Out of a total of 172,943 registered voters less than 114,000 voted. This was a good poll considering the lack of enthusiasm. Probably the illiterate voter had grown tired of politics for there were 14,830 of the 87,978 registered white voters, who were unable to write their names and 69,431 of the 84,965 registered colored voters could not write their names.[130]

The Board of Canvassers met on the last day of the year and promulgated the official vote of December 2, 1879, but the results had been known for some time.[131] The results showed that the Democrats won over the Republicans by an average of 25,000 votes. The new legislature had thirty-one

---

[125] **Annual Cyclopedia, 1879**, p. 571. Wiltz received 74,769 to 40,760 votes for Beattie; McEnery received 76,003 to 39,961 for Gillespie.
[126] New Orleans **Times**, November 30, 1879.
[127] Daily **Picayune**, December 4, 1879.
[128] New Orleans **Times**, December 3, 1879.
[129] **Report, Secretary of State, 1879**; **Picayune**, December 13, 1879. The vote for the constitution was 86,494 to 27,346. The vote for the Debt Ordinance 59,932 to 49,445.
[130] **Report, Secretary of State, 1879**, p. 8.
[131] Daily **Picayune**, January 1, 1880; New Orleans **Times**, January 1, 1880; St. Landry **Democrat**, January 7, 1880.

Democrats and twenty-five Republicans in the senate; the house of representatives contained seventy-six Democrats, seventeen Republicans, and three Independents.[132] The legislature met in New Orleans on January 12. Floods had so deranged transportation facilities that the entire delegation of North Louisiana legislators had to go by Galveston to reach New Orleans.[133]

The first general assembly under the new constitution naturally devoted most of its efforts to legislation for putting that document into effect. Governor Nicholls sent his message to a joint session of the legislature on the opening day. It was a brief message stating that he would leave to his successor the privilege of suggesting what legislation was needed. He merely reported the bills of the last session he had vetoed and gave his reasons. He also submitted a list of the appointments he had made and rendered a report on the funds appropriated for the expenses of his office.[134] The report on disbursements enumerated every penny spent, and stated that the governor held the vouchers for each expenditure plus the cash balance of $7,382.47 subject to the order of the legislature.[135]

With the induction into office of the new state officials on January 14, Francis T. Nicholls retired to private life. His retirement occasioned considerable editorial praise from city and rural press alike. The *Democrat* thought his administration would be recorded in history as one of the purest and ablest.

> No whisper has been heard of wrong or corruption in the various departments of the government, and the laws have been impartially and ably executed. The

---

[132] **Annual Cyclopedia, 1879**, p. 571.
[133] New Orleans Times, January 10, 1880.
[134] **Official Journal of the Senate of Louisiana, 1880**, pp. 5-9.
[135] Ibid., **Messages and Proclamations of the Governor; Journal of the House of Representatives of Louisiana, 1880.**

A NEW CONSTITUTION

levees have been carefully looked after and an immense amount of work well and economically done. The interests of the state have been guarded with thoughtful care, and all the public institutions conducted in a manner that reflect credit upon the administration. Surrounded at first by difficulties that seemed well nigh insurmountable, Governor Nicholls overcame them all, and leaves the office which he has honored and dignified with the proud consciousness of duty well performed and retaining the warm affection of the people.[136]

The rural press probably out-did the city press in praising Nicholls. It was generally agreed that he was the master spirit in the overthrow of Packard and that the circumstances under which he took office would retain a place in the memory of the people as one of the most momentous episodes in our history.

Governor Nicholls, we admit, has not been as much of a partisan as he might have been, but those who expected a different course from him than the one he has taken, must certainly have expected him to disregard the pledge he made when he accepted the nomination at the hands of the Baton Rouge convention of 1876. The people of the state, without respect to party, will bear witness that he has tried to keep his word.[137]

The Morehouse *Clarion* not only praised him but voiced its opinion of the machine politicians who managed to cut his term short by a full year, when it said:

Selfish newspapers and neglected demagogues have taken a wicked pleasure in heaping venomous vituperations upon the untarnished, spotless name of this mighty hero, and disgusted with the cheek and cunning of party tricksters, the maimed Nicholls has unpretentiously retired to private life, modestly announcing himself an attorney at law.[138]

---

[136] New Orleans Democrat, January 14, 1880.
[137] Opelousas Courier, January 10, 1880, copied from Catahoula News.
[138] Opelousas Courier, February 21, 1880, copied from Morehouse Clarion.

The caucus of the legislature at 9 a. m. before that body formally convened at noon January 12, was well attended.[139] The caucus declared R. N. Ogden the Democratic nominee for speaker and P. J. Trezevant the nominee for clerk of the house of representatives; the Democratic nominees were elected.[140] The governor and lieutenant-governor were inaugurated at Odd Fellows Hall at 1 p. m., January 14, in the presence of about 700 people. Governor Wiltz was still too feeble from his recent illness to make the usual address.[141] The following day the governor sent his message by his private secretary. It was a lengthy message dealing with the organization of the courts, the State House at Baton Rouge, paupers, militia, state medicine and quarantine, suffrage, Bureau of Agriculture, equality of taxation, license taxes, poll tax, levees, homestead, public education, tax for railways, corporations and labor, cruelties in punishment, charitable institutions, the state debt, debt of New Orleans, and the city charter.[142] The message as a whole was well written, and pointed out the provisions of the constitution relative to the subjects mentioned, but it was cautious in refraining from specific recommendations. When recommendations were made, they were in rather general terms. The majority of the legislature was sympathetic to the governor's message and acted in harmony with it.[143] The session was limited by law to ninety days and ended at midnight on April 10.[144]

---

[139] New Orleans Times, January 12, 1880.
[140] Ibid., January 13, 1880.
[141] Ibid., January 15, 1880.
[142] Journal of the Senate of Louisiana, 1880, pp. 14-25; New Orleans Times, January 16, 1880.
[143] An extensive discussion of the legislation of Wiltz's administration was considered beyond the scope of this study.
[144] Journal of the Senate of Louisiana, 1880, p. 364.

Chapter VII

THE LOTTERY FIGHT

THE Louisiana State Lottery Company and the fight Governor Nicholls waged against it deserve a place in the discussion of the period. It was in his first administration that Governor Nicholls began the fight against the lottery company which, years later, in his second administration, reached its well known climax and successful denouement. The events connected with the Louisiana State Lottery Company from 1876 to 1880 cannot be told properly, unless a brief sketch of the company during the preceding years is included. The lottery not only divided the people politically, but it was an important force in the economic, social, and religious life of the state.

The title of Act 25 of 1868, chartering the Louisiana State Lottery Company was, "An act to increase the revenues of the state, and to authorize the incorporation and establishment of the Louisiana State Lottery Company."[1] The charter was to run for twenty-five years and the company was to pay $40,000 annually to the treasury of the state. The payment was to be made in quarterly installments in advance beginning with January 1, 1869, and in return for this sum, the company was exempt from all taxes and other licenses. The company was required to give bond for the sum of $50,000. The capital stock was placed at $1,000,000 divided into 10,000 shares with a par value of $100 each, and the company was to begin operations when one-tenth of the capital stock had been subscribed. The board of directors was to be composed of seven stockholders.[2]

[1] Daily Picayune, July 18, 1868.
[2] **Acts of the Legislature of the State of Louisiana, 1868**, No. 25.

The act probably created the most colossal private speculative concern in the history of the state, and the company was given a virtual monopoly, as no other lottery company was to be chartered in Louisiana.

The principal arguments in favor of the bill were that the state was in need of revenue, and it was better to charter a Louisiana lottery and keep the money at home than to have the people speculate in foreign lotteries.[3] The bill was opposed for the following reasons: The immoral and corruptive influence on the community; the monopoly granted the company; the fact that there was no requirement that subscribed stock be actually paid for; and because the company was exempt from taxation.[4] The monopoly conferred by the act was hidden under the avalanche of verbiage about the objects of incorporation, which were stated as:

(1) To protect the state against losses in foreign lotteries.
(2) To establish a solvent home institution and to insure fairness.
(3) To raise funds for education and charitable purposes for the citizens of Louisiana.[5]

The poverty-stricken condition of Louisiana was used to persuade the loyal, honest, native son to vote for the bill, while the carpet-bagger and ignorant negro were bribed. There is said to be ample proof that the latter class was bribed.[6]

The man who pushed the bill through the legislature of 1868 was Charles T. Howard, who became the first president of the Louisiana Lottery Company. However, his name does not appear in the list of incorporators or anywhere else in

---

[3] Daily **Picayune**, August 4, 1868.
[4] **Ibid.**
[5] **Acts of the Legislature of the State of Louisiana, 1868,** No. 25.
[6] C. C. Buel, "The Degradation of a State," **Century** XLIII, pp. 622-623.

THE LOTTERY FIGHT

the act. Howard was born in Baltimore in 1832 and at the age of twenty, moved to New Orleans where he found employment with the steamboat interests. In 1854 he became the New Orleans agent of the Alabama State Lottery Company and retained that position until he resigned in 1861 to join the Confederate army. From 1865 to 1868 he was the New Orleans agent of the Kentucky State Lottery.[7]

Evidently the formal applicants for the charter were used as "dummies" inasmuch as nine days after passage of the act, John A. Morris, T. E. Simmons, and C. H. Murray acquired the rights of the corporation. A short time later Charles T. Howard received the shares belonging to Simmons. The other real owners held their shares intact until the corporation was legislated out of existence.[8]

The Louisiana State Lottery Company completed its organization, and was ready for business December 31, 1868. The drawings were public and every effort was made to convince the onlookers of their honesty.[9] The lottery ticket buyer failed to realize the odds were always against him, no matter how honestly the company might be managed. The daily drawings of the company began February 2, 1869.[10] The lottery company zealously defended its privileges by prosecuting agents of other lotteries[11] and defended also its exemption from taxes and licenses.[12]

The company used a variety of schemes in its drawings for several years. The published prices were for the whole tickets, but fractional parts of tickets were sold to make it

---

[7] Jewell's Crescent City Illustrated, pp. 113-114.
[8] C. C. Buel, "The Degradation of a State," Century XLIII, pp. 622-623.
[9] New Orleans Republican, January 2, 1869.
[10] Daily Picayune, January 3, 1869.
[11] Ibid.; Lottery Company vs Richoux, **23 Louisiana Annual Reports,** p. 743.
[12] Lottery Company vs City of New Orleans, **24 Louisiana Annual Reports,** p. 86; New Orleans vs Houston, **26 United States Reports,** p. 1.

possible for all who desired to play. In 1875, the company began featuring approximation prizes, or consolation prizes to those whose ticket numbers bore a resemblance to the numbers that won the larger prizes. The semi-annual drawings were differentiated from the daily and monthly by giving them such names as "Grand Golden," "Grand Extra," and "Extraordinary."[13] The company procured the services of Generals P. G. T. Beauregard and Jubal Early as commissioners to supervise the drawings and the names of these two generals created faith in the enterprise. They gave a statement testifying to the fairness of the procedure just before the "Extraordinary Drawing," June 5, 1877,[14] and a year later they again reassured the public:

> We will state if, in the drawing we have supervised, it has happened that most of the large prizes have been drawn by the Lottery Company itself, it is owing to the fact that not nearly half of the tickets have been sold.[15]

A grand jury of Orleans parish in 1872 reported that lotteries were *contra bonos mores*,[16] but no action resulted from the report. During the following two years the activities of the lottery company moved the grand jury to include in its report a request that the state legislature repeal the lottery law.[17] In a later report the grand jury thought the attorney general should institute a judicial investigation of the lottery company's claim to a legal existence.[18]

It was stated that the company had every legislature in its power from 1868 to 1892, and the truth of this statement was indicated in 1874, when the company influenced the legislature to defeat the bill providing for the creation of the

---

[13] Daily **Picayune**, June 4, 1877.
[14] Ibid.
[15] Ibid., June 13, 1878.
[16] New Orleans **Democrat**, December 26, 1875.
[17] **Ibid.**, December 19, 1875.
[18] Ibid., December 26, 1875, and June 5, 1878.

New Orleans Lottery Company.[19] The Louisiana State Lottery Company was able not only to prevent the chartering of a competitive company, but it forced through the legislature two acts designed to forestall any attempts to sell foreign lottery tickets in New Orleans. One of these acts provided a penalty of $25.00 for unlicensed selling of lottery tickets in New Orleans, one-half of the fine going to the informer.[20] The other act made it a misdemeanor to sell or draw illegal lottery tickets in the state. The penalty provided was ten to thirty days in jail and a fine of $50.00 to $200.00, and proof of sale was sufficient evidence to convict an offender.[21]

The success of the company in controlling the legislature and the growing evils of the lottery stirred the opposition in 1876 to introduce three bills: (1) to repeal the company's charter, (2) to repeal the Acts of 1874 and (3) to investigate the charges of bribery in the legislature which granted the charter in 1868.[22] The company emerged triumphant from this attack.

Friends of the lottery company were unable to understand why Nicholls did not give it his active support and accused him of breach of promise. They claimed that a joint caucus of the Nicholls legislature in January, 1877, appointed a committee to wait upon Howard, to ask him for a donation to help sustain the legislature, and that he gave several thousand dollars. A short time later a bill to abolish the lottery company was introduced but postponed indefinitely and the company then gave $34,000 additional, for the purpose of inducing a sufficient number of Returning Board men in the St. Louis Hotel to come over and join the legislature in Odd Fellows Hall.[23] Nicholls was opposed to gambling but he

---
[19] Daily Picayune, February 25 and 26, 1874.
[20] Acts of the Legislature of the State of Louisiana, 1874, No. 9.
[21] Ibid., 1874, No. 10.
[22] New Orleans Democrat, January 18, February 10 and 11, 1876.
[23] New Orleans Times, March 29, 1879.

accepted support from the lottery officials as from other people. He always contended that he made no promises in return.[24]

The opposition to the lottery was persistent. Most of the opponents were from the rural sections, some were urban church members, and a few thought the lottery took the savings of the poor without giving anything in return. A bill to abolish the Louisiana Lottery Company was introduced in the house of representatives March 7, and passed March 20, 1877, at the extra session of the legislature, but was defeated in the senate.[25] This bill was the principal cause of the breach in the Democratic-Conservative party, and led to the demand for a new constitution. The lottery crowd surmised that Governor Nicholls would like to see the lottery company abolished since the supporters of the bill were his good friends. Furthermore, the Governor had accepted donations from the company but after he was reasonably secure in office he displayed no special friendship for it. Plans were made to undermine the political power of the Governor, and at the same time make safe the status of the lottery. The lottery officials saw that if the rural people were persuaded a constitutional convention was needed and Governor Nicholls ignored the issue, he would lose his popularity. If the convention were held, the lottery men believed they could get the charter of the company sanctioned by the constitution. Such divergent viewpoints made harmony impossible between Nicholls and the friends of the lottery.

The anti-lottery men contended that the contract of 1868 was *ultra vires*,[26] and that there was nothing to prevent the

---

[24] During the first four months of 1877, Nicholls was dependent on private donations and the taxes he could collect for financing his government.

[25] **Journal of the House of Representatives of Louisiana, 1877, Extra Session**, p. 219, house bill No. 199; **Journal, Senate of Louisiana, 1877, Extra Session**, pp. 73-199.

[26] New Orleans **Democrat**, February 9, and March 1 and 7, 1878.

THE LOTTERY FIGHT 187

state's refusing to sanction any longer such a corporation. The legislature in 1878 failed to muster the necessary two-thirds vote, for a proposed constitutional amendment to abolish the company.[27] A short time later, a bill to repeal the monopoly provision of the company failed to pass.[28]

The main argument in favor of the lottery company during its first decade was that it had helped finance churches, schools, hospitals, and highways. On the other hand, the anti-lottery men condemned it as a great political evil,[29] and a licensed gambling enterprise degrading the morals of the people. The feeling against the company was well stated by the Natchitoches *Peoples' Vindicator*:

> Ever since its institution it has been a nuisance stinking in the nostrils of all good men. It had its origin in the corruption of a corrupt legislature—a legislature of thieving aliens, ignorant and debased negroes, and the depraved of our own people.[30]

The company's power was indicated by Howard's alleged statement, "Give me the monopoly of a wheel in Louisiana and I'll rule the state."[31] An opponent of the lottery with a mathematical turn of mind in 1884 figured that,

> from 1872 to 1884 there have been fourteen sessions of the legislature, at an average cost of $1,500 per day. The lottery question has retarded and occupied not less

---

[27] New Orleans **Democrat**, February 9, and March 1 and 7, 1878.
[28] Ibid., March 12, 1878. The vote was 58 yeas and 48 nays.
[29] Ibid., February 28, and May 6, 1877.
[30] The Natchitoches **Peoples' Vindicator**, June 1, 1878.
[31] The New Orleans **Democrat**, May 24, 1878. The **Democrat** pointed out: "The man who buys a ticket every day at every drawing will have only one chance in 84 years to draw even the $243.35 prize. Old Methusaleh himself had he bucked up against the lottery from his earliest childhood to the day of his death and bought a ticket every day, would have found himself winner of $2,678.85 after having spent about $250,000 on the lottery."

than ten days of each session. This represents a time expenditure of 140 days and a monetary equivalent of $200,000; with all this expenditure of wind and money, the lottery company is still impregnably behind its charter.[32]

The Louisiana State Lottery Company was involved in numerous suits. Benjamin Wood, one of the original incorporators of the company, claimed that he was defrauded of his just shares. The case was said to have been dismissed "on the exception of John A. Morris that the lottery gambling was contrary to good morals and could not be adjudicated upon by a court of justice."[33] Still another stockholder challenged the business methods of the company. This suit "was never tried, but was settled amicably out of court, and Morris's plea has been stolen from the record."[34] These cases enabled the officials of the company to realize the extent of public opposition. But the opposition reached its height during the trial of Agusti[35] who was accused by the company of selling unlicensed lottery tickets. The situation was so tense that it was reported Governor Nicholls would be requested to call out the militia.[36] This step was not necessary but four justices of the State Supreme Court sat with Judge Houston (the trial judge) in open court "to sustain by their moral countenance the dignity of the Fourth District Court and indorse the action taken in the premises by the Honorable Judge."[37] The case precipitated a controversy among the newspapers in which the *Democrat*, the mouthpiece of the administration, denounced the lottery company and charged that the lottery controlled the *Picayune* and the

---

[32] New Orleans **Times-Democrat**, June 5, 1884.
[33] J. C. Wickliffe, "The Louisiana Lottery," **Forum**, XII, p. 569. John A. Morris succeeded Charles T. Howard as president of the company.
[34] J. C. Wickliffe, "The Louisiana Lottery," **Forum**, XII, p. 569.
[35] Agusti vs Lottery Company, 34 **Louisiana Annual Reports**, p. 504.
[36] New Orleans **Democrat**, May 29 and 30, 1878.
[37] **Ibid**.

THE LOTTERY FIGHT

Times. This indicated the feeling of Governor Nicholls on the question. The city political faction and the lottery company were supported by the *Picayune* and the *Times.* The controversy became so heated that the *Picayune* said the question was "for lawyers to discuss and for judges to decide ... it would be supremely ridiculous to inaugurate a civil war to decide a question of law."[38]

The company was always on the alert for schemes and devices to attract customers despite the small chance of their winning. The charge was made that there was no just proportion between the terms and price of tickets, and the prizes drawn; that the prizes were smaller than in European countries where lotteries were in existence.[39] To offset this criticism, the lottery company induced Generals Beauregard and Early in 1878 to make a statement designed to win the public:

> As to the objection that the Louisiana State Lottery Company is a monopoly, we do not see that it is a very serious one, but are of the opinion that it is for the better that the charter confers a monopoly. If lotteries are all great evils, then it is better that they should exist as monopolies than that the right to conduct them should be general.[40]

The lottery company also launched a campaign against the opposition. The first of these was a $25,000 libel suit against the editor of the New Orleans *Democrat.* Additional suits were filed against the paper until the total amounted to

---

[38] Daily **Picayune,** May 31, 1878. A short time later the lottery company obtained control of the Democrat which turned against Governor Nicholls and put over the new constitution in 1879. The other two newspapers proceeded to reverse their position as shown in the preceding chapter. It is to be concluded that the newspapers were squabbling over the spoils.
[39] New Orleans **Democrat,** March 14 and 16, 1878.
[40] Daily **Picayune,** March 10, 1878.

$90,000 by the end of 1878.[41] The lottery company gained control of the *Democrat* before the case was decided and the suit was dropped.

Congress was appealed to for aid against the evils of the lottery, but the Federal government gave no effective help for some time.[42] The appeal was a factor though in moving the company to employ nine attorneys to defend its rights.[43]

The Louisiana Lottery Company was a live issue when the legislature met in January, 1879, and the claim was made that fifty-six country legislators came pledged to repeal the charter.[44] An act abolishing the Louisiana State Lottery Company was passed in a short time. One section made it a misdemeanor for the company to operate after March 31, 1879, and another section provided a penalty of sixty days in jail, or $100.00 fine or both for selling tickets of the company. One-half of the fine went to the informer and the other half to the parish in which the offense was committed. Possession of a ticket was made sufficient evidence for conviction.[45] Governor Nicholls studied the constitutionality of the bill two months before signing it.[46] He decided the charter of the lottery company was in legal effect nothing more than a license enjoyed and a privilege conferred for a time, and on the terms specified, subject to future legislative or constitutional control or withdrawal.[47] The United States Supreme Court in Stone *vs* State of Mississippi reached a

---

[41] New Orleans **Democrat**, May 15 and December 31, 1878.
[42] Ibid., March 6, 1878.
[43] Ibid., March 21, 1878.
[44] New Orleans **Times**, January 27, 1879.
[45] **Acts of the Legislature of the State of Louisiana, 1879**, No. 44.
[46] Daily **Picayune**, March 21, 1879; New Orleans **Times**, March 28, 1879. The bill (bill 44) passed the legislature in January and Governor Nicholls signed it March 27.
[47] Scrapbook at Ridgefield. The clipping was an article about Governor Nicholls taken from the **Annual Report of the Association of Graduates, United States Military Academy, 1912.**

similar conclusion in 1880.[48] The state refused to accept the $10,000 quarterly installment from the lottery company on April 1, 1879, on the ground that its charter had been repealed. The lottery company then asked the United States District Court for an injunction against the law (Act 44) being put into effect.[49] Judge Billings of the court granted the injuction basing his action on the ruling in the Dartmouth College case of 1819:

> Where a corporation has been called into existence by a state legislature for a definite object declared in the act creating it, and has powers and faculties given to it which are in their nature and operation pertinent to its sole object and necessary to its very existence, its rights and franchises cannot be swept away by a repealing act of the legislature of the state which created it.[50]

The injunction suspended the act of the legislature and ended the attempt to enforce it. The lottery fight shifted to the constitutional convention which contained many delegates who believed the success of the Democratic-Conservative government in 1877 was due to the funds advanced by the lottery company and were grateful for the help. Ordinances dealing with the lottery were offered on the fifth and sixth days of the convention, but the question was not agitated, according to the records, until the sixty-third day. The lottery company then became the big issue, consuming eight days of debate, with practically every member speaking. The convention forces were well balanced, but a compromise was reached by a vote of 59 to 55 which recognized the twenty-five-year charter of the Louisiana Lottery Company, re-

---

[48] United States Supreme Court Reports, Law Edition, Vol. 25, pp. 1079-1081. The case was argued March 4-5, and decided May 10, 1880, but the late Henry P. Dart inaccurately says October, 1879. See "Addenda" by the Editor, Louisiana Historical Quarterly, XVII, p. 265.
[49] New Orleans Times, April 2, 1879; Daily Picayune, April 6, 1879.
[50] Daily Picayune, May 27, 1879.

moved its monopoly, and permitted the organization of other lotteries upon the payment of $40,000 per annum.[51] The charter of the lottery was to run its full period of twenty-five years expiring January 1, 1894, after which date all lotteries were prohibited in the state.[52] The constitution further provided that the company must file a written renunciation of all its monopoly features in the office of the secretary of state within sixty days after the constitution was ratified. The company readily complied with this provision. The $40,000 license fee remained as financial support for the Charity Hospital in New Orleans, and the additional sums raised by licenses on lotteries were dedicated to the Charity Hospital at Shreveport and to the several parishes for the support of the public schools.[53]

The lottery company sought to regain the favor of the public. This was desired because during the uncertainty over what action the convention would take on the charter in 1879, the price of the stock dropped to $35.00 per share.[54] The company used two columns of a newspaper to describe the semi-annual drawing on June 17 that was supervised by Generals Early and Beauregard. General Early called the number of the ticket and General Beauregard called the sum of money that went with the ticket. It was announced that the next grand drawing would be held as usual in one of the theaters with the accustomed free concert.[55] Four of the nine principal tickets of the grand drawing were sold in New York, two in St. Louis, and one each in Louisiana, Washington, D. C., and Louisville, Kentucky. This indicated that the tickets were sold rather generally over the nation. The drawing of December 17, 1879, was held at the Grand Opera House with a concert to celebrate the "lawful renaissance" of the

[51] New Orleans Times, July 3, 1879; Daily Picayune, July 9. 1879.
[52] Constitution of Louisiana, 1879, Article 167.
[53] Ibid.
[54] Kendall, History of New Orleans, II, p. 486.
[55] New Orleans Times, June 18, 1879.

lottery. The drawing began at 11 a. m., and lasted until 2:30 p. m.[56]

Four bills to destroy or handicap the lottery company were introduced in the state legislature in 1880, but the company was successful in preventing a rival from being chartered. It boasted at the semi-annual drawing June 15, the same year, that "This is the only lottery in any state ever voted on and indorsed by the people."[57]

Nicholls retired from office in 1880 and the lottery company enjoyed its greatest financial success in the decade 1880-1890. The profits were enormous. The stockholders received 110 per cent dividends in 1887, 120 per cent in 1888, 170 per cent in 1889, and 125 per cent in 1890.[58]

The climax of the fight against the lottery came during the second administration of Nicholls, 1888-1892. The company forced through the legislature a constitutional amendment to recharter the lottery and Governor Nicholls vetoed the amendment. The message closed with,

> At no time and under no circumstances will I permit one of my hands to aid in degrading what the other was lost in seeking to uphold . . . the honor of my native state. Were I to affix my signature to the bill I would indeed be ashamed to let my left hand know what my right had done.[59]

The legislature overrode the veto and the amendment was submitted to the people. A most exciting campaign ensued culminating in a success for Nicholls. The powerful lottery company had been whipped. It only remained for the legislature to put the finishing touches to the victory.[60]

---

[56] New Orleans Times, December 17, 1879.
[57] Natchitoches Peoples' Vindicator, May 15, 1880.
[58] C. C. Buel, "The Degradation of a State," Century XLIII, p. 624.
[59] Journal of the Senate of Louisiana, 1890.
[60] The story of the lottery fight was extended beyond 1880 in order to give the outcome of the controversy. Since the end came after the period of this study the writer did not think it proper to give a full treatment of the denouement.

CHAPTER VIII.

COMMERCE AND TRANSPORTATION

THE dominating theme thus far has been political. The object of this chapter will be to supplement the foregoing with some facts concerning the financial and business activities, the efforts made to obtain the necessary transportation facilities, and the establishment of industries in the state while Nicholls was governor. The political and economic forces of society are closely interwoven and they cannot be separated. This was especially true of Louisiana during the period following the overthrow of the carpet-bag government.

By the late summer of 1877 the business outlook for the fall trade was good, and to facilitate this trade a movement was launched to make New Orleans a free port.[1] It was contended that New Orleans would be crowded with the commerce of the world if the wharfage dues were abolished.[2] The commercial houses sent their salesmen out in such great numbers, and one newspaper commented that the railroads would have no need for tickets without the "drummers."[3] It was said that no less than fifty-one insurance companies of other states or foreign countries were doing business in Louisiana.[4]

The favorable balance of trade at New Orleans was $159,486,512 for 1876; $207,514,522 for 1877; $272,827,580 for 1878.[5] These figures show a considerable increase in the excess of exports over imports for the three years and reflect returning business activity to New Orleans. The bank clear-

---

[1] New Orleans Times, August 31, 1877.
[2] Ibid., September 24, 1877.
[3] Ouachita Telegraph, November 30, 1877.
[4] Report, Secretary of State, year ending December 31, 1877, pp. 29-30.
[5] New Orleans Times, February 1, 1879.

COMMERCE AND TRANSPORTATION

ings at New Orleans for the week ending January 27, 1877, reached a total of $12,101,162.07 and from this figure declined gradually until a low of $3,779,238.82 was reached for the week ending August 25, 1877. The decline was seasonal and in the autumn the clearings increased until the week of December 29 showed a total of $12,065,178.60.[6] The bank clearings for the year 1878 were at the highest peak for the week ending January 26, and consistently declined to a low of $3,155,185.24 for the week ending September 28. The seasonal fluctuations lifted the clearings to $9,729,551.26 for the week ending December 28, which was $3,652,175.73 below the January figure.[7] This decline was due to the yellow fever epidemic of 1878 which will be discussed at greater length in another chapter. The following year, 1879, the clearings reached a sum of $12,182,755.10 for the week ending January 25. The low point of the year was $2,521,475.52 for the week of August 30, after which there was a steady increase until $12,555,192.87 was reached December 6.[8] The total bank clearings for the twelve months ending August 31, 1879, amounted to $337,303,425.07. The total clearings for the following twelve months was $421,985,005.71, which was a net gain of $84,651,580.64 for the year ending August 31, 1880, over the preceding year.[9]

During the Civil War salt was made from surface brine at Avery's Island but the surface resources were soon exhausted, and a shaft 16 feet deep was sunk to a bed of solid rock salt and the salt quarried like stone. After the Civil War deeper shafts were sunk, but the mining was not very

---
[6] New Orleans Times, January 27, and March 3 and 31, April 28, May 26, June 30, July 28, August 25, September 29, October 27, December 1 and 29, 1877. The Times published the bank clearings for the two preceding weeks.
[7] Ibid., January 26, March 2 and 30, April 27, May 25, June 1 and 29, July 27, August 31, September 28, October 26, November 30, and December 28, 1878.
[8] Ibid., January 25 to December 27, 1879.
[9] Ibid., September 1, 1880.

successful during the Reconstruction period.[10] The American Rock Salt Mining Company was organized in December, 1878, but did not succeed in making an arrangement with the Averys until February, 1879, whereby it obtained the exclusive right to work the salt mines on Avery's Island for twenty years. The company reconstructed the old salt works and sank a ninety foot shaft,[11] which inaugurated a period of successful salt mining.

Louisiana needed industries to give employment the year round to her citizens, and some manufactures were beginning to be established as shown by the census report of 1880. The manufacture of boots and shoes employed $4,261,190 of capital, foundries and machine shops had $1,005,200 invested, moss factories employed $153,000 of capital, and the cotton seed oil factories were capitalized at $2,742,000. The sugar refineries had $1,400,000 invested, the rice mills $1,505,000 additional and the slaughter houses were capitalized at $1,793,560. The cotton presses were worth $761,000, the saddle factories $356,651, carriage and wagon-making $161,100, copper and tin-smithing $181,518, marble and granite works $127,390, blacksmithing $186,000, cooperage $207,280, the flour and grist mills $350,500, candies and confectionery $388,126, artificial ice factories $158,000, the cigar makers $512,862, and other forms of tobacco an additional $432,085, the planing and lumber mills $276,280. There were many other businesses in New Orleans with less than $100,000 of capital invested.[12]

---

[10] A. E. Parkins, **The South**, p. 365; E. Q. Hawk, **Economic History of the South**, p. 307.

[11] Ouachita **Telegraph**, July 25, 1879. The salt was said to be $99 3/4$ per cent pure.

[12] **United States Census, 1880, Manufactures;** Annual **Cyclopedia, 1880,** pp. 483-484. The Louisiana **Capitolian,** April 10, 1880, tells of M. J. Williams shipping to Von Phul Plantation one of the most complete steam trains to be seen anywhere. All of it was the product of his extensive workshops, situated on Front Street, near the ferry landing, in Baton Rouge.

The economic and financial condition of New Orleans was not healthy. The debt of the city in January, 1877, was given as $22,638,779.21 divided into a floating debt of $1,983,949.81 and a bonded debt of $20,654,829.40. The city budget for 1877 estimated the receipts at $2,571,300, and the expenditures at $2,857,000.[13] A study revealed that the Metropolitan Police cost $5,983,403.73 to maintain during the preceding eight years or an average of $747,925.38 per annum; the Municipal Police Courts cost $189,317.08 for the preceding three years or an average of $263,105.69 annually; the Criminal Courts for the preceding three-year period cost $221,576.16 or an average annual expenditure of $73,858.72; the cost of the city printing averaged $24,222.33 annually for the preceding five years; to maintain the Orleans parish prison cost $95,722.53 annually for the past five years.[14] Comparatively little relief was offered the taxpayers of New Orleans in 1878, as the city budget estimated the receipts at $2,338,620 and the expenditures at $2,336,004.[15] The city found it difficult to pay its employees their salaries, which amounted to $675,542.28.[16] Clerks, laborers, teachers, and policemen realized only about forty per cent of their nominal salary.[17]

The state also found it difficult to meet its annual payroll of $604,583. One writer believed the high interest rate paid on state bonds would bankrupt the people of the state.[18] The interest coupons of the state due January 1, 1879, could not be paid[19] and the default caused some uneasiness in Washington, where the Louisiana Congressmen explained that it

---

[13] New Orleans Times, January 12, and May 20, 1877.
[14] Ibid., January 26 and 29, 1877.
[15] Ibid., December 27, 1877.
[16] Ibid., August 20, 1878.
[17] Ibid., September 22, 1878.
[18] Ouachita Telegraph, March 29, 1878.
[19] Daily Picayune, December 21 and 26, 1878.

was no fault of Governor Nicholls.[20] Professor Charles Gayarré thought the state was insolvent, and suggested the repudiation of the entire debt,[21] but the press revealed that many people were against it.[22]

The amount of the state debt was difficult to determine. In fact, the various legislative attempts to ascertain the true amount only added to the confusion. A constitutional amendment was adopted in 1869, that limited the amount of the state debt to $25,000,000.[23] In spite of this amendment, the debt increased until it was reported to be $41,000,000 in 1872.[24] This figure was undoubtedly too high for the state auditor the following year placed the amount at $24,356,-338.72, which did not include the state bonds loaned to the Citizens' Bank and to the Consolidated Association of Planters.[25]

The debt was scaled down 40 per cent in 1874 and provision was made for the funding of it by the Board of Liquidation. The funded debt was to be replaced with consolidated bonds bearing 7 per cent interest. The act also provided for a sinking fund to retire the debt thus funded.[26] The Board of Liquidation discovered that many of the bonds were of doubtful legality and a new law was passed in 1875, which did not authorize the board to fund the questionable bonds until they had been approved by the courts.[27] The funding of the debt was stopped by Kellogg when it became obvious the high interest rate of the new bonds could not be

---

[20] New Orleans Times, January 2, 1879.
[21] Ibid., February 23, 1879.
[22] New Orleans Times, February 26 and March 30, 1879; Ouachita Telegraph, June 13, 1879; quoted from the Shreveport Times; St. Landry Democrat, July 5, 1879, quoted from the Morehouse Clarion.
[23] S. A. Caldwell, A Banking History of Louisiana, p. 103.
[24] New Orleans Republican, January 17, 1872.
[25] S. A. Caldwell, A Banking History of Louisiana, pp. 104-105.
[26] Acts of the Legislature of the State of Louisiana, 1874, No. 5.
[27] Ibid., 1875, No. 11.

paid. Governor Nicholls proceeded to carry out the law and the state was forced to default on its bonds. The legislature refused to follow his suggestions and the debt question was shifted to the constitutional convention.[28]

The holders of the 7 per cent Louisiana Consolidated bonds met in New York City in October, 1879, to devise some plan of procuring from the State of Louisiana a better settlement than the one proposed by the constitutional convention, and the Bank of New York, assisted by an advisory committee of three, was appointed as agent of the bondholders.[29] As has been shown, this action was futile, and the convention plan was ratified by the electorate on the second of December.

The people were disgruntled over the amount of taxes they had to pay. Those who lived in New Orleans claimed that their tax burden was heavier than that of those outside the city,[30] but the farmers claimed that they paid a higher tax rate on livestock, land, and improvements than the merchants paid.[31] The farmers complained also over the increase in their assessments,[32] and the landowners of St. Landry parish met to consider taking suitable steps for equalizing or reducing taxes.[33] All such complaints had some influence on the politics of 1878 and were a factor in bringing about the constitutional convention the next year. An example of the political effect was the claim of Senator White that the legislature of 1878, not only saved over two million dollars in the annual expenses of government, but reduced the tax rate one and one-half mills.[34] The rate of the state

---

[28] "An Autobiography of Francis T. Nicholls," **Louisiana Historical Quarterly**, XVII, p. 258.
[29] New Orleans **Times**, October 9, 1879.
[30] Ibid., July 23, 1878.
[31] Ouachita **Telegraph**, February 1, 1878.
[32] **Weekly Advocate**, December 13, 1878.
[33] Opelousas **Courier**, February 2, 1878.
[34] Ouachita **Telegraph**, August 2, 1878.

was fourteen and one-half mills divided as follows: 5½ mills for interest and principal of public debt, 3 mills for levees, 4 mills for the general fund, and 2 mills for the schools.[35]

The people were slow in paying the 1878 taxes because the year had been so disastrous. However, the legislature seemed unable to appreciate this fact, and appropriated $200,-000 more than the state revenues during the first four weeks of the session.[36] Taxes had not been paid in full for several years past, and the auditor's books showed the amount due the state at the end of the year was $11,345,832.71, part of this dating back to 1870.[37] The constitutional convention offered the tax relief mentioned heretofore that all penalties, costs, and charges on taxes and licenses due the state and municipal corporations prior to January 1, 1878, were remitted; all the property forfeited could be redeemed by the payment of the principal and interest, and the right of redemption extended to January 1, 1881.[38]

The total sum paid into the state treasury in 1879 was $2,243,854.80 and the total expenditures amounted to $2,230,-779.72, leaving a balance of $13,075.08 for the year.[39] The auditor's warrants outstanding at the end of the year amounted to $1,130,126.97. All the registered voters were still not paying their poll taxes as the auditor's record showed only $36,959.57 collected for the year. The assessment rolls for 1879 totaled $153,486,125, and reveal something of the

---

[35] Annual Cyclopedia, 1878, p. 499.
[36] New Orleans Times, February 15, 1879.
[37] State Auditor's Report for the year ending December 31, 1879, p. 294.
[38] Constitution of Louisiana, 1879; Ouachita Telegraph, August 8, 1879.
[39] Auditor's Report for the year ending December 31, 1879, pp. 297-300.

COMMERCE AND TRANSPORTATION

economic condition of the people.[40] There was a slight improvement during the year and the assessment rolls for 1880 were $159,000,000. The total estimated receipts from all sources was $1,185,500, and the probable expenditures for 1880 were placed at $1,575,126.56. These estimated receipts and expenditures were slightly more than half of what they were the previous year. The decrease was due to the estimated savings the new constitution would bring. The state auditor reported the compensation to assessors and collectors, and unpaid taxes, usually amounted to about 25 per cent of the income from the general property tax.

Transportation was one of the urgent needs of the state in 1877, and new railroad projects occupied the time of the legislature and the governor. New Orleans voted May 25 on the proposition of levying a tax to aid the construction of the Texas-Pacific Railroad from New Orleans to Marshall, Texas, and the election resulted in 6,480 votes for and 12,059 votes against levying the tax. The Republicans endorsed the tax as it would mean work for the colored people.[41] The *Picayune* said the majority of the property owners were for the proposal and that the non-property owners were the ones who really defeated it.[42] The New Orleans, Jackson, and Northern Railroad combined during the year with the Central of Mississippi Railroad Company to form the Chicago,

---

[40] The Auditor's reports showed the assessment rolls were:

1876	$174,601,524
1877	174,633,682
1878	164,148,609
1879	153,486,125
1880	159,000,000

The decrease in the assessments for 1878 was probably due to the fact that the assessor's were more sympathetic with the taxpayers and lowered the valuation. The further decrease for 1879 was due to the havoc brought by the yellow fever of 1878.

[41] New Orleans **Republican**, May 23, 1877.

[42] Daily **Picayune**, May 26, 1877.

St. Louis, and New Orleans Railroad Company with $10,000,000 capital.[43] A citizen of Monroe declared that the city of Shreveport and the parishes along the right-of-way of the projected North Louisiana Railroad running from Shreveport to Vicksburg were interested in its construction and urged the stockholders not to rely solely on subsidies but to do something by their own exertions.[44]

Governor Nicholls realized agriculture and commerce needed transportation, but he was not willing to sacrifice those interests in order to get railroads. He vetoed an act to incorporate the Eastern Louisiana Railway Company because he believed the act conferred "unusual and exceptional privileges, powers and franchises, inconsistent with private rights and the interest of commerce."[45] The governor approved a bill authorizing the loan of state bonds to the New Orleans Pacific Railway but he believed the act was illegal because it authorized an increase of debt beyond the limit fixed by the constitution. Nevertheless, the political pressure was sufficient for him to discreetly shift the question to the courts, and he informed the general assembly of his intention to get the State Supreme Court to pass on the constitutional questions involved before he signed the bonds provided for in the act.[46] The railroad company prepared a bond which the governor rejected, and he also refused to

---

[43] **Report, Secretary of State for 1877.** The charter was filed November 8, 1877.

[44] Ouachita **Telegraph,** September 28, 1877. This road was later incorporated in the Vicksburg, Shreveport, and Pacific Railroad Company. It was completed in 1884 and is now part of the Illinois Central system.

[45] **Messages and Proclamations of Governor Francis T. Nicholls, 1878,** (January 7); **Journal of the House of Representatives, Regular Session, 1878,** p. 5.

[46] **Messages and Proclamations of Governor Francis T. Nicholls, 1878; Journal of the House of Representatives, Special Session, 1878,** p. 18; Opelousas **Courier,** March 16, 1878.

COMMERCE AND TRANSPORTATION 203

sign the state bonds to be delivered to the railroad company. The New Orleans Pacific Railroad Company applied to Judge Rodgers for a mandamus to compel the governor to sign and issue the bonds. The judge decided that the form of the bonds was a matter within the discretion of the governor and refused the mandamus; this decision was later sustained.[47]

The great need for a transportation system caused some railroads to be built that were a liability to the state treasury;[48] for example, the state never realized anything from the $2,500,000 of state bonds advanced to the Vermilionville Branch Railway.[49] A project was launched to build a railroad from Monroe northward to Monticello, Arkansas, at an estimated cost of $4,000,000. The plan was to get Morehouse and Ouachita parishes to subscribe $50,000 each for the cost of grading and laying the crossties from Monroe to the Arkansas line, in the hope that when this was done some company would gladly take over the road and complete it. But the parishes did nothing. An enthusiastic editor believed the members of the Monroe Board of Trade would subscribe $10,000 for the stock of the railroad,[50] but they did not, and the project languished. Interest in it revived several months later when Captain W. T. Hall offered to give $1,000 toward financing it. If four or five hundred other property owners in Morehouse and Ouachita parishes could give a similar amount that sum would be sufficient to begin the railroad; and the project once started would likely be completed and

---

[47] New Orleans Times, April 4, and July 24, 1878. The first contention of Nicholls that the state debt would exceed the limit of $15,000,000 if the $2,000,000 bonds for the railroad were issued was not upheld. See New Orleans Times, May 7, 1878 State ex rel. New Orleans Pacific Railway Company vs Francis T. Nicholls et al., 30 Louisiana Annual Reports, pp. 980 and 1217.
[48] The Monroe Bulletin, July 26, 1879.
[49] New Orleans Times, January 21, 1879.
[50] The Monroe Bulletin, April 19, 1879.

the land values would be increased tremendously.[51] Another optimistic editor thought that the people in Sabine parish were willing to give half of the proceeds from their entire crops for the year as a tax in order to obtain a railroad.[52] But both Monroe and Sabine had to wait a number of years before getting these railways.

The efforts of several years came to a realization with the completion of the New Orleans and Pacific Railway during the year 1880, when it was announced that South Louisiana and Texas were united by rail at 5 p. m., January 21, and regular trains would be in operation within a month.[53] Ex-Governor Mouton was one of the passengers on the first train over the section from Vermilion to New Orleans.[54] The commerce of New Orleans was influenced at once by the various railway lines for they transported 406,072,662 pounds of freight to the city and hauled away 201,424,147 pounds during the twelve months ending August 31, 1880; of the 1,728,252 bales of cotton reaching the city for the twelve months period, 400,842 bales came by railroad.[55] It was reported that Shreveport was anxiously anticipating railroad connection with Baton Rouge and New Orleans at an early date.[56]

The City Railroad Company of New Orleans had received a charter in 1860 to run for twenty years.[57] The company paid the city $227,000 for the franchise to build and

---

[51] The Monroe Bulletin, February 11, 1880.
[52] Ibid., February 25, 1880. The Bulletin quoted from the Sabine Index.
[53] Daily Picayune, January 22, 1880; New Orleans Times, August 18, 1880, gave an account of the railroad from New Orleans to Texas via Lake Charles, Louisiana.
[54] Louisiana Capitolian, March 27, 1880.
[55] New Orleans Times, September 9, 1880.
[56] Opelousas Courier, March 6, 1880.
[57] This railway was within the city connecting the various railroads with the wharves.

COMMERCE AND TRANSPORTATION 205

operate the railway within the city limits and a total of $1,433,843.86 was invested in the road. The total receipts for 1879 amounted to $499,000 and the actual running expenses were $329,962 leaving net earnings of $169,038, of which $140,000 was paid out as dividends.[58] The importance of the railroad might be shown by other statistics, as it received 323,127,008 pounds of freight and forwarded 182,792,405 pounds.[59] The twenty-year franchise would expire in 1880 and the city council advertised for bids on a new city railroad franchise. The old owners of the franchise filed the highest bid, and at a special meeting of the city council, the bid of the City Railroad was accepted.[60]

Louisiana, with more miles of navigable inland waterways than any state in the Union, has found these streams difficult to manage, especially during the spring months. The problem of flood control has been too gigantic for the state, and it has baffled the Federal engineers for years. Major H. L. Abott, in 1869, estimated it would cost $15,020,000 to repair and perfect the levees in Louisiana.[61] Various plans have been proposed to reclaim and protect the alluvial lands of the state, but among them the only practical one is a permanent levee system. Experience has shown that the levees have to be built higher and higher. Despite the importance of levees as an aid to commerce, they were neglected or made a political football during the carpet-bag regime.

The legislature of 1877 created the Board of State Engineers to construct and repair the levees, and a three mill tax was levied to meet the expense of this work. There were seventeen hundred miles of levees in the state which had to

---

[58] New Orleans Times, August 21, 1879.
[59] Ibid., September 1, 1879. Data for the freight handled for the year ending, September 1, 1879.
[60] Ibid., September 2, and October 3, 1879.
[61] House Document, 57 Congress, 2 Session, Vol. 94, **Chief of Army Engineers Report**, p. 660.

be inspected constantly, and during the flood season extra trips were necessary. The board had constructed over 2,-000,000 cubic yards of levees[62] by 1880 but it was estimated 630,000 cubic yards more were needed. The only parishes in which the police juries built levees were East Carroll, Tensas, and Concordia. East Carroll levied a five-mill special tax and the other two parishes twenty mills each for building levees.[63]

The work of the Federal government in Louisiana toward furthering water transportation was directed by the Mississippi River Commission. One of the problems was that of keeping the channels of the various streams open to navigation. The streams became clogged with snags, logs, and sand bars, and with the combination of them there was a "raft." The raft in Red river extended from Campti to the Arkansas line and almost prevented navigation of that stream except during high water. In 1874 Captain Johnston estimated the cost of removing the raft at $156,000, but Congress appropriated only $20,000 in 1875, and $48,000 in 1876 for this purpose.[64] No appropriations were made in 1877 because of the political turmoil over the election, but Congress appropriated $220,000, $175,000 and $50,000, respectively, for the years 1878, 1879, and 1880, for the work of the Mississippi River Commission.[65]

The water transportation of the entire Mississippi valley was dependent upon keeping the mouths of the river deep enough for ships to enter its channel. The project for the improvement of the mouths of the Mississippi launched in 1837 proposed to form and maintain a channel 18 feet

---

[62] Reports, State Board of Engineers, 1877, 1878, and 1879.
[63] Ibid., 1880; New Orleans Times, October 18, 1880.
[64] House Document, 57 Congress, 2 Session, Vol. 94, p. 1011.
[65] Ibid., pp. 652 and 660.

COMMERCE AND TRANSPORTATION   207

deep, through either the Southwest Pass or Pass-a-Loutre, by stirring the bottom and dredging. These projects had cost a total of $2,541,669.53 by 1878, and they were discontinued that year because of the better system demonstrated at the South Pass by the Eads jetties. Dissatisfied with the method of dredging, Congress had decided a few years earlier to experiment with the proposal of James B. Eads. The act of March 3, 1875, authorized Eads to build jetties and other works in South Pass for the purpose ultimately of obtaining and maintaining a channel 300 feet wide and 30 feet deep over the bar at the mouth of the pass and through the pass into the river above.[66] Eads began work at once deepening South Pass with jetties at least 700 feet apart, and extending from 30 feet of water within the bar to 30 feet without; the channel was to have a minimum width of 350 feet. The original act was amended by acts of June 19, 1878, and March 3, 1879, which required Mr. Eads to obtain a channel 26 feet deep, 200 feet wide at the bottom, and having through it a central depth of 30 feet without regard to width, these channels to be maintained for twenty years from July 8, 1879. Eads was eventually to receive $5,252,000 for the completed work, plus $100,000 per year for maintaining the channel.[67]

The jetties proved successful from the beginning, and South Pass had a depth of 18 feet by 1877-1878. The towboat companies[68] objected to the jetties and asked that South Pass be closed in 1878. They contended the jetties were injuring their business; and it was reported that they deliberately damaged the jetties by running their boats into them. Judge Billings ordered a grand jury investigation but no further action was taken.[69]

---

[66] House Document, 57 Congress, 2 Session, Vol. 94, p. 703.
[67] Ibid.,
[68] Daily Picayune, April 15, 1878.
[69] New Orleans Times, April 19, 1878; Daily Picayune, May 1, 1878.

The jetties were inspected from time to time by United States Army Engineers. A group of these engineers on a visit to South Pass in April, 1877, expressed confidence in the project.[70] Then in May, 1878, it was pronounced a success.[71] The jetties were completed in 1879,[72] and the government eventually paid James B. Eads $7,412,500 for them. In 1897, Major Quinn estimated that to continue the work on the jetties would cost $2,000,000 for the next three years.[73] Congress thought they were valuable enough to maintain, and they are in use today.

---

[70] New Orleans Times, April 30, 1877. The visit was made April 28.
[71] Ibid., May 16, 1878.
[72] Ibid., July 11, 1879.
[73] House Documents, 57 Congress, 2 Session, Vol. 94, p. 703.

Chapter IX.

AGRICULTURE AND THE NEGROES

AGRICULTURE was the most important occupation of the people in Louisiana, and remains so today. A report for 1875 covering fifty-three of the fifty-seven parishes of the state gave the agricultural production for that year as 300,000 bales of cotton; 100,000 hogsheads of sugar; 235,000 barrels of molasses; 175,000 barrels of rice; and over 6,000,000 bushels of corn.[1] The agricultural report for 1876 embraced forty-eight of fifty-seven parishes and gave the production as 450,000 bales of cotton; 186,000 hogsheads of sugar; 364,000 barrels of molasses; 270,000 barrels of rice; and "more than sufficient corn to supply home needs." The value of the agricultural products for the year was estimated at $55,000,000 to $60,000,000.[2] The cotton crop for the year was large but the depression of 1873 was still severe enough to affect the market, and most of the agricultural products were sold at unfavorable prices.[3] One rural editor believed the inauguration of Nicholls meant a "new era of prosperity, happiness, and political and social reform dawns upon Louisiana."[4] The editor of the New Orleans *Times* discussed various phases of agriculture, argued that Louisiana offered a fine opportunity for growing oranges, and pointed out that oranges could and were being grown in the state.[5] The editor believed the sugar cane industry was the most important in the state, as well as the most fascinating and attractive of all agricultural pursuits, with large profits in good season.

---
[1] New Orleans Times, January 2, 1877.
[2] Ibid.
[3] Ibid., April 2, 1877.
[4] **Louisiana Sugar Bowl**, New Iberia, January 11, 1877.
[5] New Orleans Times, March 8, 1877.

The sugar planters were probably more progressive than any other farmers in the state. They were trying to increase their sugar production by improving the method of manufacture, and the bagasse burner in vogue twenty years earlier was being reinstalled. Many planters bought an additional set of rollers as tests showed that a double set of powerful and well adjusted rollers would increase production enough in one year to pay for the additional expense.[6] The Sugar Planters' Association discussed at its meetings such questions as agricultural chemistry, the depressed business condition, the tenant system, and northern white labor. Some planters thought white laborers were superior to negroes. The sugar production for Louisiana had increased from 127,000 hogsheads[7] in 1877 to 250,094 hogsheads[8] in 1878. The increase was partially due to stability in political affairs under Governor Nicholls at the time the crop was planted. The prospect of the sugar crop was excellent in July, 1878,[9] but a violent equinoctial storm visited a large portion of the state in September and laid much of the cane flat on the ground. A severe frost on November 29 and 30 created much anxiety among the planters because they feared the unharvested cane was damaged. The storm of September had little effect on the yield but the frost forced the planters to convert much of the cane into molasses which resulted in an 18 per cent increase of molasses over the preceding year—the figures being 323,247 and 264,695 barrels, respectively. The production of 109.96 gallons of molasses per hogshead of sugar in 1878 was the highest ratio on record, the average being 70 gallons.[10] The production of 211,740 hogsheads[11] of sugar in

---

[6] New Orleans Times, December 8, 1878.
[7] **Report of the Commissioner of Agriculture, 1877,** p. 276. A hogshead contained approximately 1,000 pounds.
[8] Ibid., **1878,** p. 262.
[9] New Orleasn Times, July 4, 1878.
[10] **Annual Cyclopedia, 1878,** pp. 499-500.
[11] **Report of the Commissioner of Agriculture, 1879,** p. 132.

1879 was almost twelve per cent less than the previous year. The decrease was probably due to damage from frost to the planting cane and to the yellow fever[12] epidemic which undoubtedly affected the labor supply at planting time. There was an average crop of 272,980 hogsheads[13] in 1880.

The sugar planters did not spend all their time and energy trying to increase production but sought the benefits of a protective tariff.[14] The sugar importers of Baltimore, Boston, and New York objected to a tariff[15] that was low on poor grade sugar and higher on the better grades. Their efforts were directed by lobbyists but the sugar planters of Louisiana, also, knew a few political tricks and succeeded in getting the protection desired.

Rice was another important food crop but the production of the state decreased from 187,116 barrels in 1877 to 100,689 barrels in 1880.[16]

The money crop of the northern half of the state was cotton. The crop of 234,400,000 pounds[17] in 1877 decreased to 214,483,050 pounds[18] in 1878 because the yellow fever epidemic prevented much of it from being harvested. The production of 267,044,000 pounds[19] in 1879 was average but there was a decrease to 161,616,000 pounds[20] in 1880. This decrease was due to the unrest among the negro laborers and to floods of the river valleys in the spring. One editor tried to show that cotton was profitable at 10 cents per pound if

---

[12] The yellow fever will be discussed later.
[13] Report of the Commissioner of Agriculture, 1880, p. 190.
[14] New Orleans Times, January 12, 1879.
[15] Ibid., January 9 and 10, 1879.
[16] New Orleans Times, September 1, 1880. The Times of this date gave the rice production each year for the preceding ten years.
[17] Estimate made by the Department of Agriculture. (Information contained in a letter of Congressman Newt V. Mills, to the writer, April 5, 1939).
[18] Report of the Commissioner of Agriculture, 1878, p. 262.
[19] Ibid., 1879, p. 132.
[20] Ibid., 1880, p. 190.

the farm was managed properly. He assumed that a farmer ought to make his supplies and twelve bales of cotton "to the mule," and at 10 cents per pound should make a profit of $325.00 annually.[21]

Corn was an important crop on all Louisiana farms because it was a staple food for man and animals. The average crop was 14,282,430 bushels for the four-year period, 1877-1880, and varied from 12,592,000 bushels in 1879 to 16,875,000 bushels in 1878.[22] The writer was unable to account for this crop variation of almost twenty-five per cent within one year. It was probably due to variation in rains and other seasonal influences.

The hill section in the north-central part of the state was a region of small farms and these farmers "lived at home" to a large extent. They had plenty of corn, oats, Berkshire pigs, cattle, sheep, and fowls in the fall of 1877, and were anxious to pay their store accounts in order to sustain a good credit rating.[23] Cotton was sold at Trenton at the rate of 750 to 800 bales per week in the latter part of October, and the price received was nine to ten and one-half

---

[21] Ouachita Telegraph, March 22, 1878. His figures were:

Hire of 2 hands at $100.00	$200.00
Wear and tear of mule	25.00
Blacksmith bill and tools	25.00
Extra work and incidentals	25.00
Total expenses	$275.00
12 bales at 10c per pound	600.00
Profit	$325.00

[22] **Report of the Commissioner of Agriculture, 1877**, p. 162; **1878**, p. 262; **1879**, p. 132; and **1880**, p. 190.

[23] Ouachita Telegraph, October 26, 1877.

cents per pound.[24] An editor wrote about the hill farmers of Union parish in the fall of 1878 in these terms:

> I visited a young farmer the other day who may be taken as a fair sample of the thrift that follows industry in these hills. He had a fine crop of cotton, still making rapidly, a good crop of corn already made, an unlimited prospect for peas, extensive potato patches, a large patch of ribbon sugar cane, peanuts, watermelons, oats, fat mules and horses, and unnumbered poultry and numerous hogs.[25]

The farmers were beginning to see the necessity of cooperation for better markets and were organizing "Granges" and associations. The Grangers not only requested the legislature to encourage the introduction of blooded livestock in the state but they also sponsored the Gulf States Exposition to display their livestock and farm products. The exposition was held in New Orleans, February 17, 1879, and Lieutenant-Governor Wiltz made the address of the occasion.[26] The Fruit Growers' Association was active in promoting that particular branch of agriculture. The fifth annual exhibition opened in St. Patrick's Hall, New Orleans, July 18, and lasted three days.[27] There was a fine display of fruits and vegetables and the exhibition was designed to show that the orange crop was increasing annually and that a large section of the state was particularly adapted to its culture. The southern parishes produced fruit of a quality found in only a few parts of the world, but better marketing and shipping methods were needed.[28] These handicaps were not overcome

---
[24] Ouachita Telegraph, Ocober 26, 1877. Trenton, on the Ouachita river opposite the present city of Monroe, was the shipping point for the region west of it for sixty or seventy miles. The freight by boat to New Orleans was $1.25 per bale; by railroad the price was $3.00.
[25] Ibid., September 13, 1878.
[26] New Orleans Times, February 18, 1879.
[27] Ibid., July 18, 1878.
[28] Annual Cyclopedia, 1878, p. 500.

and orange growing did not develop extensively until recently.[29] The organization of the Sugar Planters' Association had proved a forward step, and its studies were helping solve the problems of the growers.[30]

The government of Nicholls had gone on record as favoring immigration, and a number of northern men investigated the farming possibilities in Louisiana.[31] Mr. W. M. Levy offered five thousand acres of hill land lying between Red River and Black Lake at seventy-five cents per acre on terms of one-fifth cash and the balance in one, two, three, and four years.[32] The state had acquired over five million acres of land by tax foreclosures and from April 30 to December 20, 1877, the state sold 45,946 acres of land for $7,742.65 and had 5,411,182 acres left unsold. During the period forty-seven homesteads were filed for a total of 6,267 acres, and patents were issued on fourteen homesteads totaling 1,801 acres of the land belonging to the Federal government.[33]

During the early summer of 1877, Federal officers seized timber in the hands of private persons and charged the individuals with taking it from government lands. The persons concerned resisted the deputy marshall, but they were arrested and the seized logs were sold at public auction.[34]

---

[29] At the present time there are extensive orange groves in St. Bernard and Plaquemines parishes. A large part of the crop is put on the market in the form of canned juice.
[30] New Orleans **Times**, January 11, 1880.
[31] **Ibid.**, April 26, and October 3, 1877.
[32] Ouachita **Telegraph**, October 26, 1877, quoted from Natchitoches **Vindicator**.
[33] **Annual Report, Registrar State Land Office, 1877.**
[34] New Orleans **Times**, May 16, 22, 23, and 27, August 31, October 2 and 4, 1877; **Annual Cyclopedia, 1877**, p. 467. The **Times** estimated the United States government would net about $10,000 out of the log sale.

The depredations upon the public lands were largely the result of the inability of the settlers to find any lines or corners and a re-survey of the lands was necessary in order to know where the government land was located. These facts prompted the citizens of Louisiana to send an address to the Senators and Representatives of the state in Congress in January, 1878. The address pointed out that one-half of the people who settled between the Sabine river and the point where re-surveys were suspended on account of the war did not know what land they were living on and had not been able to acquire titles to their homes.

> Within that region there are hundreds of valuable farms, some of which have been occupied for forty years, whose occupants know not the townships even they are situated in, and who, as a consequence, have never been able to take any steps to acquire the Federal or state title.[35]

The State Immigration Convention assembled at the State House in New Orleans, January 14, 1878, with forty-two parishes represented at the opening session. The convention undertook to frame a bill to encourage immigration for presentation to the next legislature. The bill as finally formulated was modeled after the Texas law,[36] and provided for the establishment of a bureau of immigration and prescribed its duties and powers. The convention closed its labors with an address setting forth the agricultural opportunities in Louisiana and urging white people to move to the state.[37] About the only tangible result was the migration

---

[35] **Address of the Citizens of Louisiana to the Senators and Representatives of the State in the Congress of the United States**, January, 1878, pp. 5-6.

[36] New Orleans Times, January 15, 1878; Ouachita Telegraph, January 18, 1878.

[37] New Orleans Times, January 16, 1878; Ouachita Telegraph, January 25, 1878.

of forty-five Prussian-Polish families from New Orleans to St. Mary parish.[38]

The farmers in adapting their methods to changing conditions found it necessary to make adjustments in the size of their holdings. The United States Census shows that farms of less than twenty acres decreased in number in Louisiana between 1870 and 1880. There were one hundred farms containing three acres or less in 1870, while no such farm was listed for 1880. For the same decade the farms containing three to ten acres decreased from 3,016 to 1,848; and the farms of ten to twenty acres decreased from 7,493 to 6,708. The farms with more than twenty acres all showed a fair increase for the decade; those farms containing twenty to fifty acres increased in number from 8,854 to 12,626; those of fifty to one hundred acres increased from 3,888 to 8,501; those with one hundred to five hundred acres increased from 3,753 to 15,031; the five hundred to one thousand acre size increased from 650 to 2,159; and those with a thousand acres in 1870 numbered 142, while by 1880 there were 1,319 such farms in the state.[39] The 28,480 farms of Louisiana in 1870, had a grand total of 7,025,817 acres, and ten years later the 48,282 farms had 8,273,506 acres. The farms of the state in 1870 had 4,980,177 acres unimproved, or 70.88 per cent of the total farm acreage, and in 1880 there were 5,553,534 acres unimproved, or 66.88 per cent of the total farm acreage.[40] The density of population increased from 16 to 20.69 to the square mile during the decade.[41]

In the same period the value of farms decreased from $91,303,942 to $76,707,547, the value of equipment from $7,-

---

[38] New Orleans Times, May 4, 1878.
[39] United States Census, 1890. Agricultural Statistics, pp. 118-119. It should be borne in mind that the census report of 1870 was inaccurate and unreliable. The figures used were taken from the 1870 census by the 1890 census.
[40] United States Census, 1890. Agricultural Statistics, pp. 74-107.
[41] United States Census. Compendium for 1890.

159,333 to $5,435,525 and the total value of livestock from $15,929,188 to $12,354,905. The farms decreased in value despite the fact the total acreage increased. The severe economic depression that began in 1873 swept away property values. The decline was so great that the people were reporting their property at less than its real value, or at least, the reported value did not bear the same ratio to its value in 1880 as it did in 1870. During the same decade the number of horses increased from 59,738 to 104,428, the number of mules from 61,338 to 76,674, the work oxen from 32,596 to 41,729, the number of milch cows from 102,076 to 146,454, all other cattle from 200,589 to 283,418, the number of sheep from 118,602 to 135,651, and the number of swine from 338,326 to 633,489.[42] There was a considerable increase in the number of all kinds of livestock in the state between 1870 and 1880 but the depression had caused their value to decrease. The people were probably underestimating the value of their property in order to get some relief from the heavy burden of taxation.

The negro was not only a political factor in Louisiana but he was a social and economic problem. Governor Nicholls had promised equality before the law, and he tried to make good his promise, even to the appointment of negroes to office. He expressed it thus,

> After I was recognized as Governor I set myself earnestly to work to bring about good feeling and confidence between the races . . . I was particularly anxious by kindness and strict justice & impartiality to the colored people . . . I determined that they should feel that they were not proscribed & to this end appointed a number of them to small offices sandwiching them on Boards between white men where while they were powerless to do harm they were in a position to see & know everything that was going on.[43]

---

[42] United States Census, Compendium for 1890, pp. 74-107.
[43] "Autobiography of Francis T. Nicholls," Louisiana Historical Quarterly, XVII, p. 257.

At one time 225 of the 1,085 state officials were negroes,[44] but the colored man's ignorance, backwardness, and potential corruptibility made him a serious problem. His lack of social adjustment often led him into clashes with officials,[45] and his impracticability was indicated in a letter addressed to the *Times*.

> Sir—You know we colored people of the state wish to have a place off to ourselves. We wish the President would give us transportation to some part of the country, and if he don't we will ask some other country for transportation. We cannot live under the law of a Democratic state, and so we would like to have a place to ourselves. . . .[46]

The seriousness of the social problem was presented a few months later in these words:

> The question as to what we are to do with thousands of negroes in the sugar and cotton growing parishes who refuse to work, and subsist by depredating upon property, is one of great importance to our agricultural interests and demands the earnest attention of our legislators. . . That it is almost impossible for farmers to raise poultry, fruit, or hogs in certain localities is an established fact.[47]

It was almost impossible to invoke the law for relief from thefts of fowls, fruit, and stock, because negroes were usually on the juries.

A country editor said that Nicholls had given the negro as much official patronage the first year as the Republicans

---

[44] New Orleans *Times*, April 22, 1877.
[45] Ibid., February 9, 1877.
[46] Ibid., April 27, 1877. Their lack of social adjustment was noted by the New Orleans **Republican**, March 6, 1877, and the New Orleans *Times*, June 2, 1877.
[47] New Orleans *Times*, August 9, 1877.

had during their entire regime; that the negro had found his life, liberty, and property far better protected than in the palmy days of the Republican rule. Furthermore, fewer murders had occurred in 1877 than in any previous year since the war.[48]

A case was reported where the tax collector notified a decrepit colored man to pay his back taxes on a horse assessed to him under the radical rule. When the poor fellow came to pay, the tax collector saw his condition, refused to take a penny, and sent the old "darkey" on his way rejoicing.[49] This incident was probably concocted in order to influence the negroes to leave the Republican party.[50]

The changing political lines in Louisiana saw the first definite independent movement among the negroes. Ex-Lieutenant-Governor Pinchback, then editor of the New Orleans Weekly *Louisianian,* headed the movement because he believed the Republican party had no chance with the old leaders dominating. As chairman of the Republican State Central Committee, he had endeavored to assume the leadership of the party and called all the Republican parish committees to send a list of the names of all officers and members.[51] To check the aspirations of Pinchback, the other members of the State Central Committee called a meeting for June 12, 1878. The meeting, with the negro senator, A. J. Dumont presiding, added one person from each parish and three from New Orleans to the committee, and thus weakened the power of Pinchback in the party.[52] The regular Republican leaders held many meetings throughout Louisiana during the summer, and attempted to ignore the independent

---

[48] St. Landry Democrat, January 26, 1878. The negro had composed nine-tenths of the Republican party in Louisiana before 1876.
[49] The Weekly Advocate, February 18, 1878.
[50] Ibid., April 2, 1878.
[51] The New Orleans Weekly Louisianian, Mach 30, 1878.
[52] New Orleans Democrat, June 14, 1878.

movement of Pinchback by focussing the campaign on local questions and interests.⁵³

The colored preachers should be given credit for influencing their church members to endorse the administration of Nicholls.⁵⁴ The Association of colored Baptists for the Ouachita and Bayou Macon district held a three day session, discussing politics as well as religion. The *Telegraph* understood the influence of the preachers with their flock and issued the following warning:

> May we suggest to these colored clergymen that it better befits their station and their race to tarry at Jericho and see the salvation which superior intelligence and long training—not in the jungles of Africa, or from the descendants of old Ham—can bring, if it be brought at all.⁵⁵

The political campaign of 1878 was destined to bring its tragedies before it had progressed very far. In August, four negroes were hanged on the Courthouse Square in Monroe, by an unknown mob. The hangings were thought to have had some political bearings but it was never proved.⁵⁶ The riot at Natchitoches, September 21, 1878, was undeniably an outgrowth of political feelings. It appears the Democrats announced a parish convention to be held on the same day that the Republicans scheduled theirs; two white radical leaders, Blunt and Breda, disapproved of the Democratic convention. The citizens of Natchitoches attempted to break up the Republican meeting and a riot followed in which one negro was reported killed and three wounded. Blunt and Breda were told to leave the parish and never to return,⁵⁷ because the white Democrats were determined to destroy the leaders of the negroes. Some prominent Repub-

---

⁵³ New Orleans **Democrat,** June 16, 1878.
⁵⁴ New Orleans **Times,** July 14, 1877.
⁵⁵ Ouachita **Telegraph,** August 16, 1878.
⁵⁶ **Ibid.,** August 9, 1878.
⁵⁷ New Orleans **Republican,** September 28, 1878; Daily **Picayune,** September 24, 1878.

licans called on Governor Nicholls to see what he was going to do about the Natchitoches affair and were suavely assured the governor would do his duty.[58] The Republican press in discussing the Natchitoches riot pointed out the value of colored citizens, and said they had cultivated larger crops of cotton, sugar, and rice than for many years past. The laborers on the levees, the deck hands on steamers, carpenters, cooks, and nurses performed their tasks with fidelity.[59] There were political outbreaks in Pointe Coupee, Concordia, and Tensas parishes in which lives were lost.[60] Governor Nicholls made a personal investigation and came to the conclusion that the trouble grew out of various political influences.[61] The small concern displayed by the governor was a reflection on his interest in the welfare of the colored citizens.

The younger members of the colored race had grown up without the benefits derived from slave discipline, and were vicious and dangerous. Some of these negroes were trifling and would steal before they would work. They knew little or nothing about observing the marriage laws and appeared to derive no moral benefits from Christianity; they were highly superstitious and inclined to make their religion spectacular. Notwithstanding these facts, the negro named his religion after that of "his white folks" and the majority of them were Catholics, Baptists, or Methodists.

Some whites, usually the better class, harbored no ill will toward the negro for his part in Reconstruction and realized he was the victim of unscrupulous white adventurers, while the low grade whites hated and persecuted the negro. The former white masters and mistresses held a real affection for their ex-slaves, but the younger generation of whites

---

[58] Daily Picayune, September 27, 1878.
[59] New Orleans Republican, September 28, 1878.
[60] Senate Reports, 45 Congress, 3 Session, No. 855, p. 1, Election 1878; Ouachita Telegraph, October 18, 1878.
[61] Daily Picayune, January 9, 1879; New Orleans Times, January 9, 1879; Weekly Advocate, January 10, 1879.

appeared indifferent. Most of the negroes lived on large plantations in the parishes along the rivers in the southern half of the state, since the hill section had few slaves in 1860. The planters were dependent upon the negroes for labor, and gave them a fair wage and kind treatment. The colored man was also granted the privilege of participating in political affairs, for thirteen of the one hundred thirty-one delegates to the constitutional convention were negroes.[62] The press commented on the peaceable and friendly relations between the white and colored people in the various parishes. During the yellow fever epidemic of the previous year, it was said that each race was ready to help the other; and white men proclaimed that the negroes, with full and ample protection for life and property, were living among their friends.[63]

The census of 1880 reported 454,954 whites and 483,655 colored people in Louisiana.[64] The great majority of the negroes were lacking in habits of thrift and industry, and these shortcomings were not the result of legislation, nor of mistreatment by the whites. The condition was due, in a large measure, to the fact that 82 per cent of the colored population over twenty-one years of age, and 80.2 per cent of all colored males over twenty-one years of age were illiterate.[65] This meant that the negroes were dependent for information upon their political and religious leaders.

The negroes were not as contented as the white people said they were, otherwise the colored people would not have gone to Kansas in such numbers in 1879 and 1880. They were dissatisfied because they thought that Kansas would be

---

[62] **Journal of Proceedings of Constitutional Convention of Louisiana, 1879;** New Orleans **Picayune,** April 21, 1879; New Orleans **Times,** April 21, 1879.

[63] The Louisiana **Capitolian,** February 15, 1879; Weekly **Advocate,** February 21, 1879.

[64] **Negro Population 1790-1915,** Bureau of the Census, p. 44.

[65] **United States Census, 1880,** Compendium, p. 1653.

AGRICULTURE AND THE NEGROES   223

better for them. The improvident had nothing; and the demagogues convinced some that they were denied their political rights.[66] The discontented held a convention in New Orleans to consider their condition and the discussions lasted two days.[67] One month later 1500 negroes and whites gathered at Lafayette Square in New Orleans to hear ex-Governor Harry S. Foote of Kansas tell of the wonderful opportunities of that state.[68] The lure of Kansas became so strong among the colored people of Avoyelles parish that they held a meeting to determine whether they should emigrate and many joined the "exodusters."[69]

It was reported that the negroes in Pointe Coupee parish were told the constitutional convention would put them back in slavery so they prepared to go to Kansas.[70] It was shown that there was nothing in the proposed constitution to indicate hostility towards the colored race. The negro leaders in the constitutional convention praised the fair and courteous treatment they received on the floor of the convention, and approved the guarantees embodied in the constitution.[71] In Madison parish the pastor and deacons of a colored Baptist church were reported to have led the entire church membership of 300 to Kansas.[72]

The organizers of the Kansas movement misled the negroes with alluring circulars and posters of good times in Kansas. One poster showed a large banana tree filled with fruit and darkies eating the fruit with the inscription, "This

---

[66] New Orleans Times, March 15, 1879. Editorial on "Colored Exodus."
[67] Ibid., April 19, 1879.
[68] Ibid., May 23, 1879.
[69] Marksville Bulletin, May 16, 1879.
[70] Weekly Advocate, June 13, 1879. Quoted from the Pointe Coupee Pelican.
[71] New Orleans Democrat, October 31, 1879. Pierre Landry, Henry Demas, and P. B. S. Pinchback were the negro leaders quoted.
[72] Weekly Advocate, September 26, 1879.

is the way we live in Kansas."[73] A circular claimed the Colored Colonization Society had been organized by the government to provide each family in Kansas with 160 acres of land free.[74] The charge was made that the exodus was the work of sharpers making money out of the poor negroes, and a number of newspapers in Kansas were reported as demanding punishment of the perpetrators for swindling. The Labor Convention at Vicksburg, May 6, 1879, gave the causes of the emigration as (1) low price of cotton and poor economic conditions, (2) irrational system of planting in some sections and the pressure to make profits, (3) the vicious system of credit, (4) apprehension on the part of many colored people, (5) false rumors of free land, mules, and money from the government for those who went to Kansas.[75] An old darkey offered the explanation that the negro just wanted to ramble.[76]

The movement was ill-advised and hasty since most of the negroes set out for Kansas without any definite idea or purpose of what they would or could do when they reached their destination. The people of Kansas were not as congenial as the people of Louisiana and it was reported that the white working-men in Kansas were alarmed over the great influx of laborers as there was not work enough for all.[77] Governor St. John of Kansas was quoted as saying that four thousand negro refugees in Kansas were on relief, and the labor market was over-supplied with them. It would be impossible to obtain employment for any more and it would

---

[73] Weekly **Advocate,** May 2, 1879. Another poster showed a giant potato labeled, "Grown in Kansas."
[74] Ibid., May 9, 1879. The **Advocate** quoted from the St. Louis Globe Democrat, The Topeka **Commonwealth,** the **Star,** and Kansas **Commercial,** as papers denouncing the exodus.
[75] Ibid., May 9, 1879.
[76] Ibid., May 16, 1879.
[77] Ibid., April 25, 1879.

be a cruel outrage on the colored man to send more to Kansas to suffer.[78]

When the exodus began, the planters of Louisiana gave it little consideration and regarded the movement as an effort of a few malcontents to disorganize labor and make the colored people dissatisfied with their condition. The seriousness of the movement soon became evident. One paper denounced the New Orleans convention of colored people in ill-tempered language as:

> a dastardly attempt by certain scoundrels in the pay of Northern radical demagogues, to demoralize Southern labor and injure agricultural interests of the South.[79]

The same paper continued to evade the real cause of the exodus and considered the leaders vagabonds spreading the seeds of dissension among the colored people in many parishes.[80] The exodus reached such proportions that the men engaged in the cotton business in New Orleans formed the Mississippi Valley Immigration Company to turn the tide of immigration from the Old World into the Southern States to replace the departing negroes. The company undertook to ascertain the needs of the planters and to procure whatever labor they desired at a fair wage from Europe. The police jury of Tensas parish subscribed $10,000 for the enterprise —the money was to be raised by a special tax.[81] The company spent most of its energy in propaganda and brought in very few immigrants.

The whites used a variety of arguments to get the negroes to remain in Louisiana. It was pointed out that they would meet keen competition from the whites of the North, whereas, in Louisiana they lived together among friends, had

---

[78] Weekly Advocate, August 8, 1879.
[79] Ibid., April 25, 1879.
[80] Ibid., May 2, 1879.
[81] Daily Picayune, May 26, 1879.

their own churches, schools, amusements, societies, and could find employment easily. The negroes had a monopoly of labor on the plantations and rivers, and in New Orleans they worked as stevedores, draymen, warehousemen, and laborers. The women could usually find housework as cooks, maids, and nurses. Moreover, the South was the place where the negroes were numerous enough for their political influence to be felt.[82] A report was published that a negro by the name of Ben Moore in East Feliciana parish, with the assistance of his wife, made fifteen bales of cotton in 1879, and a good crop of corn and potatoes.[83] Another means of influencing the negroes to remain where they were was a purported dispatch from Topeka, Kansas, to the effect that a number of deaths had occurred among the colored refugees at the barracks there and that the bodies had been left at the burying ground three or four days before being interred.[84] Furthermore, the negro was told of the poverty and suffering of the "exodusters" in all the river towns and railway stations.[85] Letters were published ostensibly from negroes in Kansas to their former employers. The negroes begged for a transportation ticket back to Louisiana, and were usually quoted as writing such statements as ,"I hope and pray that I may come back to you again."[86]

An Irishman of New Orleans proposed to bring his countrymen into the state to replace the colored laborers. He wrote that the New York *Herald* reported 316,000 Irishmen were in want of food and clothing. He urged the formation of an immigration society to bring these needy people to the sugar and cotton plantations of Louisiana. Several

---

[82] Louisiana Capitolian, January 10, 1880.
[83] Ibid., January 24, 1880.
[84] Louisiana Capitolian, January 31, 1880.
[85] Ibid., February 21, 1880.
[86] Ibid., Letter from William Walker (colored) in Kansas City, February 11, 1880, to Mr. John Laycock of West Baton Rouge parish.

newspapers of the state were quoted as favoring the idea of bringing in the Irish laborers.[87]

In some of the parishes there were labor troubles involving not the rising of the blacks against the whites, but of employees against employers. The negroes, during March, (1880) in the parishes of St. James, St. John the Baptist, and St. Charles, went from plantation to plantation, forcing the negroes to quit work or leave the parishes. They rode about in armed bands, spreading terror by breaking into cabins, taking quiet laborers from their work in the fields, and whipping them.[88] A proclamation from the governor did not quiet the rioters and the militia was called out at a few points. One hundred white men in St. John the Baptist parish organized a cavalry troop to catch and arrest the leaders. The leaders when caught were taken to New Orleans, and a committee was appointed to arrange their differences with the planters. The conferences brought out the fact that the negroes had a false conception of their rights.[89] The solution of the exodus and unrest was to give the negro a square deal, for the planter and laborer inevitably rose or fell together.

---

[87] Louisiana Capitolian, January 17, and March 6, 1880. The newspapers that endorsed the idea were the Shreveport Times, Country Visitor, Thibodaux Sentinel, Sabine Index, Farmerville Gazette and Jackson Clarion.

[88] Weekly Advocate, April 9, 1880; Louisiana Capitolian, April 10, 1880.

[89] Annual Cyclopedia, 1880, p. 482.

CHAPTER X.

EDUCATION AND HEALTH

EDUCATION was recognized as an essential business of the state government in 1877, but the records of the state superintendent for the preceding years were not available, because of the political turmoil.[1] The legislature enacted a general school law[2] which provided for a state board of education composed of the governor, lieutenant-governor, secretary of state, attorney general, superintendent of education, and two citizens appointed by the governor for a term of four years. The state board was to appoint the parish school boards, which were to consist of not less than five and not more than nine members. Each parish board was to appoint the district boards, and the school funds were to reach the districts on the basis of the number of educable children. The parish boards were authorized to issue certificates to the teachers. The salary of the parish superintendent was limited to $200.00 per year. The law provided for a New Orleans school board of twenty members, eight appointed by the state board and twelve by the city council. The New Orleans board was allowed a city superintendent at $3,000 per year, and a secretary at the same salary. The state school tax was placed at two mills and the local school taxes of New Orleans were limited to $300,000 per annum. Separate schools for white and colored children were authorized.

The work of reorganizing the school system was in progress by May of that year.[3] The Democrats said the public

---

[1] Daily **Picayune**, January 11, 1877. The **Picayune** gave the educational statistics for 1875.
[2] **Acts of the Legislature of the State of Louisiana, 1877,** No. 23.
[3] New Orleans **Times**, May 8, 1877. The boards in fifty-seven parishes had been appointed. In the larger parishes six white and three negroes were put on the board, while in the parishes in which the negroes were dominant five white and four negroes were appointed.

school system was a political machine under Radical rule and that the new law was designed to take the public schools out of politics,[4] but the law really put them in politics, as the governor and other elected state officials controlled the state school boards and all the other school officials. The law made it impossible to have good educational leadership in the parishes without which there could be no efficiency in the schools. The parish superintendent was intended to be a mere clerk to keep an account of the school funds, issue checks, and make an annual report to the state authorities. Another defect of the law which handicapped education was the division of the parishes into school districts and the distribution of all school funds on the basis of the number of educables in the district. Still another defect was the failure to require the parishes to provide a definite minimum public school support.[5]

The school board of New Orleans in July decided to separate the schools of that city into white and colored.[6] A colored citizen sought an injunction to prevent such action on the ground that it was an abridgment of the privileges and immunities of citizens of the United States. The Sixth District Court granted an injunction but it was later dissolved on the grounds that the plaintiff's petition disclosed no injury to himself and no cause of action.[7] A negro mass meeting was held in July to protest against separate schools for white and colored children, but the meeting was tinged with politics and nothing was accomplished.[8]

An effort to arouse the citizens against the educational system the government was instituting came to light in the published correspondence between a citizen, "G. K.", and Mitchell, Catholic member of the school board. Mitchell was ac-

---

[4] New Orleans Times, September 15, 1877.
[5] T. H. Harris, The Story of Public Education in Louisiana, p. 58.
[6] New Orleans Times, July 4, 1877.
[7] Ibid., September 27, and October 24, 1877.
[8] Ibid., July 11, 1877.

cused of "advocating a sectarian division of the schools for the purpose of aiding "fat priests and lazy nuns" and replied:

> if the gentleman will point out when, where, and under what circumstances, any language was uttered by me conveying that I approved of a sectarian division of the pupils, I shall not only be exceedingly obliged to him, but will immediately resign as a member of the board.[9]

The following day "G. K." replied that at the school board meeting July 3, Mitchell said,

> If Catholic parents objected to sending their children to the public schools, it would be the duty of the board to separate them.[10]

Mitchell made no published reply to this citation and did not resign from the school board.

State Superintendent Lusher took a census in August of the educable youth of the state between six and twenty-one years of age because such a census had not been taken in eight years. The school census showed 266,033 youths between six and twenty-one years of age in the state with 68,918 of these in the city of New Orleans,[11] and only 54,390 of the educables were enrolled in the public schools of the state. The 1,004 school houses were valued at $627,305.00 and the furniture at $109,269.90 which means the average school house was valued at slightly more than $600.00 and had about $100.00 worth of equipment. Most all the schools were one-teacher affairs, and they only required 1,507 teachers. The public schools were aided by 306 private schools employing 638 teachers and enrolling 20,693 pupils.[12] The

---

[9] New Orleans Times, July 11, 1877.
[10] Ibid., July 12, 1877.
[11] Ibid., August 17, 1877.
[12] Report, Superintendent of Education for the year ending December 31, 1877, pp. 314-315.

EDUCATION AND HEALTH 231

total public school revenues for the entire state were $467,-368.45 and the total disbursements were $361,830.73.[13]

The Peabody Educational Fund withdrew financial support from the state in September, 1875, because the agents of the fund worked under such disadvantages and accomplished very little of a permanent character, but the financial aid was resumed in 1877.[14] School conditions were deplorable especially in the rural parishes,[15] and local fairs were used to stimulate interest in education.[16] School money was not free from the grasping hands of politicians as was indicated by the arrest of state senator J. H. Burch, who was charged with embezzling the school funds of Baton Rouge.[17] Superintendent Lusher wrote that the year 1877 was:

> a period of careful reorganization of the public school system, rather than of marked success in achieving decided results in the educational work of the state, and the teachers were compensated at rates far below the value of their services, and inadequate to their support as respectable members of society. The mission of conscientious teachers, who blend moral with intellectual enlightenment, is second in importance only to that of the expounders of religion.[18]

The State Board of Education decreed that the public schools of the state should be open for twenty-four weeks of the year and made rules and regulations for the government of the schools, dealing with such subjects as: examinations, vacations, holidays, teachers, principals, discipline, admission, attendance and deportment of pupils. Plans were matured

---

[13] **Report, Superintendent of Education for the year ending December 31, 1877**, pp. 318-319.
[14] Ouachita **Telegraph**, October 26, 1877. Louisiana was given $55,-578 by the Peabody Educational Fund in 1877.
[15] Opolousas **Courier**, October 20, 1877.
[16] New Orleans **Times**, September 4, 1877.
[17] Ibid., July 5, 1877.
[18] **Report, Superintendent of Education for the year ending, December 31, 1877.**

for the management and improvement of the free public school fund by: (1) the recovery of the trust fund for the cause of education in Louisiana, (2) a poll tax, and (3) increasing the current school fund with a two and one-half mill local tax.[19]

Public education made as much progress in 1878 as could have been expected under the circumstances. The legislature was informed that the poor school teachers experienced considerable difficulty in obtaining their pay and the warrants were worth only a fraction of their face value when the teachers did get them.[20] The state contributed that year only 76¼ cents for the education of each child of school age.[21]

The citizens of New Orleans held a mass meeting in the interest of education while the legislature was in session in 1879.[22] A move was made in the constitutional convention of that year to abolish the office of state superintendent of education. This was construed as an attack upon the existing system of free public schools and the schemers were warned that the people would not permit the destruction of the free public school system.[23]

The constitution of 1879 provided for a state superintendent of education to be elected by popular vote for a four-year term. His salary was $2,000 per year, plus an expense account not to exceed $1,000 annually.[24] The general assem-

---

[19] Report, Superintendent of Education for the year ending December 31, 1877. The trust fund came from the proceeds of sale of school lands donated by the Federal government to the state. When the lands were sold the proceeds were invested in state bonds. Act number 81, of 1872, abolished the fund, but it was decided in 1879 that the state owed the public school fund $1,130,867.51. See Harris, **The Story of Education in Louisiana**, p. 53.
[20] New Orleans Times, January 7, 1879.
[21] Ibid., January 20, 1879.
[22] Ibid., January 29, 1879.
[23] New Orleans Times, May 31, 1879.
[24] **Constitution of Louisiana, 1879**, Article 225.

bly was to provide for the establishment, maintenance, and support by taxation or otherwise of free public schools for the children of the state between six and eighteen years of age.[25] All money for education raised by the legislature, except the poll tax, was to be distributed to the parishes in proportion to the number of children of school age. The poll tax was to go to the schools of the parish in which collected, and no public funds were to be used for sectarian schools.[26] The English language was to be used in the general exercises of the school and in the elementary branches taught, but the French language might be used in sections where French predominated, if no extra expense was incurred thereby. The parish school boards were empowered to appoint the parish superintendents whose salaries could not exceed $200.00 per year, except the parish of Orleans.[27]

The educational provisions of the constitution were a slight improvement on the previous laws. The two-mill tax on the assessments should have amounted to $342,000 in 1879, but the amount actually collected and apportioned to the parish boards was $208,159.69. The funds suffered because of high fees paid for collecting the tax. The aggregate amount of the poll tax on "all male inhabitants of the state" paid into the state treasury was $14,620, which showed only a few of the registered voters were actually required to pay a poll tax and only one-fourth of the amount paid in went to the free public schools.[28] The remainder of the poll tax fund was diverted to other purposes.

An attempt was made in the courts to compel the school board of New Orleans to allow colored children to attend the same schools as white children. The constitution of 1879 did not mention mixed or separate schools. The framers of

---
[25] Constitution of Louisiana, 1879, Article 224.
[26] Ibid., Article 228.
[27] Ibid., Article 225.
[28] Annual Cyclopedia, 1879, p. 563.

the constitution probably omitted the question as part of a conciliatory policy toward the negroes.[29] The whites knew they could put the negroes in separate schools without a constitutional provision. The new constitution contained a provision for a separate university in New Orleans for colored students, and fixed the maximum annual legislative support at $10,000.00. The legislature established the school in January, 1880, and named it Southern University.[30]

It was recognized in some, but not in all, parts of the state that funds were necessary for an efficient school system and the public schools were an essential part of a democratic state. With such conditions prevailing, the state superintendent received no report from a number of the parishes in 1880, and the reports that were received lacked uniformity. The 874 schools for white children enrolled 16,624 boys and 15,018 girls, and the schools were in session from one to eight months during the year. The average monthly salary of the teachers in the parishes was $25.62, and in New Orleans the average was $52.50. The teachers in the 91 private schools were paid from $14.00 to $45.00 per month. The schools for the colored children enrolled 11,746 boys and 10,924 girls.[31] The total receipts for education for 1880 amounted to $444,-979.44, and the disbursements for teachers' wages were $352,208.45. Other expenditures left a balance of $29,186.44 at the end of the year with $6,065.42 in outstanding obligations.[32] New Orleans paid two-thirds of the school taxes of the state which meant that New Orleans paid for schooling

---

[29] **Constitution of Louisiana,** 1879, Article 231.
[30] **Survey of Negro Colleges and Universities,** Bureau of Education, Department of the Interior, Bulletin No. 28, p. 390. After two years the college was moved from New Orleans. It is now located at Scotlandville, (near Baton Rouge) and is known as Southern University and Agricultural and Mechanical College.
[31] **Report of the State Superintendent of Education for 1880.**
[32] Ibid.

the children in the city and a large portion of the remainder of the state.[33]

The colleges were reorganized but economic conditions prevented adequate financial support. The legislature of 1877 combined the State University and the Agricultural and Mechanical College and located them temporarily at Baton Rouge. The combined institution had the residue of the Morrill fund in state bonds of $196,200 par value bearing seven per cent and $138,000 from the Seminary fund in bonds bearing six per cent interest.[34] The Board of Supervisors of the new institution directed the secretary of state and state treasurer, who were custodians of the bonds, to present them to the Board of Liquidation for funding, but these officials refused, and when they were forced to present the bonds, the board rejected them as not fundable.[35] The question was presented to the State Supreme Court and that body ordered the funding.[36] The Seminary fund was then scaled from $138,000 at six per cent to $85,800 at seven per cent. The faculty in 1877 consisted of President David F. Boyd and three professors. The Sugar Planters' Association requested the new institution to conduct experiments and researches in sugar culture and manufacture.[37] This was probably the beginning of the well known School of Sugar Chemistry of the University.

The enrollment of the Louisiana State University increased from 75 in October, [38] 1877, to 135 in January,

---

[33] New Orleans Times, January 23, 1880.
[34] W. L. Fleming, Louisiana State University, 1860-1898, pp. 320-322. The Morrill fund belonged to the Agricultural and Mechanical College, and the Seminary fund was from the coffers of the University.
[35] Annual Cyclopedia, 1877, p. 466.
[36] State ex rel. Board of Supervisors, et al., vs the Board of Liquidators, 30 Louisiana Annual Reports, p. 816.
[37] Report, Board of Supervisors of Louisiana State University and Agricultural and Mechanical College, session 1877-1878, pp. 105-130.
[38] W. L. Fleming, Louisiana State University, p. 308.

1879.³⁹ The supervisors of the University and Agricultural and Mechanical College made a sharp statement of facts concerning the revenues to the constitutional convention in 1879. The United States government donated to the State of Louisiana for the endowment of a free school for instruction in the higher branches, land which sold for $464,000, and the money was invested in state bonds. The state government during the administrations of Kellogg and Nicholls reduced the amount to $282,000. The constitutional convention raised the value of the bonds to $318,313.

The state library had been for years without appropriations for books, and was forced to depend upon voluntary contributions and such exchanges as could be effected with the duplicates on hand. The librarian wrote in his report of 1877 that he was not permitted to enter upon the discharge of his duties until the seventeenth of March because of the political situation. There were 22,931 books in the library, but exclusive of duplicates the number was 16,859, and of these 11,189 were in English and 5,670 in French.⁴⁰ The total number of volumes, exclusive of duplicates, was 27,951 in 1879.⁴¹

Statistics on health were as inadequate as those for education. Births and deaths were seldom reported except in New Orleans and the State Board of Health in 1877, recorded only 2,675 births, 6,708 deaths, and 1,270 marriages for the entire state.⁴² The health department of New Orleans inspected 35,317 premises, which included 28,602 dwellings and 4,607 stores. The dwellings contained 142,091

---

³⁹ New Orleans Times, January 25, 1879. There were 108 boarding and 27 day students.

⁴⁰ Annual Report, State Librarian, 1877, pp. 2-24. The report covered the period from March 17 to December 31, 1877.

⁴¹ Ibid., 1879.

⁴² New Orleans Times, January 9, 1878. The deaths were reported as 3,976 white and 2,732 colored; divided as to sex—3,650 males and 3,058 females.

rooms for the population of 158,705. Only forty-three people were reported for non-compliance with the health laws which indicated that the laws were not rigidly enforced. There were 2,087 cases of smallpox and 18,921 people were vaccinated. The prevalence of smallpox prompted the Board of Health to ask for a smallpox hospital,[43] but no such institution was obtained.

Governor Nicholls complied with the recommendation of the Board of Health and issued a quarantine against yellow fever, effective June 15, 1877. The proclamation required all officers, crews, passengers, and cargoes arriving from Rio de Janeiro, Havana, Sagura la Grande, Cardenas, Santiago de Cuba, Kingston, Porto Rico, San Juan, Santo Domingo, and Vera Cruz to undergo a quarantine of ten days.[44] With the approach of autumn the quarantine was lifted.

New Orleans suffered one of the worst yellow fever epidemics on record in 1878. The fever was supposed to have reached the city with the ship, "Borussia", which arrived May 21, and was detained ten days at quarantine; two days later the purser of the ship died of what was thought to be yellow fever, and a member of the crew was ill but recovered; May 30, another death occurred.[45] The governor, upon the recommendation of the Board of Health, had already declared a general quarantine effective May 14, on all vessels arriving from all West India ports, all ports along the coast of the Gulf of Mexico, south of Texas, and all ports along the Atlantic Coast of South America as far as the city of Buenos Aires.[46]

---

[43] Report, New Orleans Board of Health for the year ending December 31, 1877.
[44] Messages and Proclamations of Governor Francis T. Nicholls, Issued June 4, 1877.
[45] Kendall, History of New Orleans, I, p. 406.
[46] Messages and Proclamations of Governor Francis T. Nicholls, 1878, p. 307.

The press gave considerable attention to the epidemic. It was reported July 30 that yellow fever had been raging for several days with one hundred and four cases and thirty-four deaths.[47] The papers on August 19, began giving daily reports of new cases, deaths the preceding twenty-four hours, total cases, and total deaths. Such daily reports were given until November 4. The page facing this one gives this data in graph form for the period.[48] It will be seen from the graphs that three hundred twenty-seven new cases occurred September 3, and the fever reached its climax September 11, when ninety people died. By November 4, no less than 3,954 deaths and 13,213 cases had been reported in New Orleans.[49] This is to say, approximately thirty per cent of those contracting the fever died. During the epidemic music was forbidden and church bells were not rung. In one square, one hundred and three cases occurred, and an entire family of seven died and were buried in one day.[50] When the fever was declared epidemic, there was a general exodus from New Orleans, and this spread the infection to other parts of the state.[51] Donaldsonville reported 1,322 cases and 168 deaths,[52] Baton Rouge had 2,463 cases and 159 deaths.[53] The fever spread so extensively that the crops went unharvested in many sections.[54]

The problem of caring for the afflicted and destitute was great, but the entire nation responded generously; gifts came from North, East, and West, as well as from neighbor-

---

[47] Daily **Picayune**, July 30, 1878.
[48] New Orleans **Times**, August 19 to November 4, 1878, inclusively.
[49] The population of the city was 154,132. By November 8, the dead reached 3,975 and the number of cases 13,317, according to the Daily Picayune, November 8, 1878.
[50] Kendall, **History of New Orleans**, I, p. 406.
[51] New Orleans **Times**, October 14, 1878.
[52] **Ibid.**, November 1, 1878.
[53] Weekly **Advocate**, November 15, 1878.
[54] New Orleans **Times**, October 20, 1878.

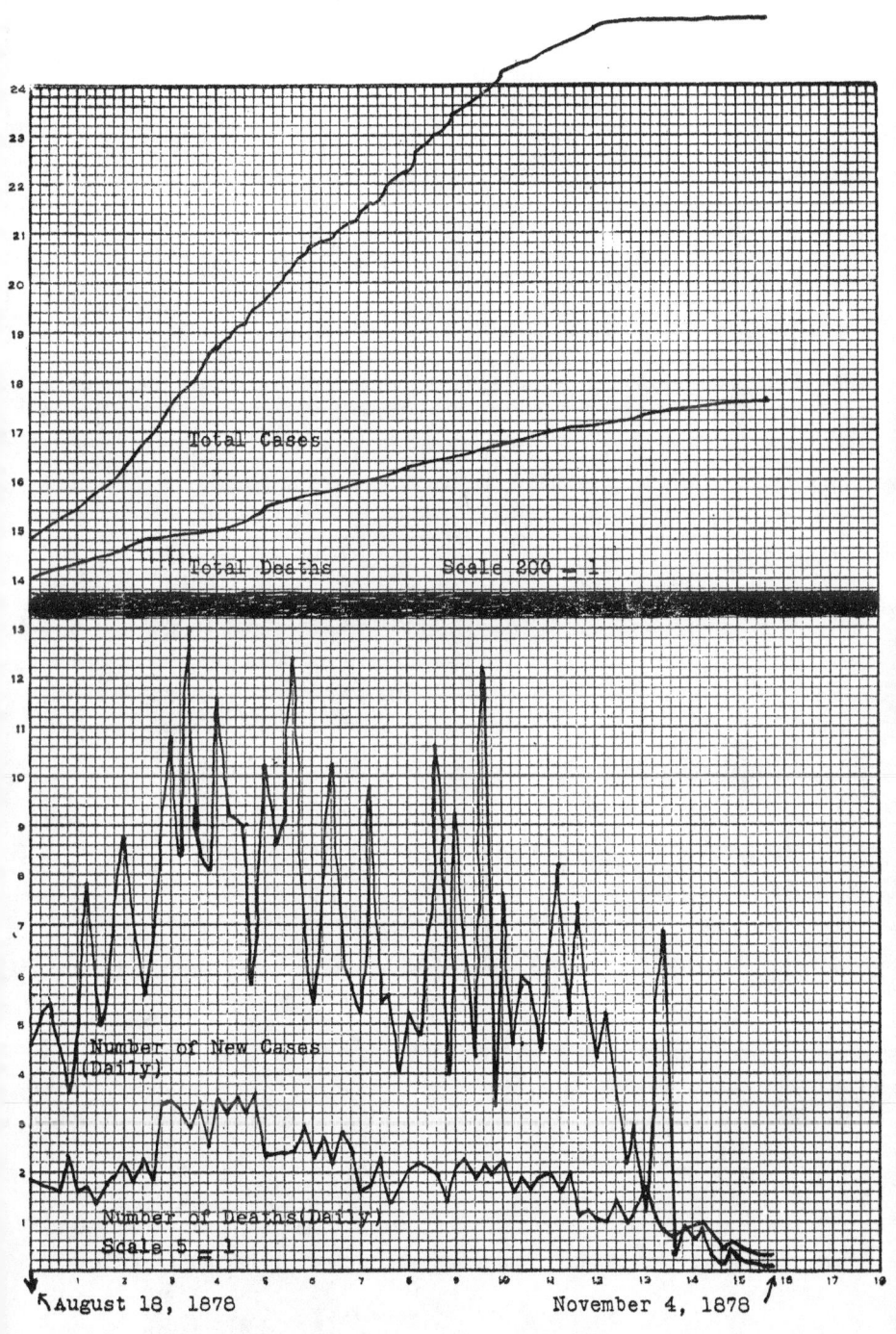

ing states. The railroads transported all supplies *gratis* to New Orleans during the epidemic. The magnitude of the relief prompted a meeting of the citizens at Turner's Hall on September 8. They discussed these questions:

(1) By what means can this timely aid be made to benefit all of those and only those who most need it.

(2) By what means can the distress of thousands who are out of employment be averted after the epidemic has ceased and the distribution of provisions will be stopped.[55]

The Central Relief Committee asked to borrow wagons with which to distribute relief provisions. By October, no less than fifty thousand people were suffering for the necessities of life. The government lent its aid in the work of relief and Governor Nicholls ordered rations for 40,000 people shipped to New Orleans.[56] Port Collector Smith telegraphed the Secretary of the Treasury, John Sherman, October 6, that a meeting of the chairmen of thirty charitable associations had been held to consider the supplies on hand, the necessities of the people, and more especially the ability of existing organizations to supply what was absolutely needed. A few thought the societies they represented could supply relief for another week. It was their unanimous opinion that the means in the possession of the Howard Association had been greatly over-estimated. Port Collector Smith thought 500,000 rations would not be too much for the 50,000 people in the city suffering for the necessities of life.[57] At one

---

[55] New Orleans Times, September 8, 1878.
[56] Ibid., September 9, 1878. The governor's order of September 4, was for 20,000 pounds of ribbed sides, 19,000 pounds shoulders, 20,000 pounds flour, 16,000 pounds corn meal, 21,000 pounds sugar, and 20,000 pounds salt.
[57] Ibid., October 7, 1878. Senator Sherman was appointed Secretary of Treasury by President Hayes. Smith was collector of customs at New Orleans.

time the Howard Association had one thousand destitute cases on hand and it cared for a total of more than 24,000 persons.[58] The St. George Society reported giving relief to 4,946 families and 15,843 persons. Most of this was for food, but 617 families or 1,041 persons were furnished with money, doctors, nurses, and medicine. To these should be added the 8,508 fed at the soup house, making a grand total of 24,351 persons relieved and 122,493 rations issued.[59]

There was a woeful lack of sanitary information and it appears that certain officials were negligent. The *Times* came out with the following statement:

> It comes to our knowledge, upon authority abundantly reliable, that 4,000 loads of kitchen garbage which had been hauled to the dumping grounds by the city carts have been brought back by the contractors and used to fill up streets in the front part of the city.[60]

Medical science did not know the causes of many diseases, and the people attributed the yellow fever epidemic to the lack of the ordinary principles of sanitation. Dr. J. Holt reported August 8, as follows:

> Neglect unutterable has characterized the whole system of street cleaning. The carelessness and neglect in the removal of garbage, the dumping of garbage by hundreds of cart loads into populous streets, the most horrible outrage ever perpetrated upon a civilized community, the bad state of some of the markets, especially the Magazine market, and above all the pernicious method of pretend-

---

[58] Kendall, **History of New Orleans**, I, p. 406.
[59] The New Orleans **Times**, November 2, 1878. The St. George Society reported that of the 15,843 persons relieved, 13,100 were Irish, 1,840 English, 238 Scotch, 300 from Jamaica, 144 Canadians, 191 from Hong-Kong, and 30 Americans. Of the 8,508 fed at the soup house, 55 per cent were Irish, 25 per cent English, 5 per cent Canadian, 5 per cent other nations, and 10 per cent Americans.
[60] **Ibid.**, September 18, 1878.

EDUCATION AND HEALTH   241

ing to clean the streets and gutters by gangs of men employed in throwing their contents into the streets, under a blazing sun to putrefy and presently to be washed back again by a passing shower; all of these causes have been combined to prepare the community for the inevitable and legitimate result of such flagrant disobedience of all sanitary laws, the appearance and rapid spread of some malignant contagion.[61]

The Sanitary Commission reported that yellow fever was indigenous under favorable conditions. The fever proceeded from a combination of filth, heat, and moisture, and if these conditions did not exist, it was not contagious. The commission declared every epidemic of yellow fever had been proved by investigation to have originated in such conditions.[62]

The yellow fever epidemic was so alarming that the President appointed the United States Yellow Fever Commission to investigate the causes and prevention of yellow fever.[63] The investigation began the first of the year in New Orleans and much testimony was taken, but time has proved its conclusions unsound and unscientific. As the press said, it threw "no light on this subject of vital interest to the people of the South."[64]

As the epidemic of yellow fever showed signs of subsiding the governor proclaimed October 9 as a day of prayer and thanksgiving. He called on the people to recognize their

---

[61] New Orleans Times, September 20, 1878.
[62] Ibid., September 25, 1878.
[63] Ibid., October 7, 1878. The commission consisted of the following: Dr. S. M. Bemiss (New Orleans), Dr. Jerome Cochran (Mobile), and Professor E. Lloyd Howard (Baltimore).
[64] St. Landry Democrat, January 18, 1879; New Orleans Times, January 4, 5, 7, 8, and February 4, 1879. The New Orleans Times of January 17, 1879, said the estimated damage to New Orleans from the yellow fever was $12,000,000 to $100,000,000.

dependency upon God and to exhibit their faith in His power and mercy. Every person was requested:

> to repair to some place of public worship, and there humbly invoke our Heavenly Father to stay His chastening hand and deliver us from the scourge which, baffling human skill and all that devotion, courage, and charity can bring to its assistance, still spreads desolation throughout our own and sister states.[65]

They were to invoke God's blessings also upon those who had so generously manifested their devotion, courage, and humanity in the dark hours of the supreme distress. The Thanksgiving proclamation of Governor Nicholls contained the following reminder:

> The summer which has passed has left many of our households in Louisiana desolate, but even through the sadness of the year there is no one among us but who has cause to recognize God's kindness and mercy. In humble recognition of that fact, I do recommend to the people of Louisiana that on the day suggested they unite with the people of the entire country in a common expression of gratitude to their maker.[66]

Governor Nicholls in his mesage to the legislature January, 1879, spoke of the destructive epidemic of yellow fever, the spontaneous exhibition of sympathy, Christian charity, and brotherhood of a common country. Lieutenant-Governor Wiltz, also referred to the yellow fever epidemic, the philanthropic contributions from all classes of people in all sections of the nation and from cities abroad. He suggested that

---

[65] **Messages and Proclamations of Governor Francis T. Nicholls, 1878,** p. 418. Proclamation was issued October 1, 1878; Daily **Picayune,** October 9, 1878; New Orleans **Times,** October 5, and 9, 1878. The mayor of New Orleans issued a proclamation also naming October 9, as a day of prayer.

[66] **Messages and Proclamations of Governor Francis T. Nicholls, 1878,** issued November 31.

suitable resolutions should be passed to let the world know that the people of Louisiana were not ungrateful.[67] The legislature passed an appropriate joint resolution of thanks for the contributions which reached $1,100,000.[68]

The people of New Orleans feared a return of the yellow fever in 1879, and Governor Nicholls took the precaution to declare a quarantine of twenty days beginning April 30 on all vessels arriving from West India Ports, all ports along the Gulf of Mexico south of Texas, all ports along the mainland bordering on the Caribbean, and all ports along the Atlantic coast of South America as far as the city of Buenos Aires.[69] The Mississippi Valley Transport Company entered a vigorous protest against the quarantine order, and claimed disastrous consequences would entail on merchants, producers, and shippers throughout the Mississippi Valley.[70] The New Orleans Medical and Surgical Association opposed the quarantine. Governor Nicholls thought some of the opposition to the preventive measure was political.[71]

Rumors soon spread to cities and towns of the South that New Orleans had another epidemic of yellow fever, which caused those cities to establish quarantines against New Orleans. Louis A. Wiltz, while acting governor, issued a proclamation that the people of New Orleans had enjoyed as good health during the preceding ninety days, as ever before known during the summer months. No case of yellow fever had occurred in the city since July 29, 1879, and all towns and cities were urged to raise the quarantine against

---

[67] **Journal of the Senate of Louisiana, Regular Session, 1879**, p. 3 and pp. 7-20; Daily Picayune, January 6, 1879; New Orleans Times, January 6, 1879.
[68] **Journal of the Senate of Louisiana, Regular Session, 1879**, p. 24.
[69] **Messages and Proclamations of Governor Francis T. Nicholls, 1879**, issued April 17.
[70] New Orleans Times, April 18, 1879.
[71] Ibid., May 3, 1879.

New Orleans, as Mobile and Montgomery had done, because it was a needless obstruction to travel and commerce. Citizens who were absent from New Orleans were asked to return to their homes.[72] Such action would prove that the residents of the city did not fear an epidemic.

---

[72] **Messages and Proclamations of the Governor, 1879.** Issued by the acting governor, L. A. Wiltz, August 17, 1879.

CHAPTER XI.

THE SIGNIFICANCE OF THE CHANGE FROM RADICAL TO DEMOCRATIC RULE

BY 1876 Louisiana had had fourteen years of Reconstruction—longer than that of any Southern state. Its people were weary and discouraged, but the approaching election offered a ray of hope. The nation seemed to be disgusted with the Republican regime and the use of the army to hold the South within partisan ranks. The time came for action and the native whites met the challenge with renewed courage. It was not enough to get every white citizen within the ranks of the Conservative-Democratic party—the negro voter must be won over and that must be done by peaceful means. Unity within the ranks of the whites was obtained by nominating the governor from the rural section and the lieutenant-governor from New Orleans. The campaign plans were laid wisely and carried out, for the most part, peaceably. Fortunately, the nominee for Governor, Francis T. Nicholls, understood the colored men and won the confidence of enough of them to turn the scales in his favor on election day.

But experience was to show again that it was more important to count the ballots than to cast them. The Returning Board was completely in the control of the Republican party. The Democrats were acquainted with its partisan methods and took precautions to procure a duplicate set of returns from the election officials. When the Board arbitrarily threw out enough votes to claim a Republican victory, the Democrats possessed evidence to dispute the action, and made a determined fight to hold what they had won. The Federal government, after the inauguration of Rutherford B. Hayes, had the wisdom not to force the Republican minority upon the state and the government of Nicholls came into undisputed control.

The native white government was faced with vexing problems. Many people had supported Nicholls in hopes of being rewarded with the spoils of office, they were soon disappointed and the discontented element formed the nucleus of a faction that opposed the administration. A considerable number of young men had reached voting age since 1860 and all their political training consisted of opposition technique. Their conception of politics was to oppose every thing favored by the Republican party. They were not aware that the responsibility for solving the complicated social and economic problems would rest on them should the carpet-bag government be overthrown.

The opposition to the administration of Nicholls was strengthened by his attitude toward the Louisiana Lottery Company, and crystallized in a movement for a new constitution. The anti-administration forces were triumphant in the convention, not only in having the new constitution guarantee the lottery for the length of its charter, but they also succeeded in cutting off a full year from the term which Nicholls was elected to serve.

The post-Reconstruction period had its economic problems. Banking and business capital were lacking, and transportation facilities had to be reconditioned. Rivers and harbors needed dredging, levees were necessary to keep the streams within bounds, old railroads had to be repaired, and new lines built. The credit of the state was pledged for much of these improvements in transportation. Agriculture was in a pitiful condition. The livestock was depleted, the buildings were dilapidated, and the machinery was worn out. The farms needed complete renovation and the labor force had to be readjusted to the changed conditions.

The rebuilding of the social order was not an easy task because it had been turned upside down during the war and Reconstruction. The colored man had to learn what freedom meant and many formerly wealthy whites, who had never worked with their hands before the war, were forced to do manual labor. The public school system, inadequate before the war, was woefully handicapped for the problems to be solved. Medical knowledge was insufficient and the scourge of disease brought more suffering and hardships.

The period of transition signified the break-down of the Republican party in Louisiana. The Republicans decreased in numbers until they were an insignificant minority party. From that day until the present they have ceased to be a positive force in the politics of the state. Their function has been that of frightening potential recalcitrant Democrats into party harmony. Many a Democratic candidate for office made much of the fact that he or his father helped destroy the Republican regime in the state. Such an appeal was effective in rallying voters to the support of the Democratic nominee.

The change resulted in undermining the political power of the negroes. The native whites sought the vote of the negroes in 1876, because their votes were necessary to overthrow the Republicans. Once the native whites were established in office, plans were made to undermine and destroy the political power of the colored man. His political influence waned until it was destroyed, for all practical purposes, by the "Grandfather Clause" of the Constitution of 1898.

The political change was not very pronounced either for better or for worse. The old Republican political order, supported by colored votes and Federal soldiers, was replaced by a Democratic ring, based upon white votes. The Democrats hungered for the spoils of office and were about as extravagant with public funds. They partially repudiated the public debt which did not enhance their reputation for honesty. The change of political control did not bring forth any outstanding modification of political principles nor any great improvement in public morals. With the exception of Governor Nicholls and a few others, the new public servants were not especially concerned with improving the lot of the masses.

The transition calmed the agitation of the native whites and many of the carpet-baggers left the state. The colored man was docile by nature, and he readily settled down into the routine pattern of life arranged for him. Thus, the state enjoyed comparative political peace.

The Bourbon class of native whites, once more in office, made some effort to solve the economic problems, but the educational and social maladjustments were left undisturbed until recent years. These gigantic economic, educational, political, and social problems could not be solved during this short period of transition, but greater effort might have been put forth if all the public servants had possessed a profound devotion to the public good. In short, the most significant factor in the transition was the absence of any outstanding change.

BIBLIOGRAPHY

PRIMARY SOURCE MATERIALS
Public Documents (Federal)

Congressional Globe, 1862-1873.
Congressional Record, 1873-1893.
Executive Documents of the House of Representatives 40-46th Congresses.
Executive Documents of the United States Senate, 40-46th Congresses.
Miscellaneous Documents of the House of Representatives, 37-46th Congresses.
Miscellaneous Documents of the United States Senate, 37-46th Congresses.
Journal of the House of Representatives, 37-46th Congresses.
Journal of the Senate of the United States, 37-46th Congresses.
Journal of the Executive Proceedings of the Senate of the United States, 40-46th Congresses.
Reports of the Committees of the House of Representatives, 37-46th and 51 Congresses.
Reports of the Committees of the United States Senate, 37-46th Congresses.
Statutes at Large of the United States, 37-46th Congresses.
United States Supreme Court Reports, (U. S. Reports, Wallace), Vols. 98-105.
United States Department of Agriculture. *Reports of the United States Commissioner of Agriculture, 1877-1880.* Washington, Government Printing Office, 1877-1880.
United States Department of Agriculture. *Report on the Cotton Production of the State of Louisiana.* Washington, Government Printing Office, 1880.

United States Department of the Interior, Bureau of Education, *Survey of Negro Colleges and Universities.* Washington, Government Printing Office, 1929.

Address of the Citizens of Louisiana to the Senators and Representatives of the United States from Louisiana, January, 1878. Washington, Government Printing Office, 1878.

Bureau of the Census, Department of Commerce. *Negro Population, 1790-1915,* by John Cummings, Expert Special Agent. Washington, Government Printing Office, 1918.

Eighth Census of the United States (1860), *Statistics of the Population. Statistics on Agriculture.*

Ninth Census of the United States (1870), *Statistics of the Population. Statistics on Agriculture.*

Tenth Census of the United States (1880), *Statistics of the Population. Statistics on Agriculture.*

Eleventh Census of the United States (1890), *Statistics of the Population. Statistics on Agriculture.*

Compendium of the Tenth Census of the United States (1880).

Counting the Electoral Votes. Speech of Honorable L. W. Ballou in the House of Representatives, January 25, 1877. Washington, Government Printing Office, 1877.

Counting the Electoral Votes. Speech of Honorable H. C. Burchard in the House of Representatives, January 18, 1877. Washington, Government Printing Office, 1877.

Counting the Electoral Votes. Speech of Honorable John L. Burleigh in the House of Representatives, January 25, 1877. Washington, Government Printing Office, 1877.

Index to Reports of Chief of Engineers, 1866-1900, 3 Vols. Published as a House Document of 57 Congress, 2 Session.

In the Matter of the Count of the Electoral Votes of Louisiana, 1877. Washington, Government Printing Office, 1877.

Journal of the Joint Committee on Reconstruction. Edited by B. B. Kendrick, New York, Columbia University Press, 1914.

Ku Klux Klan. Senate Committee Report on Alleged Outrages in the Southern States, with the minority report. Washington, Government Printing Office, 1871.

The Nation and Louisiana. Speech of Honorable Roscoe Conkling in the Senate of the United States. Washington, Government Printing Office, 1875.

Proceedings of the Electoral Commission, 44 Congress, 2 Session, 1877.

RICHARDSON, JAMES D., *A Compilation of the Messages and Papers of the Presidents, 1789-1897,* 10 Volumes. Washington, Government Printing Office, 1900.

Statement of Facts Relating to the Election in Louisiana, November 7, 1876, by E. A. Burke of Counsel for the Democratic and Conservative Party. Washington, Government Printing Office, 1877.

Testimony Taken by the Committee on Privileges and Elections, in regard to the late election in Louisiana. Washington, Government Printing Office, 1877.

War of the Rebellion: A Compilation of the Official Records of the Union and Confederate Armies, 53 Volumes. Washington, Government Printing Office, 1880-1898.

Public Documents (Louisiana)

Acts of the State of Louisiana, 1864-1880. New Orleans, New Orleans Republican, 1864-1877, and George W. Dupree and the New Orleans Democrat, 1877-1880.

Louisiana Annual Reports, 1870-1880. New Orleans, New Orleans Republican, 1870-1877, and F. F. Hansell, 1877-1880.

Constitutions of the State of Louisiana, 1868 and 1879. New Orleans, New Orleans Republican, 1868; and New Orleans Democrat, 1879.

Constitutions of Louisiana (1812-1921), Compiled by Huey P. Long. Baton Rouge, Ramires-Jones Printing Company, 1930.

Executive Documents of the State of Louisiana, 1870, and 1877-1880. New Orleans, New Orleans Republican, 1870; George W. Dupree and the New Orleans Democrat, 1877-1880. (These volumes contained the Reports of the State Auditor, Adjutant General, Attorney General, Secretary of State, Superintendent of Education, State Printer, Treasurer, and the reports of the authorities in charge of the state boards and institutions).

Intimidation and the number of White and colored Voters in Louisiana in 1876 as shown by Statistical Data Derived from Republican Official Reports. Compiled by Stanford E. Chaillé. New Orleans, Picayune Office Job Print, 1877.

Legislative Documents of the State of Louisiana, 1869-1880. New Orleans, New Orleans Republican, 1869-1877; G. W. Dupree and New Orleans Democrat, 1877-1880. (These volumes contained the reports of various committees of the legislature).

Official Journal of the Proceedings of the Constitutional Convention of the State of Louisiana, 1879. New Orleans, Cosgrove, Official Printer, 1879.

Official Journal of the Proceedings of the House of Representatives of the State of Louisiana, 1869-1881. New Orleans, New Orleans Republican, 1869-1877; G. W. Dupree and New Orleans Democrat, 1877-1881.

Official Journal of the Proceedings of the Senate of the State of Louisiana, 1868-1881. New Orleans, New Orleans Republican, 1868-1877; G. W. Dupree and New Orleans Democrat, 1877-1881.

Official Journal of the Proceedings of the Senate of the State of Louisiana (Republican), January-April 13, 1877. New Orleans, New Orleans Republican, 1877.

Proceedings of the Returning Board of the State of Louisiana, Election of 1876. New Orleans, New Orleans Republican, 1877.
Records of Louisiana Confederate Soldiers and Louisiana Confederate Commands, 3 Volumes, compiled by A. B. Booth. New Orleans, Commissioner of Louisiana Military Records, 1920.

Autobiography

"An Autobiography of Francis T. Nicholls, 1834-1881," edited by Barnes F. Lathrop, *Louisiana Historical Quarterly,* XVII, pp. 246-274.

Manuscripts

Private Letters of Francis T. Nicholls, 1850-1856. (Family collection at "Ridgefield," the Nicholls home).

Magazines

Army and Navy Life, June, 1912. (150 N. Nassau Street, New York).
Atlantic Monthly, Vols. 27-46. (Boston, 1871-1880).
Harper's Weekly, Vols. 37-61. (New York, 1868-1880).
Louisiana Historical Quarterly, Vols. 1-22. (New Orleans, 1917-1939).
The Mississippi Valley Historical Review, Vols. 1-24. (Cedar Rapids, Iowa, 1914-1938).
Southern Historical Society Papers, Vols. 1-9. (Edited by Reverend J. William Jones, Richmond, 1876-1881).

Magazine Articles

BONE, FANNY, "Louisiana in the Disputed Election of 1876," *Louisiana Historical Quarterly,* (New Orleans), XIV, pp. 408-440, and 549-566; XV, pp. 93-116, and 234-267.

BONHAM, M. L., "Financial and Economic Disturbance in New Orleans on the Eve of Secession," *Louisiana Historical Quarterly*, (New Orleans), XIII, pp. 32-36.

BUEL, C. C. "The Degradation of a State," *Century*, (New York, XLIII, pp. 618-632.

BURNS, F. P. "White Supremacy in the South: The Battle for Constitutional Government in New Orleans, July 30, 1866," *Louisiana Historical Quarterly*, (New Orleans), XVIII, pp. 581-616.

By a Member of the Louisiana Historical Society, "The Nicholls Family in Louisiana," *Louisiana Historical Quarterly*, (New Orleans), VI, pp. 5-18.

COMSTOCK, ANTHONY, "Lotteries and Gambling," *North American Review*, (New York), CLIV, pp. 217-224.

GREER, J. K., "Louisiana Politics, 1845-1861," *Louisiana Historical Quarterly*, (New Orleans), XII, pp. 381-425, and 555-610; XIII, pp. 67-116, 257-303, 444-483, and 617-654.

JOHNSON, M. W., "The Colfax Riot of April 1873," *Louisiana Historical Quarterly*, (New Orleans), XII, pp. 257-303.

KENDALL, L. C., "The Interregnum in Louisiana in 1861," *Louisiana Historical Quarterly*, (New Orleans), XVI, pp. 175-208, 374-408, and 639-669; XVII, pp. 124-138, 246-267, and 524-536.

KING, GRACE, "Remembrance of New Orleans and the Old St. Louis Hotel," *Louisiana Historical Quarterly*, (New Orleans), IV, pp. 128-129.

LESTAGE, H. O., JR., "The White League in Louisiana and Its Participation in Reconstruction Riots," *Louisiana Historical Quarterly*, (New Orleans), XVIII, pp. 617-695.

MCGINTY, G. W., "Changes in Louisiana Agriculture, 1860-1880," *Louisiana Historical Quarterly*, (New Orleans), XVIII, pp. 407-429.

MOODY, V. A., "Slavery on Louisiana Sugar Plantations," *Louisiana Historical Quarterly*, (New Orleans), VII, pp. 191-301.

SCHULER, K. R., "Women in Public Affairs in Louisiana During Reconstruction," *Louisiana Historical Quarterly*, (New Orleans), XIX, pp. 668-750.
SCROGGS, W. O., "Materials for Research in Louisiana History," American Historical Association, *Annual Report*, (Washington), 1912.
SELLERS, J. L., "The Economic Incidence of the Civil War in the South," *Mississippi Valley Historical Review*, (Cedar Rapids), XIV, pp. 179-191.
SPOFFORD, A. R., "Lotteries in American History," American Historical Association, *Annual Report*, (Washington), 1912.
STEPHENS, E. L., "Education in Louisiana in the Closing Decades of the Nineteenth Century," *Louisiana Historical Quarterly*, (New Orleans), XVI, pp. 38-56.
WHITE, M. J., "The Influence of Agricultural Conditions Upon Louisiana State Politics During the Nineties," American Historical Association, *Annual Report*, (Washington), 1922.
WICKLIFFE, J. C., "The Louisiana Lottery: A History of the Company," *Forum*, (New York), XII, pp. 569-576.

Newspapers

The Daily Picayune, New Orleans, 1862-1881. (Library of the Louisiana Historical Society, New Orleans, and the Archives of the City Hall, New Orleans).
The Louisiana Capitolian, (Weekly) Baton Rouge, 1879-1880. (Louisiana State University Library, Baton Rouge).
The Louisiana Democrat, (Weekly) Alexandria, 1875-1876. (A few numbers found in the Louisiana State University Library, Baton Rouge).
The New Orleans Bee, 1876. (Library of the Louisiana Historical Society, New Orleans).
The New Orleans Bulletin, 1874-1876. (Library of the Louisiana Historical Society, New Orleans).

The New Orleans Democrat, (Daily) 1878-1881. (Library of the Louisiana Historical Society, New Orleans).

The New Orleans Republican, (Daily and Weekly) 1874-1878. (Library of the Louisiana Historical Society, New Orleans).

The New Orleans Times, 1875-1881. (Library of the Louisiana Historical Society, New Orleans).

The Opelousas Courier, (Weekly) Opelousas, 1875-1880. (Scattered numbers in Louisiana State University Library, Baton Rouge).

The Ouachita Telegraph, Monroe, 1875-1880. (The Public Library, Monroe, Louisiana. These papers are a private collection and unbound).

The St. Landry Democrat, (Weekly) Opelousas, 1878-1881. (Louisiana State University Library, Baton Rouge).

The Weekly Advocate, Baton Rouge, 1878-1881. (Louisiana State University Library, Baton Rouge).

The Weekly Democrat, New Orleans, 1866-1881. (Library of the Louisiana Historical Society, New Orleans, and Archives of the City Hall, New Orleans).

SECONDARY WORKS
(General)

American Annual Cyclopedia, Vols. 9-21. New York, D. Appleton and Company, 1869-1881.

Annual Report of the Association of Graduates of the United States Military Academy. Saginaw, Michigan, Seeman and Peters, Inc., 1912.

Appleton's Cyclopedia of American Biography. New York, D. Appleton and Company, 1888.

BADEAU, ADAM, *Grant in Peace*... Hartford, S. S. Scranton and Company, 1887.

BEALE, HOWARD K., *The Critical Year*. New York, Harcourt, Brace and Company, 1930.

BEARD, J. M., *Ku Klux Klan*. Philadelphia, Claxton, Remsen and Haffelfinger, 1877.

BIGELOW, JOHN, *Life of Samuel J. Tilden*. New York, Harper and Brothers, 1895.

BLAINE, JAMES G., *Twenty Years of Congress*, 2 Volumes. Norwich (Conn.), The Henry Bill Publishing Company, 1884-1886.

BOUTWELL, GEORGE S., *Reminiscences of Sixty Years in Public Affairs*. New York, McClure, Phillips and Company, 1902.

BOWERS, CLAUDE G., *The Tragic Era*. Boston, Houghton, Mifflin and Company, 1929.

BOYLE, JAMES E., *Cotton and the New Orleans Cotton Exchange*. Garden City (New York), The Country Life Press, 1934.

BROWN, WILLIAM G., *The Lower South in American History*. New York, Peter Smith, 1902.

BUTLER, BENJAMIN F., *Autobiography and Presonal Reminiscences*. ..Boston, A. M. Thayer and Company, 1892.

Cambridge Modern History, Vol. 7, "The United States." New York and London, Macmillan and Company, 1903.

The Case Between the Presidential Candidates. Compiled by A. M. Hart. Washington, John L. Ginck, 1876.

CHANNING, EDWARD, *History of the United States*, 6 Vols. New York, Macmillan, 1925.

CHURCH, WILLIAM C., *Ulysses S. Grant and the Period of National Preservation and Reconstruction*. New York, G. P. Putnam and Sons, 1897.

The Cipher Dispatches, Tribune Extra No. 44. New York Tribune, 1879.

CONKLING, A. R., *Life and Letters of Roscoe Conkling*. New York, C. L. Webster and Company, 1884.

COUCH, W. T., *Culture in the South*. Chapel Hill, The University of North Carolina Press, 1934.

CROSS, NELSON, *The Modern Ulysses and His Political Record*. New York, J. S. Redfield (Printers), 1872.

DAVIS, JEFFERSON, *The Rise and Fall of the Confederate Government*, 2 Vols. New York, D. Appleton and Company, 1881.

DEWEY, DAVIS R., *Financial History of the United States*. New York, Longmans, Green and Company, 1912.

Dictionary of American Biography, Vol. 13, Dumas Malone, editor. New York, Charles Scribner's Sons, 1934.

DU BOIS, W. E. B., *The Negro Farmer*. Special Report of the Twelfth Census.

DUNNING, W. A., *Essays on the Civil War and Reconstruction*. New York, P. Smith, 1931.

DUNNING, W. A., *Reconstruction, Political and Ecomonic*. New York, Harper and Brothers, 1907.

ECKENRODE, H. J., and WIGHT, P. W., *Rutherford B. Hayes, Statesman of Reunion*. New York, Dodd, Mead and Company, 1930.

The Encyclopedia Britannica, Vol. 17, (Eleventh Edition).

EVANS, C. A., *Confederate Military History*, Vol. 10. Atlanta, Confederate Publishing Company, 1899.

FIELD, DAVID D., *The Vote That Made the President*. New York, D. Appleton and Company, 1877.

FLEMING, WALTER L., *Documentary History of Reconstruction*, 2 Vols. Cleveland, Arthur H. Clark Company, 1906-1907.

FLEMING, WALTER L., *The Sequel of Appomattox*. New Haven, Yale University Press, 1919.

GARNER, JAMES W., *Reconstruction in Mississippi*. New York, Columbia University Press, 1901.

GARFIELD, JAMES A., *Counting the Electoral Vote*. Washington, R. O. Polkinhorn (Printer), 1877.

GIBSON, A. M., *A Political Crime*. New York, W. S. Gottsberger (Printer), 1885.

HACKER, LOUIS M., and KENDRICK, BENJAMIN B., *The United States Since 1865*. New York, F. S. Crofts and Company, 1932.

HAWORTH, PAUL L., *The Hayes-Tilden Election of 1876*. Cleveland, The Burrows Brothers Company, 1906.
HAWK, E. Q., *Economic History of the South*. New York, Prentice-Hall, Inc., 1934.
HENRY, ROBERT S., *The Story of Reconstruction*. Indianapolis, Bobbs-Merrill Company, 1938.
HERBERT, H. A., *Why the Solid South*. Baltimore, R. H. Woodward and Company, 1890.
HESSELTINE, WILLIAM B., *Ulysses S. Grant, Politician*. New York, Dodd, Mead and Company, 1935.
HOAR, GEORGE F., *Autobiography of Seventy Years*, 2 Vols. New York, Charles Scribner's Sons, 1903.
HOLDEN, E. S., *The Cipher Dispatches*. New York, A. S. Barnes and Company, 1879.
JOHNSON, C. S., EMBREE, E. R. and ALEXANDER, W. W., *The Collapse of Cotton Tenancy*. Chapel Hill, The University of North Carolina Press, 1935.
LYNCH, J. R., *Facts of Reconstruction*. New York, Neale Publishing Company, 1913.
MCCLURE, A. K., *The South: Its Industrial, Financial, and Political Condition*. Philadelphia, J. B. Lippincott and Company, 1886.
MCMASTER, JOHN BACH, *A History of the People of the United States*, 8 Vols. New York, D. Appleton and Company, 1913.
OBERHOLTZER, E. P., *The History of the United States Since the Civil War*, 5 Vols. New York, Macmillan Company, 1917-1922.
PARKINS, A. E., *The South, Its Economic-Geographic Development*. New York, John Wiley and Sons, 1938.
POOR, HENRY V., *Manual of the Railroads of the United States*, (Fourteen Annual Numbers). New York, Poor's Publishing Company, 1868-1881.
RAMSDELL, CHARLES W., *Reconstruction in Texas*. New York, Columbia University Press, 1910.

RANDALL, JAMES G., *The Civil War and Reconstruction.* Boston, D. C. Heath and Company, 1936.

RHODES, JAMES FORD, *History of the United States,* 8 Vols. New York, Macmillan Company, 1920.

RUSSELL, C. E., *Blaine of Maine; His Life and Times.* New York, Farrar and Rhinehart, 1931.

Samuel J. Tilden, Writings and Speeches, 2 Vols., edited by Bigelow. New York, New York Public Library, 1882.

SCHOULER, JAMES, *The History of the Reconstruction Period, 1865-1877,* (Volume 7 of Schouler's *History of the United States*). New York, Dodd, Mead, and Company, 1913.

SCOTT, W. A., *Repudiation of State Debts.* New York, Thomas Y. Crowell and Company, 1893.

SHERMAN, JOHN, *Recollections of Forty Years in the House, Senate, and Cabinet.* Chicago, Werner Company, 1895.

STANWOOD, EDWARD, *A History of the Presidency.* Boston, Houghton, Mifflin Company, 1898.

STAPLES, T. S. *Reconstruction in Arkansas.* New York, Columbia University Press, 1923.

The Supreme Court and the Electoral Commission, (an open letter to the Honorable Joseph H. Choate from John Bigelow). New York, G. P. Putnam and Sons, 1903.

The South in the Building of the Nation: The History of the Southern States, 12 Vols. Richmond, The Southern Historical Publication Society, 1909.

TATUM, GEORGIA LEE, *Disloyalty in the Confederacy.* Chapel Hill, The University of North Carolina Press, 1934.

TAYLOR, RICHARD, *Destruction and Reconstruction.* New York, D. Appleton and Company, 1879.

THOMPSON, HOLLAND, *The New South,* Volume 42 in Chronicles of America. New Haven, Yale University Press, 1910.

TROWBRIDGE, J. T., *The South, Its Battlefields and Ruined Cities.* Hartford, L. Stebbins, 1866.

VANCE, RUPERT, *Human Geography of the South: A Study in Regional Resources and Human Adequacy.* Chapel Hill, The University of North Carolina Press, 1932.

WHITE, HORACE, *Life of Lyman Trumbull.* Boston, Houghton Mifflin, 1913.

WILSON, WOODROW, *A History of the American People,* 10 Vols. New York, Harper and Brothers, 1918.

WOODSON, C. G., *A Century of Negro Migration.* Washington, Associated Publishers, Inc., 1918.

WINSTON, ROBERT W., *Andrew Johnson, Plebeian and Patriot.* New York, Henry Holt and Company, 1928.

Secondary Works on Louisiana

BELISLE, JOHN G., *The History of Sabine Parish.* Many, (Louisiana), The Sabine Banner, 1914.

BIGNEY, MARK F., *Poetical History of Louisiana.* New Orleans, E. A. Brandao and Company, 1885.

Biographical and Historical Memoirs of Louisiana, 2 Vols. Chicago, The Goodspeed Publishing Company, 1892.

Biographical and Historical Memoirs of Northwest Louisiana. Nashville and Chicago, Southern Publishing Company, 1890.

Biographical Sketches of Louisiana Governors from D'Iberville to McEnery, by a Louisianaise. New Orleans, A. W. Hyatt (Stationer and Printer), 1883.

BREAUX, J A., *Francis T. Nicholls.* (An Address by the President of the Board of Curators of the Louisiana State Museum Upon the Presentation to the Museum of Certain Mementos of Francis T. Nicholls, 1912). New Orleans, Louisiana State Museum, 1912.

CABLE, GEORGE W., *The Creoles of Louisiana.* New York, Charles Scribner's Sons, 1885.

CALDWELL, STEPHEN, A., *A Banking History of Louisiana.* Baton Rouge, Louisiana State University Press, 1935.

CARPENTER, M. H., *Counting the Electoral Votes of Louisiana, 1877.* Washington, McGill and Witheraw, 1877.

CHAMBERS, HENRY, E., *A History of Louisiana*, 3 Vols. Chicago and New York, American Historical Association, 1925.

CLINE, RODNEY, *The Life and Work of Seaman A. Knapp.* Nashville, George Peabody College, 1936.

DENNETT, DANIEL, *Louisiana As It Is.* New Orleans, Eureka Press, 1876.

Did Louisiana Vote For Hayes or Tilden? By an Ohio Lawyer. Kanesville (Ohio), C. Morehead (Printer), 1878.

FICKLEN, JOHN R., *History of Reconstruction in Louisiana Through 1868.* Baltimore, John Hopkins University Press, 1910.

FICKLEN, JOHN R., and KING, GRACE, *History of Louisiana.* New Orleans, The L. Graham Company, 1902.

FLEMING, W. L., *Louisiana State University, 1860-1896.* Baton Rouge, Louisiana State University Press, 1936.

FORD, ALMA LOUISE, *The Negro in Louisiana Politics, 1878-1898.* An M. A. Thesis, 1933, in the University of Texas Library.

FORTIER, ALCEE, *A History of Louisiana*, 4 Vols. New York, Manzi Joyant and Company, 1904.

FORTIER, ALCEE, (Editor), *Louisiana*, comprising sketches of towns, parishes, events, institutions, and persons, 2 volumes. Atlanta, Southern Historical Association, 1909.

GAYARRE, CHARLES, *A History of Louisiana*, 4 Vols. New Orleans, F. F. Hansell and Brother, 1903.

GRAHAM, KATHLEEN, *Notes On A History of Lincoln Parish, Louisiana.* Ruston, Louisiana Polytechnic Institute Printing Department, 1934.

HARRIS, THOMAS H., *The Story of Public Education in Louisiana.* New Orleans, Delgado Trade School (Print Shop), 1924.

JEWELL, EDWIN L., (Editor), *Jewell's Crescent City, Illustrated.* New Orleans, The author, 1873.

KENDALL, JOHN S., *History of New Orleans*, 3 Vols. New Orleans, Lewis Publishing Company, 1916.

KING, GRACE, *The Creole Families of New Orleans*. New York, The Macmillan Company, 1921.

KING, GRACE, *Memoirs of A Southern Woman of Letters*. New York, The Macmillan Company, 1932.

LONGINO. LUTHER, *Thoughts, Visions, and Sketches of North Louisiana*. Minden (Louisiana), Privately printed by L. Longino, 1930.

Louisiana: Statistics and Information Showing the Agricultural and Timber Resources. Compiled by the Missouri Pacific Railway Company. St. Louis, Woodward and Tiernan Printing Company, 1900.

LONN, ELLA, *Reconstruction in Louisiana After 1868*. New York, G. P. Putnam and Sons, 1918.

McLURE, LILLA, *The Election of 1860 in Louisiana*. New Orleans, A reprint from the Louisiana Historical Quarterly, October, 1926.

McLURE, LILLA, and HOWE, J. E., *History of Shreveport and Shreveport Builders*. Shreveport (Louisiana), Published by J. E. Howe, 1937.

McLURE, LILLA, *Louisiana Leaders, 1830-1860*. Shreveport, The Journal Printing Company, 1935.

MAGRUDER, HARRIETT, *A History of Louisiana*. Boston, D. C. Heath and Company, 1909.

MARCHAND, SIDNEY A., *The Flight of a Century*, 1800-1900, *in Ascension Parish, Louisiana*. Donaldsonville (Louisiana), Privately published, 1936.

MARTIN, FRANCOIS X., *The History of Louisiana and the Annals of Louisiana*. New Orleans, James A. Gresham (Printer), 1882.

MURPHY, WILLIAM M., *Notes from the History of Madison Parish, Louisiana*. Ruston, Louisiana Polytechnic Institute Printing Department, 1927.

New Orleans Price Current Report of Louisiana Sugar and Rice Crops, 1875-1876. New Orleans, Bright and Company, 1878.

PARTON, JAMES, *General Butler in New Orleans.* Boston, Houghton, Mifflin Company, 1892.

PHELPS, ALBERT, *Louisiana: A Record of Expansion.* Boston, Houghton, Mifflin Company, 1905.

REYNOLDS, GEORGE M., *Machine Politics in New Orleans, 1897-1926.* New York, Columbia University Press, 1932.

RIGHTOR, HENRY, *History of New Orleans.* New Orleans, Lewis Publishing Company, 1900.

THOMPSON, MAURICE, *The Story of Louisiana.* Boston, D. Lothrop Company, 1888.

The Ursulines in New Orleans, 1727-1925. Edited by Henry C. Semple, New York, P. J. Kennedy and Sons, 1925.

WARMOTH, HENRY C., *War, Politics, and Reconstruction.* New York, Macmillan Company, 1930.

WILKERSON, MARCUS M., *Thomas Duckett Boyd: The Story of a Southern Educator.* Baton Rouge, The Louisiana State University Press, 1935.

Films from Hayes Memorial Library

(Freemont, Ohio)

Micro-films of Documents Relating to Francis T. Nicholls in Hayes Memorial Library.

Micro-films of Documents Relating to S. B. Packard in Hayes Memorial Library.

Micro-films of Documents Relating to Louisiana in Hayes Memorial Library.

INDEX

INDEX

Abott, H. L., 205.
Agriculture, 26, 27, 209, 210.
Agusti Case, 188.
Allen, Henry Watkins, 3, 4.
American Rock Salt Mining Company, 196.
Anderson, T. C., 55, 56, 64, 65, 126;
    Tried and Convicted, 131, 132;
    Freed by Supreme Court, 134.
Antoine, C. C., 12, 30.
Association of Colored Baptists, 220.
Avery Island Salt Mines, 195, 196.

Bank Clearings, 195.
Banks, General N. P., 3.
Baton Rouge Advocate, 154.
Battle of New Orleans, 15.
Bayou Lafourche, 39.
Beattie, Taylor, 176.
Beauregard, P. G. T., 184, 189, 192.
Belden, Simeon, 8.
Bill of Rights, 7.
Black League, 14.
Board of Canvassers, 87, 105, 177.
Board of Equalization Proposed, 136.
Board of Liquidation, 198.
Board of State Engineers, 205, 206.
Bossier Banner, 153.
Bovee, George E., 8.
Boyce, Henry, 4.
Burke, E. A., 79, 80, 82, 83, 106;
    Defends Hayes, 121;
    Nomination for State Treasurer, 148.
Bush, Louis, 87, 88.
Business Outlook, 194.
Butler, Gen. B. F., 1.

Caffery, Don, 175.
Campaign of Nicholls, 1876, 41, 42, 45, 51.
Capitol at Baton Rouge, 167.
Casanave, Gadane, 55, 56.
Central Relief Committee, 239.
Chandler, W. D., 146.
Chandler, Zach, 99.
Charity Hospital, 192.
Citizen's Conservative Association, 150, 151.
City Railroad Company of New Orleans, 204, 205.
City Railroad Franchise, 205.
Claims of Fraud, 52, 53.
Colored Colonization Society, 224.
Commission sent to Louisiana to Represent President Hayes Unofficially, 117, 118;
    Reports, 119, 121.
Committee of House of Representatives, 70, 72;
    Democratic Majority Report, 72;
    Investigation of 1878 Report, 74.
Committee on Public Debt, 162, 163.
Committee of United States Senate, 72, 73.
Concordia Parish, 206.
Congressional Committee, 6, 16.
Corn, 212.

Constitutional Amendments, 143, 145; Defeated, 149, 150.
Constitution of Louisiana, (1852), 2; (1864), 5; (1866), 6; (1868), 7; (1879), 152-170.
Constitutional Convention, Proposed, 152;
    Press Comment, 152, 156;
    Before Legislature, 158;
    Called, 159; Address of Governor Nicholls, 160;
    Expenses of, 168, 169.
Cotton, 211, 212.
Count of Electoral Vote, 75;
    Louisiana Vote Given to Hayes and Wheeler, 80. ;
Coushatta Tragedy, 15;
    Twitchell shot at, 48.
Converse, W. F., 133.
Conway, T. W., 8.

Daily Picayune, 109, 113, 139, 141, 152, 155, 163, 164, 173, 174, 188, 189, 201.
Debt, State, 137.
Democratic Barbecue at Opelousas, 149.
Democratic Campaign, 176.
Democratic Caucus, 180.
Democratic-Conservative Association, 174.
Democratic-Conservative Electors, 67.
Democratic Convention of (1876) 34; platform of, 35, 40; (1879), 174, 175.
Democratic Legislature, 87, 88; at Odd Fellows Hall, 89, 105;
    Extra Session, 1877, 112;
    Resolutions of, 119.
Democratic Party Splits, 127, 128; 152, 157.
Democratic State Central Committee, 148.

Democratic Visitors, 56;
    Report of, 63, 70.
Democrats, 6, 8, 9, 12, 16, 17, 28; 33, 41, 43, 48, 50, 61;
    Steps Taken, 66.
Dinkgrave shot at Monroe, 49.
Dubuclet, Antoine, 8, 17.
Dumont, A. J., 219.
Dunn, Oscar J., 8.
Durell, E. H., 5.

Eads, James B., 207, 208.
Eads Jetties, 207, 208.
Early, Jubal, 184, 189, 192.
East Baton Rouge Parish, 48, 60, 140, 141.
East Carroll Parish, 206.
East Feliciana Parish, 48, 60.
Economic Problems of Post-Reconstruction, 246, 248.
Educational Provisions of Constitution of 1879, 232, 234.
Educational Reorganization, 228, 229.
Election (1876) Importance of 33;
    Early Returns, 52; (1879), 177, 178.
Electoral Commission, 76-80, 84.
Electoral Vote Counted, 84, 85.
Ellis, E. J., 173.
Ellis, G. T., 101.
Eustis, J. B., 112.

Farms, Size of, 216;
    Value of, 216, 217.
Federal Lands, 215.
Ferry, Thomas W., 75, 77, 84.
Ficklen, John Rose, 1.
Filibuster, 81, 84.
Flanders, Benjamin Franklin, 1.
Flood Control, 205, 206.
Foote, Harry S., 223.
Foster, Charles, 81, 82.

Franchise, Committee on, 165, 166.
Free State Party, 1, 2.
Fruit Growers' Association, 213, 214.

Garfield, James A., 56, 57, 83, 134.
Gayarre, Charles, Approves President Hayes' Southern Policy. 114, 115; On State Debt, 198.
Gibson, R. L., 100.
Gillespie, James M., 176.
Grandfather Clause, 166.
Grangers, 213.
Grant, Ulysses S., 8, 12, 13, 14, 15, 25, 53, 82, 90, 98; Orders Troops Withdrawn, 111.
Gulf States Exposition, 213.
Gunpowder Plot, 109, 110.

Hahn, Michael, 1, 2; Report on Republican Party, 147.
Hale, Eugene, 134.
Hall, W. T., 203.
Hancock, W. S., 133, 134.
Harris, John S., 8.
Harris, W. H., 160.
Hayes, Rutherford B., 81, 83; Appointments, 126; Inaugurated, 85; Sends Commission to Louisiana, 116.
Holt, Dr. J., 240, 241.
Howard Association, 239, 240.
Howard, Charles T., 155, 182, 183, 185, 187.
Howell, R. K., 5.
Hunt, Randell, 4.

Immigration, 214, 215.
Irish Immigration, 226, 227.

Johnson, President Andrew, 2, 6.
Johnson, George B., 135.
Jonas, B. F. 158.

Kellogg, William Pitt, 8, 11, 12, 13, 14, 15, 17, 19, 21, 29, 39; 78, 79, 86, Message, 88, 146.
Kenner, L. M., 55, 56.
Kidd, Captain, 172.
Knights of White Camelia, 10.
Ku Klux Klan, 10.

Lafayette Square, 91, 94; Mass Meeting, 116.
Land Sales, 214.
Legislature's Extravagance, 19, 22.
Legislature, (1876) 17; (1877), 86; (1878), 139-145; Special Session (1878), 145, 146; (1879), 157, 159.
Levee Taxes, 161.
Levees, 205, 206.
Levy, W. M., 175, 214.
Lincoln, President Abraham, 1, 2.
Lincoln Parish, 47.
Log Stealing, 214.
Logan, M. D., 168.
Lonn, Ella, 1, 100.
Louisiana's Jubilee of Deliverance, 124.
Louisiana—
Readmitted to Union, 8; Condition of in 1876, 25.
Louisiana Lottery Company, 155; Donations, 185-186; Open for business, 183; Act to Abolish, 190; Obtains an Injunction, 191; Profits of, 193, 246.
Louisiana State University, 235, 236.
Louisville Courier Journal, 121.

McCrary, George W., 121.
McEnery, John, 12, 13, 14, 21, 66, 173.
Machine Politics, 172, 173, 175.
Manufacturing, 196.
Mass Meeting at Lafayette Square, 172.
Matthews, Stanley, 82, 83, 134.
Mechanics Institute Riot, 6, 7.
Metropolitan Police, 9, 15.
Mississippi River Commission, 206.
Mississippi Valley Immigration Company, 225.
Monroe Board of Trade, 203.
Monsour, J. C., 157.
Moore, Ben, 226.
Morehouse Clarion, 179.
Morehouse Parish, 47, 60.
Morris, John A., 183, 188.
Murray, C. H., 183.

Natchitoches Parish, 102.
Natchitoches Peoples' Vindicator, 187.
Natchitoches Riot, 220, 221.
Negroes, 18, 40;
    Appointed to Office, 217, 218;
    Citizens, 221, 222;
    Clubs, 46, 47;
    Constitutional Convention, 160, 161;
    Dissatisfied, 102, 104;
    Exodus, 222-227;
    Illiterate, 222;
    Political Party, 219, 220;
    Riots, 227;
    Social Problem, 218.
New Orleans, Battle of, 15;
    Economic Condition, 197;
    Protest of People, 65, 66;
    Suffering, 21, 26, 39, 40;
    Voters, 44.

New Orleans Democrat, 173, 178, 188, 189, 190.
New Orleans Evening Democrat, 92, 170.
New Orleans Item, 170.
New Orleans Republican, 92, 104;
    Valedictory, 147, 148.
New Orleans Sanitary Commission, 241.
New Orleans Times, 92, 109, 113, 124, 125, 149, 153, 156, 158, 164, 166, 172, 173, 189, 209, 218, 240.
New Orleans Trade Balance, 194, 195.
New Orleans Weekly Louisianian, 219.
Nicholls, Francis T., 34, 36, 79, 83, 87, 171, 214, 239, 245, 246;
    Appeal to the People, 66;
    Attitude toward Railroad Bonds, 199;
    Effort to Equalize Taxes, 136;
    Inaugural, 90, 92;
    Interpretation of Lottery Charter, 190;
    Messages to the Legislature, 139, 140, 142, 145, 157, 178, 193, 242, 243;
    Nominated Governor, 37;
    Metropolitan Police Organized, 94;
    Press Praises, 127, 175, 176, 179;
    Proclaims Day of Deliverance, 124;
    Reform Program, 142, 145;
    Refused to take State House, 96.
    Strategy, 93, 94;

Thanks the People, 115;
Thanksgiving Proclamation, 242;
Veto of Lottery Bill, 193.
Nicholls, Thomas Clark, 35.

Odd Fellows Hall, 89, 93, 120, 180, 185.
Ogden Campaign Committee, 174.
Ogden, Fred N., 94, 173, 175.
Ogden, H. N., 66.
Ogden, R. N., 180.
Ohio State Journal, 81.
Opelousas Courier, 152, 154.
Opposition to Lottery, 185-189.
Orleans Parish Grand Jury Report on the Lottery, 184.
Ouachita Parish, 49, 50, 60, 101, 102.
Ouachita Telegraph, 153, 220.

Packard, Stephen B., 11, 13, 30, 31, 43;
Address to Republicans, 123;
Evacuates St. Louis Hotel, 122;
Inauguration, 90;
Proclamation, 115;
Shot, 109;
Supreme Court, 126.
Peabody Educational Fund, 231.
Penn, Davidson B., 12, 173.
Pinchback, P. B. S., 13, 24, 28, 30, 103, 104; Calls Republican Executive Committee, 147, 219.
Pinkston Eliza, 50.
Pinkston, Henry, 50.
Pointe Coupee Parish, 223.
Pointe Coupee Pelican, 154.
Political Campaign of 1878, 220, 221.
Political Job Seekers, 125.

Political Outbreaks, 1878, 221.
Political Parties, 1, 2, 4, 8, 10, 11, 12, 16, 17, 22, 28, 29, 151.
Press Comment on Inauguration of Nicholls, 92.
Property Bank Bonds, 140.

Quarantine, 237, 243.

Railways, 27, 201-204.
Records Left by Radicals, 138.
Red River Raft, 206.
Republicans, 8, 10, 11, 12, 16, 29, 32, 47, 50, 52.
Republican Electors, 67, 68.
Republican Executive Committee Meeting, 147.
Republican Legislature, 87, 89, 99, 102, 104, 105, 123, 124.
Republican Party, 247, 248.
Republican Platform, 177.
Republican Politicians, 127.
Republican State Convention, 176.
Republican Visitors, 56, 64. 70.
Returning Board, 10, 16, 17, 25, 130, 245;
Abolished, 105;
Attitude toward Congressional Committee, 71;
Canvass of Election Returns, 54, 55;
Forged Returns, 69;
Jury, 131;
Members, 55, 56;
Power, 68, 69;
Proceedings, 59, 63;
Trial of, 128-134.
Rice Production, 211.
Riots, of 1868, 10; Colfax, 14.

St. George Society, 240.
St. Landry Democrat, 141, 145.
St. Landry Parish Taxes, 136.

St. Louis Hotel (State House), 104, 105, 122, 167, 185.
St. Patrick's Hall, 87, 90.
Salaries, 167-169.
Salary of Teachers, 234.
Savings of New Constitution, 168.
School Census, 230, 231.
Schools, Public, 23, 24, 27, 46.
Sewing Machine Swindle, 44.
Shaw, Alfred (Judge), 67.
Shepley, General, 1.
Sheridan, Philip, 6.
Sherman, John, 56, 134.
Simmons, T. E., 183.
Smith, George L., 59, 127.
Sniffen Telegram, 84.
Spofford, Judge, Elected to United States Senate, 112.
State Board of Education, 228, 231.
State Board of Health, 236, 237.
State Debt, 88, 161-165, 198, 199.
State House, 89, 90, 96; Besieged, 97, 110, 112; Evacuated, 124.
State Library, 236.
Status Quo, 98, 106, 107, 108.
Strong, W. A., 138; Calls roll of Constitutional Convention, 160.
Stubbs, Frank P., 153.
Sugar Planters' Association, 210, 214.
Sugar Production, 210, 211.
Supreme Court of Nicholls, 94, 95.

Tax Assessments, 136, 137.
Taxes, 20, 26, 46, 135, 136, 199, 200.

Tensas Parish, 206, 225.
Tissot, A. L. (Judge), 66.
Trezevant, P. J., 87, 180.
Troops Withdrawn From Louisiana, 121, 122.
Twenty-second Joint Rule, 75, 76.

Union Association, 1.
Union Parish Farmer, 213.
Unionist Party, 1, 2, 4, 5.
United States Yellow Fever Commission, 241.

Vagrant Law, 4.
Vicksburg Labor Convention, 224.
Voting Qualifications of, 166.

Wallace, General Lew, 57.
Ware, Henry, 114.
Warmoth, Henry Clay, 7, 11, 13, 19, 20, 29, 30.
Wells, J. Madison, 2, 6, 55, 60, 61, 68, 131.
Wheeler Compromise, 17.
Wheeler, William A., 116.
White, Edward Douglas, Jr., Defends Legislature, 156, 157.
White, Harry, 134.
White League, 15, 94, 99.
Wickliffe, G. M., 8.
Williamson, George, 127.
Wiltz, Louis A., 34, 35, 87, 126, 127, 160, 170, 171, 175, 180, 213, 242, 243.
Wood, Benjamin, 188.
Woodlawn, 36, 37.
Woman's Rights, 166.
Wormley Hotel Conference, 83, 109.

Yellow Fever, 237-244.

www.ingramcontent.com/pod-product-compliance
Lightning Source LLC
Chambersburg PA
CBHW022106150426
43195CB00008B/289